The Ministry of Women in the Church

Cover: *Female Saints* by Fr. Theodore Jurewich. Icon used with permission from The Sign of the Theotokos Church, Montreal, Quebec, Canada.

Front row, l. to r., ANNA, Mother of the Theotokos (first century); ELIZABETH, Mother of the Forerunner (first century); MARY MAGDALENE, Equal to the Apostles and Myrrhbearer (first century); NINA, Equal to the Apostles and Evangelizer of Georgia (ca. +337).

Back row, l. to r., JULIANA of Lazarevski (+1604); IRENE, Great Martyr of Thessalonica (second century); Great Martyr BARBARA (ca. +306); ALEXANDRA the Empress, Wife of Diocletian (+303).

The Ministry of Women in the Church

Elisabeth Behr-Sigel
Translated by Fr. Steven Bigham

Ωakwood ΠPublications
Redondo Beach, California

Originally published in French under the title:
Le ministère de la femme dans l'eglise
by Les Editions du Cerf, 1987

616 Knob Hill, Redondo Beach, California 90277
Telephone: (213) 378-9245

Published by Philip Tamoush
Translation reviewed and approved by Elisabeth Behr-Sigel
Typeset by Hope Publishing House, Pasadena, California
Proofing by Gerald Fong
Distributed by Source Books, Box 794, Trabuco Canyon, CA 92678

ISBN: 0-9618545-6-1

LC: 89-063746

But you are a chosen race, a royal priesthood, a holy nation, God's own people, that you may declare the wonderful deeds of him who called you out of darkness into his marvelous light (1 P 2:9).

Dedicated to the unheralded women of the "royal priesthood" who through the centuries accepted the Lord's call with courage and to the women who today are dedicated to a faithful contemporary expression of their personal ministry in the Church in unbroken continuity.

TABLE OF CONTENTS

PREFACE TO THE ENGLISH EDITION

This splendid translation of Elisabeth Behr-Sigel's essays on issues related to the ministry of women in the church is a cause of joy and gratitude for English-speaking people interested in Orthodox Christianity. Its appearance is a special joy for the members of the Orthodox Church for whom English is their primary, and often exclusive, theological and liturgical language.

Elisabeth Behr-Sigel is well known to those involved in intra-Orthodox and ecumenical theological discussion, particularly, though by no means exclusively, on the subject of women and men in Christian thought and practice. Those new to these concerns will meet in these pages Eastern Orthodoxy's premier woman thinker; a learned, noble and courageous woman whose years of life have already passed the psalmist's "fourscore" (surely not without her share of "toil and trouble"), who has contributed significantly to contemporary Orthodox historical and theological scholarship.

Elisabeth Behr was converted to Orthodoxy in her youth while studying theology. For a short time she ministered to a small Protestant community in France. She has by now spent well more than a half century within the Orthodox Church. She knows what Orthodox Christianity is; both in its theological vision, spiritual experience and ecclesial realization in history, as well as in the faults, foibles and failures of its earthly adherents. In a sense, this is what the essays in this present volume are about. They reveal Madame Behr-Sigel's inevitably *two-fold* experience as a member of the Orthodox Church: her experience of the Church as a theanthropic mystery full of grace and truth, and her experience of the various Orthodox churches as ecclesiastical institutions composed of sinful people tried and often conquered by the passions, prejudices, ignorances and evils of this fallen world.

The essays in this volume testify to what Elisabeth Behr-Sigel sees as being of the Church's divine life and teaching as Christ's body and bride incarnate in human history. And they witness as well to what she identifies as deviations and distortions of the Church's genuine doctrine and practice in ecclesiastical history, a history which for her, as for all Orthodox Christians, is radically different from the Church's Holy Tradition understood as the Church's divinely-inspired life hidden in Silence and yet testified to in the community's canonized scriptures, sacraments, liturgical services and saints.

Although the emphasis of the essays in this volume is on the ministry of women in the church, the contributions published here, which were written on various occasions for different reasons, cover a broad range of information and reflection on the subject of women and men in Christian life and teaching generally. Each of the essays treats the same basic issues, albeit from different perspectives and for different purposes. There is, therefore, an inevitable, though not at all regrettable and often enlightening, repetition of themes, materials, references and quotations. None of the essays deals in depth with any one issue. Their nature and purpose do not allow it. And perhaps at this primitive stage of discussion on the subject, at least among the Orthodox for whom the real discussion has not yet really begun, this is as it should be, and only can be.

Because of the nature of her various tasks in the essays comprising this volume, the author opens herself to various questions and criticisms. She can and will—and of course even *must*—be challenged about her choice of sources and references in dealing with her questions, as well as about her interpretations of biblical, liturgical and patristic texts, her theological conclusions and her practical applications. She herself expects this to happen; and she welcomes it. She has spoken and written, as she herself says, for this very purpose. Her decision to do so will remain to her honor whatever the evaluation of her work when—as Orthodox Christians hope and believe—

consensus on the essential issues concerning women and men, particularly the issue of ministry, is attained by those who recognize each other's faith, life and worship as consonant with that of the Orthodox Church everywhere and always.

In greeting these English translations of Elisabeth Behr-Sigel's writings, I dare to express the hope of many people, Orthodox and non-Orthodox, that other Orthodox women will follow this leading lady's example and take up the issues which she opens in these pages. There is no doubt that women's voices must be heard if Orthodox Christianity is going to be heard on these (and virtually all other) issues today.

In our American scene we begin to see a small number of Orthodox women who have published and are planning to publish on subjects treated in this book. We have heard and read, and are waiting to read and hear more from such women as Deborah Belonick, Sophie Daniels, Mary Ann DeTrana, Kyriaki FitzGerald, Elaine Hanna, Verna Harrison, Susan Harvey, Elizabeth Moberly, Constance Tarasar, Eva Topping, Stephanie Yazge, Valerie Zahirsky and others who have spoken and written on gender-related issues. Their work ranges from scholarly theological, historical and psychological research to spiritual reflections and popular manuals intended for religious education, catechetical instruction and ecumenical discussion. Those interested in the questions treated in this volume should look for their writings.

If the present volume did nothing more than to widen and deepen discussion among the Orthodox concerning the community and ministry of women and men in the church, this alone would be sufficient reason to offer its author, and its English translators and publisher, our greatest gratitude. The fact that Madame Behr-Sigel provides insights to be reckoned with in an intelligent, clear and forthright manner (unlike some of the few other writings which we have to date in English relating to "women's issues") makes her work all the more valuable. For what we have here is not only a book unique in its historical significance as the first work of a single Orthodox thinker, man or woman, devoted to this most essential and contested issue of our day. We have a book which must be read, reflected upon and responded to by all, particularly all Orthodox Christians, who care about the identity, continuity and integrity of Christian faith and life through history from apostolic times to our own, and into the awesome days of our daughters and sons yet to be born.

—***Fr. Thomas Hopko***
St. Vladimir's Seminary
Feast of St. Catherine of Alexandria, 1990

PREFACE TO THE FRENCH EDITION

With great joy I recommend this book to all serious readers, to those who are ready to put aside their prejudices. May it be the "first swallow that announces the coming of spring." It will, I hope, open a new horizon for many Churches, for many fearful spirits that are afraid of rethinking ideas that have been accepted without reflection. In society and in the Church, we are used to giving women a secondary place, thus making their social condition, in antiquity as well as in our own time, the basis of a theology that, it seems to me, has its roots in Genesis 3. We forget, is it a Freudian slip, the creation of the total Man, undifferentiated, which contains all masculinity and all femininity. In this unique Man (*anthrôpos*), masculinity and femininity attain a maturity that requires for its perfect development and fulfillment the separation into two entities at the moment of Eve's birth. We too easily forget that God created Eve for Adam so she would be a "partner," not a subordinate. She was to be his "half." Did God take just a rib [*une côte*] or a whole side [*un côté*] of Adam for Eve's creation? When he saw her, Adam proclaimed both his difference from her and the fact they were one. The Churches that call themselves "traditional" never cease referring to the fact that in Christ God showed himself as man (*anêr*, male), and they forget that he is the total and perfect Man (*anthrôpos*) who contains and reveals the totality of the human being and not just the "virile" side for "what he did not assume, He did not save."

As for the continual reference to the humility of the Mother of God, to her absence, always "standing back," this reference makes us easily forget that without her giving of herself the incarnation would have been as impossible as without the will of God. Twice, Mary had a properly priestly ministry: once when she carried her son who was destined to be sacrificed to the Lord and once when, at the foot of the cross, she completed the offering by uniting her will, in a heroic abandoning of self, to the will of the heavenly Father and to that of the Son of God who by her had become the Son of Man and the sacrificial Lamb.

The Orthodox, and Roman Catholics too, must rethink the problem of woman in the light of the Scriptures. They must not make hasty statements about her being and her place in the work of salvation to which God has called us to be witnesses. The question of the ordination of women to the priesthood has only recently been asked. For us Orthodox, the question comes "from the outside." It must become for us a question that is asked "from the inside." This question requires of us all an interior freedom and a deep communion with the vision and will of God, in a prayerful silence. I hope that this book will be the beginning of a humble but bold awakening on the part of men and women.

—***Anthony Bloom***
Metropolitan of Sourouzh (Great Britain)
London, July 15, 1987

INTRODUCTION

The studies brought together in this small book are sign posts along the road of a personal reflection which has been going on for several years. This reflection has also been subject to the ups and downs of events and circumstances and is therefore somewhat unsystematic. It is, nonetheless, a reflection which is quite open ended. The point of departure was the Consultation of Orthodox Women jointly organized by the World Council of Churches and the Orthodox members of the Council in September, 1976, at the Agapia Monastery in Rumania.[1]

This was the time when women's protests were beginning to have an impact on ecumenical circles. The breakthrough was the result primarily of the North American feminist movement, but the voices of European, and even African women, were also being heard. The problem of women's ordination suddenly appeared as one of the main stumbling blocks in the various dialogues between the Churches.

In Accra in 1974, the Faith and Order Commission of the World Council of Churches took note of this new situation. In response to the reproach that the Churches were acting as if they were made up only of men, the Commission launched a study project on "the community of women and men in the Church." The following year, the project was adopted by the General Assembly of the WCC in Nairobi. At the same time, a motion was passed asking the Churches "to make room for women at all levels of the decision-

---

[1] On the Agapia consultation, see *Orthodox Women: Their Role and Participation in the Orthodox Church*, World Council of Churches Publications, Geneva, 1977; E. Behr-Sigel, "Femmes et Hommes dans l'Eglise" [Women and Men in the Church], *Service Orthodoxe de Presse*, Supplément 64.

making process."[2] It was in the optimistic climate of the initial successes of the feminist cause that an audacious idea was born: to organize an international consultation of Orthodox women under the auspices of the WCC. Having received the agreement of the local Orthodox Churches, the Patriarchate of Rumania offered its hospitality to the consultation members. The project, initially conceived under the palm trees of Nairobi, became a reality less than a year later within the walls of the historic Agapia Monastery, a place dear to the heart of the Rumanian writer Virgil Geoghiu.

All the agitation and tension that swirled around the question of women certainly took the Orthodox Churches by surprise. They quite rightly denied being anti-feminist. Is it not true that in the Orthodox Church, a woman, the Mother of God, is venerated as the creature closest to God? Is she not an eschatological sign of humanity saved and transfigured by grace? At the same time, however, it is true that feminism as a cultural and specifically Western phenomenon–as ideology and militancy–is foreign to the Orthodox Churches. For many reasons, both sociocultural and spiritual, the feminist movement has not really affected the societies of Eastern Europe and the Mediterranean basin where the Orthodox Churches have their deep historical roots. These Churches have little contact with feminism except on their fringes, in their diasporas in Western Europe and North America, in groups that have a tendency to turn in on themselves like all minorities anxious to preserve their identity. Even in the diaspora, the feminism of the first heady years appeared to be a foreign virus that the Churches had to protect themselves against. Among Orthodox theologians and moralists, Paul Evdokimov, a French-speaking Russian thinker, was for a long time the only person to consider the woman's movement with interest and sympathy. We should also mention,

---

[2] *The Ordination of Women in Ecumenical Perspective*, Constance F. Parvey, ed., World Council of Churches, Geneva, 1980, p. 25.

of course, "A Monk of the Eastern Church," who was Evdokimov's friend and often his inspiration.[3] Evdokimov was the spiritual heir of the prophetic Russian religious philosophy which he tried to synthesize with patristic theology. He discerned in the women's revolt, beyond the "sound and fury," a legitimate ethical imperative, one of the "signs of the times" which Christ exhorted his disciples to be attentive to. In an important and stimulating book, *La Femme et le Salut du Monde*[4] [Woman and the Salvation of the World], although certain points are debatable, Evdokimov meditated deeply on the spiritual vocation of women. Like Simone de Beauvoir, whose book *Le Deuxième Sexe* [The Second Sex] Evdokimov had read, he denounced the alienation that women were victims of during the centuries of so-called Christian civilization. This repression, he notes, has produced the reaction of an aggressive and often atheistic feminism. But this kind of feminism, by confusing the equality of the sexes with their identity, denied their difference and richness. Has it not ended up by producing a new alienation? By becoming part of the masculine world, "women risk losing their nature." According to Evdokimov, the key to the mystery of women is to be found in the Person of the Holy Spirit whose hypostatic maternity extends to the virginal maternity of the Theotokos and prefigures, for all eternity, the vocation of every woman to spiritual maternity.

---

[3] On Paul Evdokimov, see "Paul Evdokimov, témoin de la beauté de Dieu," [Paul Evdokimov: Witness to God's Beauty], special number of *Contacts* 1/2, 1971; Olivier Clement, *Orient-Occident, Deux Passeurs: Vladimir Lossky, Paul Evdokimov* [East-West, Two Passers-By: Vladimir Lossky and Paul Evdokimov], Labor et Fides, Geneva, 1985. Archimandrite Lev Gillet, 1893-1980, took the pen name A Monk of the Eastern Church and was the author of various works on spirituality. For more than fifty years, he was a discrete but profound influence on a great number of Orthodox intellectuals in France, England, Greece, and the Middle East. See also "Un Moine de l'Eglise d'Orient" [A Monk of the Eastern Church], *Contacts* 4, 1981.

[4] P. Evdokimov, *La Femme et le Salut du Monde* [Woman and the Salvation of the World], reedited by Desclée de Brouwer, Paris, 1978.

Whatever we may make of these speculations and of the consequences he draws from them,[5] Evdokimov has undoubtedly been a voice rousing many from sleep. Under his influence, which his writings are perpetuating now that he is dead, certain Orthodox theologians have understood the necessity of a creative reflection on the role and ministries of woman, and of women, in the Church. These thinkers, like Evdokimov during his life, are also close to the World Council of Churches. These friends and disciples of Paul Evdokimov were members of the WCC staff and in 1975-76 were the ones urging forward the apparently revolutionary project of an international and interjurisdictional consultation of Orthodox women. In spirit and through his prophetic inspiration, the great Franco-Russian Orthodox theologian was present at Agapia.

I first met Paul Evdokimov and his first wife, Natacha, in 1929. I was at the beginning of my theological studies, and he had just finished his at St. Sergius Orthodox Theological Institute in Paris. He had been a disciple of Fr. Sergius Bulgakov whose sophiology had made a great impression on both of us. We sometimes disagreed about things, especially about women, for it seemed to me that his idealization of women often came close to mystification. Nonetheless, he and I were dear friends for forty years. Because our friendship was known to some of the organizers of the Agapia consultation, I was given the honor of being invited not only to come but, to my total surprise, even to make the opening address. This address started and oriented my subsequent reflection.

When I received the invitation in the spring of 1976, I was stunned and filled both with joy and apprehension. I took great pleasure in the fact that the ancient Orthodox

---

[5] On the special relation that he believed he could establish between women and the Holy Spirit, Paul Evdokimov concluded that the priesthood which is essentially "Christic" was not suitable for women: *op. cit.*, pp. 214-22. See also *La Nouveauté de l'Esprit* [The Newness of the Spirit], Editions de Bellefontaine, 1977, p. 265.

Church, heir to the Tradition of the undivided Church, had shown itself ready to consider one of the great questions of modern time. On that question, it was willing to consult women as responsible members of the Christian people in search of a creative response. But, being near the end of my life, would I have the strength to take on what I sensed would be a whole new battle? Unbelieving, like the aged Sarah at the announcement of Isaac's birth, I just wanted to laugh. When the initial shock had passed, I nonetheless accepted. While this invitation was a new beginning for me, it was also a return to the sources, and a coming face to face with my own past.

The reader will forgive me, I hope, if I make a personal digression here. Even if ideas sometimes fall from heaven, they nonetheless germinate in the ground of concrete existence.

I was not born into a traditionally Orthodox family. My father was a Lutheran from Alsace and my mother, a very assimilated Austrian Jew, but they maintained only distant relations with their own religious backgrounds. I was all the same baptized at the age of one by a Lutheran pastor friend of my father. I received no religious education in my family, but thanks to the religious instruction in the Protestant school, I was very early on made aware of the main texts of the gospels. As a teenager and young adult, I, like many others, went through a metaphysical crisis. I was able, however, to meet some great believers, both men and women, in the Protestant youth movement, and through them, my crisis ended with a personal acceptance of Christ as master of my life and giver of the true life which is "love as strong as death." When I was twenty years old, with my philosophy diploma in hand, I decided to begin my theological studies. In 1927, coincidentally, the theology faculty of the University of Strasbourg had just opened its program to women. If my memory serves me well, we were only three or four girls in the first year and, on the whole, rather well received by our fellow male students and future pastors. Only our fellow students, the seminarians of the Catholic faculty of theology seemed a bit surprised when they met us in the hallways. But they too got used to seeing us.

We girls naturally asked ourselves many questions: What were we going to do after our studies? Would the Churches accept our services? In what capacity? We were nonetheless confident; the Lord had already helped us cross the first obstacle. We felt that since He had called us, He would look after the rest. For my Protestant sisters, this hope would not be disappointed. As for me, it was also to be fulfilled but in a different way. During the ten years that followed the opening of theological studies to women at the University of Strasbourg, the two local Protestant Churches, the Alsace-Lorraine Church of the Augsburg Confession (Lutheran) and the Alsace-Lorraine Reformed Church, both decided, though by different means, to give pastoral ministries to woman who had acquired an adequate theological training.[6]

I was one of the first of these women who had to face this question, and I did so with "fear and trembling." The president of the Reformed Synod asked me to take over a rural parish that had not had a regular minister for several years because of the lack of pastors after the slaughter of the First World War. I was to be interim pastor "without being ordained" (which I did not want to be in any case). I accepted to try things out. Thus, for eight months between 1931 and 1932, I was in charge, all alone, of a small Reformed community sitting between the Vosges and the Alsatian plain. My official title was "pastor-administrator." I lead the Sunday worship, announced the Word of God, gave religious instruction to the children and teenagers, and visited the sick and the very numerous isolated people. It was a humble ministry which made very little noise and caused no scandal. The parishioners, for the most part

---

[6] H. Mehl, "La condition des femmes-pasteurs en France," [The Condition of Women Pastors in France], *Le Supplément* 157, July, 1986, p. 109.

simple people, adopted me. Some of them, women mostly, showed great confidence in me. I would not dare draw any general conclusions from such a limited experience. I felt though that I had to put an end to it and start off in another direction. I nonetheless have always kept a glowing and grace-filled memory of that pastoral ministry. It has made me feel a deep solidarity with all the Christian women who, from the beginning of the Church, from Prisca, Phoebe, Lydia, Junias, the woman co-workers with the Apostle Paul "worked, toiled, and labored" (this is the meaning of the verb *kopian* used by St. Paul) to announce the Gospel of Christ.

An old Portuguese proverb says that "God writes straight with curved lines." Paradoxically, my theological studies had begun under the sign of Protestant liberalism, but they were to lead me to the Orthodox Church, to that community which still preserves the Tradition of the undivided Church, to that common root onto which we must be regrafted if we hope to come to the unity Christ prayed for. Unfortunately alas, that Tradition is far too often obscured by human sin and ignorance. This short introduction is not the place, even if it were possible, to explain a complex spiritual evolution which was influenced by many factors: the mind, the heart, a theological as well as ecclesiological reflection, and deep personal encounters. I was not like the ambassadors of the Grand Prince of Kiev;[7] I was not in Hagia Sophia when I saw "the true Light," that the liturgical hymn sings about. I was instead in a humble community of Russian emigrés on Easter night when we shared the "tearful joy" of Pascha. There I knew in my heart the foretaste of the beatitude that is the Kingdom of Heaven.

---

[7] According to the account of the ancient Russian chronicles, the ambassadors of Prince Vladimir of Kiev thought they were "transported from earth to heaven" when they attended the Holy Liturgy in Hagia Sophia in Constantinople. Their testimony is what made Vladimir adopt the Christian faith in its Oriental form under the authority of the Patriarchate of Constantinople.

For the last half century, the Orthodox Church has been my spiritual home on earth. The Orthodox Church I have known was first of all the Church of the pathetic Russian emigration of the first years of this century. Then it was the Church which through the years has tried to enroot itself in the reality of Western European, especially French, culture. I have tried, as much as I could, to contribute to this process of cultural adaptation. In this Church, my spiritual home, I have been nourished by the eucharistic mystery, and have received grace on grace. In it, I have also known surprises and disappointments.

Having been introduced to Orthodoxy by great free-spirited thinkers such as Fr. Sergius Bulgakov and Archimandrite Lev Gillet, I was particularly shocked to discover that in its empirical reality, Orthodoxy is often weighted down with archaic prejudices and Old Testament taboos about women. One would think that the Light of Christ would have dissipated these shadows. Today these leftover beliefs of a neolithic age are being fought against, but they die hard. It would be a good thing if the pastors of the Church got more involved in this struggle.[8] Even more serious, it seems to me, is the cleavage between an ecclesiology of communion and conciliarity and the often heavy clericalism which excludes laymen, and especially laywomen, from participating in important responsibilities and decision making. Strangely, it was this very ecclesiology of communion, the *sobornost* of the 19th century Russian Slavophiles, that put such an emphasis of the royal priesthood of the whole Christian people. The situation no doubt varies from place to place since the spirit of conciliarity blows where it wants bringing with it some measure of progress. Nonetheless, one of our more clear-minded bishops recently felt obliged to sound the alarm:

---

[8] See the annexed document, *Questions sur l'homme et sur la femme dans le peuple de Dieu* [Questions about Men and Women in the People of God] by a task force of Orthodox people in France: *Service Orthodoxe de Presse* 46, July, 1979, and *Supplément* 64.

"We have made of the Church a clerical plaything, a hierarchical structure that betrays our theology . . . a heresy from the point of view of Trinitarian as well as liturgical theology."[9] The malaise resulting from this practical "heresy" concerns the whole Christian people but especially Christian women.

Must we simply submit to this state of affairs? Must we put up with the dust and deposits that disfigure the face of the Church as we have to put up with the wrinkles of age on the face of a loved one? But the Church is called to stand before the Lord as a bride forever young, "cleansed . . . by water and the word . . . in splendor, without spot or wrinkle or any such thing . . ." (Ep 5:26-27). Does not this vocation imply for the Church, as well as for each of us personally, the duty to reform ourselves ceaselessly—*semper reformanda*? Or better still, does not this vocation contain the call to a conversion to the Gospel, a conversion that is forever to be renewed?

The customs I mentioned earlier are, as Metropolitan Anthony Bloom so forcefully said, "an insult to women."[10] They are customs that do not spring from the teachings of Christ but are leftover from the Old Testament, archaic beliefs. When confronted with these beliefs and practices, I have always been pulled in two directions: one is a longing to fight them in the name of the authentic Tradition which, as Vladimir Lossky said, is the "critical spirit of the Church." The other is just to give up, pretend to accept them in order not "to scandalize the weak ones." In doing this, however, I run the risk of scandalizing other "weak ones" who may draw back and run away from the Church as fast as they can. To say that these customs are not important, that they do not represent what is essential

---

[9] Metropolitan Anthony Bloom, "L'Eglise, communauté eucharistique" [The Church as a Eucharistic Community], *Service Orthodoxe de Presse* 111, Sept.-Oct., 1986.
[10] *Ibid.*

is certainly true in a sense.[11] But is that not also the easy way out for a privileged woman, an intellectual? It is too easy just not to take them too seriously, to play with them as with baroque trinkets inherited from great grandparents. I am afraid I have sometimes given in to this temptation.

Because I already had a very full personal life, I was all the more pulled toward the second reaction, perhaps a cowardly and fearful way out. I was a wife, mother, then grandmother, teacher, something of a theologian, a founding member of a French-speaking Orthodox community, and also very much involved in ecumenical dialogue. I did not feel called upon to participate personally in the feminist struggle. I followed it only from afar and with a critical eye. The invitation to participate in the Agapia consultation was for me a turning point. I had not solicited it in any way. Through the voices of certain of her pastors, the Church herself was giving me the right to speak in the name of those women who for nearly 2000 years had been invited to keep silent.

It goes without saying that the Agapia consultation in 1976 was only a modest beginning, though far from being unimportant or insignificant. The women who participated in the consultation came from all parts of the Orthodox *oikumene*: the great traditional Orthodox Churches of the Mediterranean basin and Eastern Europe, the diasporas of Western Europe and America, the newly born Orthodox communities in black Africa, and the ancient Oriental Churches. Although invited by the WCC, these women did not in any official sense "represent" their home Churches. They lived in countries having very different political regimes and were very unevenly prepared to discuss freely and publicly problems bearing on Church life. United in the same faith, sharing the same spirituality, or very similar spiritualities, they had extremely varied cultural

[11] See the chapter on Orthodox women in Monique Hebrard, *Les Femmes et l'Eglise* [Women and the Church], Paris, 1984.

backgrounds. Between the young shy Russian girl, student from the Leningrad Academy, and the casual American graduate from the New York Orthodox seminary, between the Finnish lady in jeans and the Indian woman from Kerala majestically draped in her sari, the differences in mentalities were very great. The miracle was, however, that the meeting took place at all. For all the women present, the Agapia consultation was experienced as an important event in their personal lives as well as in the life of the Church. For the first time in Christian history, women were called upon to reflect together, in dialogue with bishops and theologians, on their vocation and specific ministry. Wishes were formulated, and above all, a reflection was started, a reflection whose goal was twofold: first of all, rediscover under the deposits of the past, the authentic ecclesial Tradition about women, as it sprang forth from the liberating Gospel of Christ, and secondly, apply that Tradition creatively to new situations. Despite all sorts of obstacles and impediments, this reflection has continued and is beginning to bear some concrete fruit. Some of us are wondering about the date for Agapia II.

In the wake of the Agapia consultation, between 1977 and 1981, I was invited to participate in a study sponsored by the Faith and Order Commission on "The Community of Women and Men in the Church." I thus took part in the conferences in Strasbourg-Klingenthal (1978) on the "Ordination of Women" and in Niederaltaich (1979) on "Theological Anthropology." I was also present at the Sheffield congress (1981) which marked the provisional final stage of the study, its climax, and, at the same time, its partial failure. The debates on the ordination of women took place in a highly charged atmosphere, and this question became the sore point around which crystallized many hopes and disappointments. It also brought out some of the existing antagonisms between the different Christian communities, and often, as in the case of Sweden, within the same community. The Sheffield congress was not, however, limited to a duel between the partisans and adversaries of the ordination of women. It was also the arena of fertile exchanges, even serene ones. Despite the real divergences that their dialogue ran up against, the Christian women and men who gathered together on this occasion had a real foretaste, maybe for only a few moments, of the new community of men and women which the Church carries within herself as a seed and a hope shining with the mystery of the Holy Trinity.

For various reasons, the participation of the Orthodox Church in the study "The Community of women and men in the Church" was insufficient, from the point of view both of numbers and of ability. The Orthodox had the feeling of not being able to make themselves heard, but the responsibility for this situation, it seems to me, must be shared. The Orthodox underestimated the importance of the problem of the ordination of women for their Protestant partners who, in turn, believed that they could treat the Orthodox hesitation with scorn. Following the Sheffield congress, the crisis exploded at the meeting of the central committee of the WCC held in Dresden, August, 1981. The report of the congress as well as its "Letter to the Churches," written in a style that intended to be prophetic, was severely criticized by several representatives of the Orthodox Churches. A rather complete dossier on the study was published by the WCC in English and German,[12] but I fear that except in North America, few Orthodox had any knowledge of it. From the ecumenical point of view and on the surface, the results may appear disappointing, but however slowly, the ideas are spreading and growing in people's minds.

Throughout my participation in the WCC study on "The Community of Women and Men in the Church," I was

---

[12] Constance F. Parvey, ed., *The Community of Women and Men in the Church*, WCC, Geneva, 1983. Texts from different consultations in the American journal *Mid-Stream*, July, 1982. On the Niederaltaich consultation, see Janet Crawford and Michael Kinnamon, ed., *In God's Image*, WCC, Geneva, 1983.

called upon to give an account of my work in lectures, articles, and seminars, in places as different as the Ecumenical Institute of Tantur in Jerusalem and the Dominican College of Philosophy and Theology in Ottawa, Ontario, Canada. Having thought over my experience in terms of dialogue, it seemed that the reflection would be fruitful in the longer term. Its first results were, however, rather disappointing. The communication breakdown, hopefully only temporary, has forced us to think more deeply about the problems raised, especially the ordination of women. We need to rethink them in a more global fashion and in relation to their complexity. But above all, we need to reflect on them in relation to what is essential. And what is essential is the fiery mystery of the Church's faith, the mystery of the Trinity, of one God in three Persons illuminating the mystery of the new human community of men and women. The Church, according to her vocation, is the matrix and womb of this new community.

To indicate the circulation of life and of mutual service which unite the Three who are one single God, the Fathers of the Church used the word *perichoresis*. Its etymological origins suggest images of a dance in which, as Metropolitan Anthony of Souroge recently said, "each person is simultaneously in the place of the other: a total unity in which each person, while not being the other persons, is what the others are."[13] The Lord of the dance invites us all, both men and women, to join by grace in the divine dance.

The different chapters of this small volume are the fruit of the reflection and dialogues I have just mentioned. They come from published articles in various journals or collected works.

On rereading the material, I felt I needed to make some changes here and there, so I cut out some repetitive parts. Perhaps I should have cut more, but I ask my readers to be

---

[13] Metropolitan Anthony Bloom, *op. cit.*, p. 22.

forgiving. The order of the material is not chronological but rather thematic. It is meant to show the internal logic of a process I progressively became aware of. What we have are bits and pieces of thoughts, but, like the little white stones dropped in the forest by Tom Thumb, these bits and pieces have a meaning and they point the way.

The problem of the place and status of women in the ecclesial assembly is not new. Though it is absent in the gospels, it has a prominent place in Paul's letters. Despite certain Gospel-based advances, subsequent history was to resolve the problem of women's place in a progressively restrictive way. As the expectation of the immediate end of the world faded, the Church settled in to the world as we know it. It found itself in the midst of societies that considered the submission of women to men to be written in the order of nature. In turn, this order was nothing other than the divine order reflected in that of the city and the family.

Today, on the other hand, we find ourselves in the midst of a technical and scientific culture that is spreading over the entire planet. The idea of a natural and static order of things is being swept away by an immense tidal wave. We are seeing a mutation that is affecting the physical and biological sciences as well as the human sciences and ethics. For many, the only remaining foundation for ethical thinking, the only "faith that remains," is the respect of the human person regardless of race, sex, or social condition.

In this context, the question of the status of women in the Church has become the criterion, or at least one of the main criteria for judging the credibility of this Church which is accused of having a double language with regard to women. But is not the question of the status of women above all a call, in a new historical form, to be converted to the Gospel? This is finally the basic question which has inspired and oriented my quest and given unity to the whole process.

At the beginning of this collection of essays, I thought it useful to consider the otherness of men and women. The idea of the physical and intellectual inferiority of women has been an uncontested axiom for a long time. For centuries, it has been used to justify the hierarchy of the sexes in the order of the family and society. Today this idea has been discredited, at least in those societies that have been influenced by Christianity. It has been replaced by the notions of the otherness and complementarity of men and women. Each sex has its own domain and its own specific, but complementary, virtues. Though these ideas should apparently be less offensive to women than the notion of their inferiority, are they not, however, just a mystification which leads to a new form of discrimination? The otherness of women has been violently denied by certain feminists because they feel it is merely the result of social pressures. They suspect that it is only being used to advance a new form of inferiority. Is the ideal then to be masculinized Amazons in a society where men and women are merely interchangeable parts? Does difference exclude equality? Or rather, can equals be different?

The first chapter of the book is an attempt to answer these questions by examining what the Word of God in the Scriptures has to say to us about them. The second chapter completes the first with a rather elementary investigation of the meaning of "image of God" in the Cappadocian Fathers, the 4th century founders of Christian anthropology. According to them, women as well as men bear that image.

The third chapter studies two icons, images that are guides and sign posts, according to the Tradition of the Orthodox Church, serving to found the new reconciled community which is the Church according to her divine vocation. The Church is a community of equal although different persons within the radiant mystery of the Trinity. All members, both men and women, are turned toward Christ who saves and reconciles all human beings.

This, in any case, is the vision rooted in the depths of the ecclesial consciousness. But what about the living reality? As individual persons, but also as a historical collectivity, can we say with the Apostle Paul, "I was not disobedient to the heavenly vision" (Acts 26:19)?

In keeping with this line of questioning, which was in fact that of the Agapia consultation, the fourth chapter about the place of women in the Orthodox Church follows an existential, rather than theoretical, perspective. I wanted to encourage Orthodox Christians to take notice of a problem which "they have not yet even become aware of," to quote Metropolitan Anthony of Sourozh.[14] Going beyond the attitude that sees the past through rose colored glasses, an attitude that is often confused with faithfulness to Tradition, we must try to consider the problem as it presents itself today at the dawn of the third millennium. Let us try to respond to it, not on the basis of prejudices or of canonical texts quoted out of their historical context but rather on the basis of the authentic ecclesial Tradition. Let us reappropriate that Tradition, scraped free of the dust and deposits that have disfigured it for so long. We can then apply it to our own present situation.

The same theme is taken up in the following chapter, the 5th, but this time in a wider context, not merely limited to Orthodoxy as a historical and institutional reality.

The question of the status of women is thus placed in relation to ecclesiology and more precisely in relation to two conceptions of the Church as they coexist, more or less, inside all historical Churches. The one is patriarchal and hierarchical, and the other is conceived and lived essentially as a mystery of communion. This latter is a communion of persons equal in dignity, and indignity, and saved only by grace. At the same time, each person is ineffably unique and called upon to serve God and men according to his or her own vocation and special charisms. These are certainly colored by the person's sex but not determined by it.

In this chapter, the burning question of the ordination of women is taken up more openly but still in the context of

---

[14] *Ibid.*, p. 23.

ecumenical dialogue. The question is this: is the fact that some Churches ordain women to the priestly ministry to be necessarily considered as a breach of the faith and the Tradition of the *Una Sancta Catholica*, a rupture such that no communion is possible between the communities that have women priests and those that strictly maintain the *Catholic* Tradition? Is the ordination of women an acceptable difference, in keeping either with the diversity of cultures that the historical Church has known on her way toward her final end beyond history? Or is it in line with different, but not exclusive, theological emphases? Does the difference in discipline in this area affect the essence of the apostolic faith, as some think? Or is it compatible with ecclesial communion as expressed by the patristic saying: "In necessary things, unity; in doubtful things, liberty; in all things, charity."? The reader will realize that I lean toward the second alternative.

There is no doubt that the evolution in my thinking on the question of women priests is evident in this book itself. It has shocked, even scandalized, some.[15] My position, however is the result of an effort to rethink the problem honestly and in an ecumenical perspective. I feel that I should make myself clear on this matter.

In an essay written in 1977, after the Agapia consultation, I took up for the first time the question of the ordination of women to an ecclesial ministry. Since that time, this problem, as I said at Agapia, has appeared to me as an unavoidable question. In the present cultural and ecumenical context, Orthodox Christians can no longer escape from it on the pretext that it is foreign to their Tradition and that, in any case, the question is not being raised in their Churches. A valid answer, we said, can only be the fruit of a deepening reflection and must be sought in a spirit of *conciliarity*. We must listen to the Word of God

---

[15] J. Hourcade, *La Femme dans l'Eglise* [Women in the Church], Paris, 1986, p. 120.

and try to find the real *meaning* of the ecclesial Tradition. We must also be attentive to others in a spirit of brotherly charity. In 1977, this serious reflection had only just begun in Orthodox circles. At Agapia, it was timid and stammering. When asked by their ecumenical partners about women priests, most Orthodox theologians and decision makers justified their opposition by an argument based on Tradition which is opposed to the ordination of women. A small number, Paul Evdokimov in Europe and Fr. Thomas Hopko in the United States, tried to justify the Tradition by using arguments not too offensive to women. These justifications took the form of speculation on the femininity of the Holy Spirit. In this line of thinking, woman closely reflects the Holy Spirit while man (*vir*, the male) is potentially priest and the image of Christ.[16] I have stated elsewhere my reaction to these arguments. Although generous and even containing some sound insights, they seem to be without explicit Scriptural basis, in my opinion. This speculation seems to get tangled up in confusion and contradiction especially when applied to the problem of the ordination of women.[17]

As for the argument from Tradition brandished about without discernment, it has always seemed to me not only insufficient but also offensive to the Church and the Spirit that is at work in her. This argument denies to both any creativity or capacity to adapt to new situations—without, of course, denying the essentials. According to this argument, it seems sufficient to say that "the Church has never ordained women in the past; she cannot therefore do it in

---

[16] P. Evdokimov, *La Femme et le Salut du Monde*, pp. 214-16; P. Evdokimov, *La Nouveauté de l'Esprit*, Ed. de Bellefontaine, 1977; "Les charismes de la femme" [The Charisms of Woman] and "Le Saint-Esprit et la Mère de Dieu" [The Holy Spirit and the Mother of God], T. Hopko, "On the Male Character of Christian Priesthood" in *Women and the Priesthood*, T. Hopko, ed., New York, 1983. See also my review of this book in *Contacts* 126, 2/1984, pp. 207-214.

[17] *Ibid.*

the present or in the future." The conclusion results from two premises, one explicit and the other implicit. The first refers to a belief that a serious historical study would lead us to modify somewhat, at least in the case of the deaconesses of the ancient Church. The second is the axiom that the future of the Church is nothing more than its past indefinitely repeated. The whole history of the Church reveals, however, that even though the life of the Church is continuity, it is also dynamism and creativity. Authentic faithfulness to Tradition is creative and requires each generation to respond to new needs and challenges according to the dynamic of Tradition. Faithfulness to Tradition is the work of the Spirit in the Church, raising the heavy dough of humanity. I am thinking of Jesus' conversation with the Samaritan woman near Jacob's well. Two traditions are highlighted in this episode: the one of the Jews and the Temple of Jerusalem opposed to the other, that of the heretical Samaritans. By confiding to the Samaritan woman the revolutionary secret of worship "in spirit and in truth," Jesus transcended this opposition. In his person, the tradition is both accomplished and gone beyond in an unimaginable way.

This passage must certainly not be used to justify any evanescent and anarchical spiritualism or giving in on the substance of the faith, the rock on which the Church is built. The call is to worship in spirit and *in truth*; we are to deepen the ecclesial spirit under the inspiration of the "Spirit of truth," to deepen the meaning and the implications of the faith. In the light of this progressive discernment, the question is to determine whether the masculinity of the priest is part of the dogmatic truths in so far as they express the essence of the Church's faith. Or is it possible, in the light of a deepening of the meaning of Christian ministries, to entertain the possibility of an evolution in this area? Or, at least, is it possible that different local practices could be compatible with the unity of faith?

In the face of blind submission to Tradition, I have always felt it necessary to appeal to the intelligence of the faith, being inseparable from brotherly love. In so doing, I follow in the steps of Alexis Khomiakov, the founder of modern Orthodox ecclesiology, who always strongly stressed this point.

Nonetheless, in the spirit of this necessary discernment, I was for a long time impressed by the argument of liturgical symbolism which requires a male priest. This point of view was set out in the Roman document *Inter insignores* (1976) and is also used in a slightly different form by Orthodox theologians who are otherwise quite sensitive to the questions raised by the feminist movement.

In the liturgical action, and especially in the Eucharist, the male priest, according to this point of view, *represents* Christ. Modern Orthodox spokesmen have taken up an expression of St. Theodore Studite who said that the priest is the *icon* of Christ. The common doctrine of the Church, without any doubt, says that the Word of God became incarnate and assumed the totality of humanity, but historically the Word of God was a male. This masculinity is not without significance. Does it not designate the Word as the Bridegroom, the husband, of the Church? Can the Church renounce the profound language of symbols? Does not traditional biblical symbolism require the masculinity of the priest who represents Christ?

This line of argument is not without a certain weight. It is given a prominent position by Orthodox theologians with whom I feel united by respect and love, such as Bishop Kallistos Ware.[18] I took it into account in the study published in 1977 and also after the Agapia consultation. However, as I continued to reflect on the problem of the ordination of women to a ministry officially validated by the Church, eventually a priestly or presbyteral ministry, I found the argument of symbolism to be less and less convincing and not decisive. This is especially the case in the perspective of ecumenical or bilateral dialogues with

---

[18] K. Ware, "Man, Woman and the Priesthood of Christ," in *Women and the Priesthood*, T. Hopko, ed., pp. 23-27.

Churches such as the Anglican Communion. This dialogue has in fact revealed a very wide consensus between the Anglican Communion and the Orthodox Church on the essence, the unchangeable core of the ecclesial faith. It no longer seems evident to me that the symbolism of masculinity of the priest is part of that core. On the one hand, the meaning of how the priest "represents Christ" and the way this "representation" is mediated need to be made more precise. On the other, we are faced with the question of whether the priest, in the exercise of his ministry, and in particular his eucharistic ministry, represents only Christ. Does he not also represent the Church, that community gathered together under the breath of the Spirit? Hoping to get an indispensable clarification on the matter, I reread Hebrews 7 and 10 as well as certain authors who are as respected in the Church as St. John Chrysostom and Nicholas Cabasilas, the author of a commentary on the liturgy. I also benefitted from the reflections of a contemporary spiritual father who was also a great theologian.[19]

On the basis of my renewed reflection, a reflection however that sought to be faithful to the authentic Tradition of the Church, I concluded that in the Orthodox perspective, the priest does not represent Christ and is not the "image" of Christ in the sense of naturalistic realism. Like the painted icon, but in another manner and by other means, which have to be made clear without falling into the snare of words, the priest is the instrument for making the invisible presence of Christ real and active. The priest points to Christ the one great High Priest who stands before the Father and in the Spirit, from whom he is distinct but inseparable (Heb 9:11-14). As John Chrysostom so strongly said, "It is the Father, the Son, and the Spirit who accomplish everything. The priest only contrib-

[19] See *Sois mon prêtre, quelques mots sur l'appel du Christ à ses prêtres* [Be My Priest: Some Words on the Call of Christ to His Priests], by a priest, Beiruth, 1962. The author was Fr. Lev Gillet.

utes his tongue and offers his hand."[20] "He stands before us, makes the gestures that Christ made, pronounces the words that Christ pronounced, but the power and the grace come from God."[21] Thus the symbolic mediation consists in the action of the priest and in the words of the divine Word pronounced by him, or rather pronounced "through him" and placed on the bread and the wine, fruits of man's labor. Neither St. John Chrysostom nor Cabasilas spoke of the symbolism of the priest's masculinity. Moreover, the priest lends his voice and suppliant hand to the Church as well, that is, to the Bride, according to the symbolism of marriage. He lends himself to the Christian people whose common priesthood he activates in communion with Christ's unique priesthood. According to Orthodox sacramental theology, the epiclesis is the summit of the eucharistic prayer, and in this invocation of the Spirit, the priest asks that the Holy Spirit be expressly sent "on us" and on the gifts here present. The priest is the voice of the Bride longing for union with the Bridegroom. Here also, and even more so, the symbolism of sex does not determine his role.

My reflections on these points have led me to relativize both the theological significance of the male priesthood and a symbolism that is never rigorously "natural." This symbolism, however, is always based on an interpretation of nature according to a variable cultural grid. As a result of the evolution of my thinking, I propose, in chapter 5, a pluralism in the practice of the local Churches on the question of women's ordination to the priestly ministry. Ordination is never a right for anyone but rather a confirmation by the Church of a call that comes from God in the succession-transmission of the call addressed to the Apostles.

---

[20] St. John Chrysostom, *Homily 77 on John 4*, PG 59, 472, quoted by K. Ware, *op. cit.*, p. 23.

[21] St. John Chrysostom, *On the Betrayal of Judas*, PG 49, 380 and *Commentaries on Galatians*, PG 61, 663.

In addition, attentive to the Churches that ordain women, I am conscious of the question implicit in the title of a book by Pastor Elizabeth Schmidt, *Quand Dieu appelle des femmes* [When God Calls Women].[22] I knew Elizabeth Schmidt very well. She was a pastor in Algeria during the worst times of the decolonization and the civil war. Later she exercised a blessed ministry in France in the service of the French Reformed Church. Faced with cases like hers, we Orthodox and Roman Catholics, along with the pastors of our Churches, find ourselves put in the question box. We certainly recognize in our leaders the responsibility and the charism of discerning and eventually of orienting vocations, but can they, can we, state with absolute certainty that God never calls women to the Christian priesthood? If we refuse to examine a vocation because a woman claims to have it, do we not run the risk of falling under the judgment of the Word of God which says, "Do not quench the Spirit . . . but test everything with discernment; hold fast what is good . . ." (1 Th 5:19-20).

To certain Orthodox (and Catholics), the questions that I have raised will seem sacrilegious, but I would not be doing my duty as a responsible member of the people of God if I did not ask them, seeing how I have consciously reflected on them myself. I leave it to the Church, to the bishops and faithful together, to answer with prudence and courage.

The book comes to an end with a meditation on Mary, the Mother of God, *Theotokos*, as she is shines in the piety of the Orthodox Church. The title *Theotokos* was proclaimed by the 3rd Ecumenical Council of Ephesus in 431.

Is it possible that the ancient Christocentric Mariology of the 4th and 5th century councils–Chalcedon completing Ephesus–may enlighten our present-day research concerning the status and ministries of women in the Church?

---

[22] E. Schmidt, *Quand Dieu appelle des femmes* [When God Calls Women], Cerf, Paris, 1978, and *J'étais pasteur en Algérie* [I Was a Pastor in Algeria], Cerf, Paris, 1976.

When this question was asked of me at a conference organized by the World Lutheran Federation in 1985, I felt able to give a positive answer. The ancient formulas and the traditional expressions of ecclesial veneration of Mary are clarified if we know how to extract from them their profoundly existential and theological meaning.

According to the great ecclesial vision, Mary is not the "model" only for women, the prototype of submissive, passive, and oversweet femininity which women today are no longer able, no longer want, to identify themselves with. Mary is not a goddess either, a symbol of a feminist Christianity which is implicitly or explicitly opposed to a masculine Christianity centered on Jesus. This is what a certain type of recent feminism has proposed, but the roots of such a feminist Christianity go deeply into a very ancient paganism, often carried along by popular piety. According to the Orthodox understanding, Mary is fully human and represents all of humanity, the complete humanity which God, in his grace, wanted to freely associate with the realization of his loving plan. She is a sign, the anticipation of a human person entirely given to the Lord, the ultimate eschatological realization of man-*anthropos*. Walking ahead of us all, she accompanies us along the way which, ever since Easter morning and the pouring out of the Spirit at Pentecost, leads to the glorious Second Coming. There is no doubt a deep meaning in the fact that this whole and complete humanity carries the features of a woman, a mother. In Mary and with her, we are all called, men and women, to a "feminine" attitude of welcoming grace, of giving and offering ourselves so that the new man, the total Christ, *totus Christus*, can be born in the Spirit in each one of us and in all of us together in the Church.

If this is the message of the Mother of God, does it not give a proper weight to our questions about the respective ministries of men and women in the Church setting them in their true place and perspective?

—The Annunciation, March 25, 1987

CHAPTER ONE

The Otherness of Men and Women in the Context of a Christian Civilization*

The Otherness of Men and Women in Traditional Societies

For Socrates, surprise and wonderment were at the basis of philosophical thinking and, in a general way, of all efforts at thinking the world and man. His pedagogical method consisted in leading people to wonderment, to a confession of their ignorance in the face of what they thought they understood, or what was, for them at least, unquestioned and unquestionable. Now we have to admit that for centuries, even millennia, the otherness of men and women has provoked very little surprise. For pagan religions, this otherness has its place in the extension of the sexual organization of the cosmos, even including the gods. It appeared to be part of the natural order. Based on this accepted order, society defined different models of behavior and different social standings for males and females. These models and standings are obviously not the

---

* This presentation was given at a multi-disciplinary conference during the celebration of the 75th anniversary of the Dominican College of Philosophy and Theology in Ottawa, Ontario, Canada, October 4-6, 1984.

same everywhere. They vary according to societies and ages, but the otherness of men and women always tends to appear as an absolute in relation to some unchanging, divino-cosmic hierarchy. This order is reflected in the organization of the city and assigns to each man and woman a place and a role in the hierarchy of family, society, and religion. The fate of women in this order is by no means necessarily an unhappy or degrading one, but her status nearly always implies a subordination to the male, and her otherness is expressed in terms of inferiority. This is a consequent result of confusing the natural order with the divine. Moreover, does not this inferiority result from what we know, or think we know, about womanhood? Are not women weak? Do they not lack the virtues of intelligence, reasoning, force of character? After all, the very word *virtue* comes from the Latin *vir* meaning *male*, and are not these virtues the very characteristics that make the virile man the paradigm of humanity? This virile man certainly appreciates the feminine tenderness of his mother, wife, or mistress. Social inferiority can even go hand in hand with the romantic idealization of the *Eternel Féminin.* Men willingly agree that women are beautiful, and that beauty has always entranced them, but they do not concede that women are intelligent. And is not intelligence the organizing principle of the world? "Be beautiful and be quiet!" This injunction has never stopped being addressed to women, either explicitly or implicitly.

The belief in the existence of a sacred order does not imply contempt for women but only requires their subordination. Certain fears, more or less openly acknowledged, go with this belief. Men are afraid of the opposite sex. Women are in a sort of unholy alliance with the dark forces of life which masculine intelligence cannot penetrate. Men fear feminine charm, according to the strong etymological meaning of the Latin *carmen.* Does not the presence of women risk confusing masculine minds, mixing up the cards held by the male players who control the institutions of society? It is therefore better to keep women away from the game.

In traditional societies, biological facts, that is, sexual differences, combine with economic necessities, beliefs, and simple prejudices to give birth to a division of labor and an assignment of domains and roles that are determined principally by sex. Each person finds his place in this structure, a place that has, on the whole, already been determined. Motherhood is the axis around which feminine existence is built. The woman's place is the home in which she is the "mistress." Her essential task is to give birth to children and to educate them as long as they need her care. To the male is given the organization of the city, the creative work in the realm of culture, and especially thinking for which women are not generally thought to be very qualified.[1]

The picture I have just drawn is painted in broad strokes and therefore somewhat over simplified. It should be more finely shaded and diversified according to various eras and cultures, for the structures of so-called "traditional" societies are far from being uniform. I especially had in mind a certain common western conception of men and women's otherness that has been perpetuated across very diverse social, economic, and political systems from the dawn of the Middle Ages up to our own time, systems that blend influences as different as Roman law and Christian preaching. I have purposefully not mentioned the Christian or ecclesial thinking, but I will come back later on to its ambivalence on this question. I limited myself to setting out an inevitably incomplete and not very detailed framework, one that aims at giving a general mental and cultural picture. The preaching of the Gospel in this cultural

---

[1] The inferiority of women in the domain of cultural creation is artlessly proclaimed even by thinkers who try to emphasize the value of "feminine charisms." Paul Evdokimov: "Man creates science, philosophy, art. . . . Woman is at the opposite end of every objectivation for she is in the perspective not of creation but of birth-giving." *La Nouveauté de l'Esprit* [The Newness of the Spirit], Bégrolles, Abbaye de Bellefontaine, 1977, p. 244.

context certainly introduced a tension. It introduced a seed of newness, a word that changes the meaning of traditional categories, a light that sometimes transfigures them. All this, however, does not destroy the framework that continues to form the individual, as well as the collective, psyche. Now, it is this framework, for a long time thought to be unchangeable, that is breaking down around us as a result of a great cultural mutation. All Christian reflection on the otherness of men and women must take this cultural earthquake into account. If it does not do so, it will simply appear to be irrelevant. We are not saying that we should just surrender in the face of a changing world. Jacques Maritain, the "peasant from the Garonne," warned us against that tendency. We must, however, deal with this mutation in the light of the Word who, coming into the world, "enlightens every man" (Jn 1:9), and consequently every human being, with a light that is both charity and spiritual discernment.

A Profound Cultural Mutation

One of the most spectacular manifestations of modern culture, at the same time of great significance, is the radical transformation of the status of women. As a result, new ways of being male and female have appeared, along with new relationships and a different perception of their otherness, going even as far as denying the reality of otherness. Rightly or wrongly, some people claim that women are becoming masculine. Women are nonetheless assuming numerous roles which up until recently were men's preserves. On the masculine side, men are no longer afraid to show emotions that used to be thought of as feminine: loathing of war and violence, for example. They dare to choose professions that used to seem altogether foreign to their vocation. There are now even male "maieuticians," a word coined to indicate the ancient profession of midwifery. Everywhere that modern western civilization has triumphed, women are progressively gaining equality with men. This is true in legal matters that touch on areas of action and responsibility, in society as well as in the family, but these transformations do not concern just the juridical personality. They go hand in hand with a profound change in the status of women in people's minds. For a century now, women have massively been entering the professions, and as far as they are given a chance, they are showing that they are just as capable as men. In the 19th century, the movement was limited to the working class, but it has now touched the middle and bourgeois classes in so far as women have had access to higher education. In turn, higher education has opened up carriers that confer material comfort, power, and prestige. Not being happy just to be doctors, jurists, and teachers, women have broken down the best protected bastions, such as in France the army and the high level graduate schools. It used to be claimed that women were not able to carry on without male guidance, but we now see women promoted to be heads of state, ministers, directors of research laboratories, and leaders of industry and labor. Women used to be described as inspirers of great men, sometimes even brilliant interpreters of such men's works; on a more prosaic level, these women were devoted secretaries or housekeepers. We now see them quite capable of being creative in all areas of literature, science, and the arts. Nowadays, a woman, just like a man, has the right to aspire to material independence if she has a good job. Even so, she may still run up against numerous difficulties of a social and psychological nature. She can, nonetheless, hope for personal development in a job that corresponds to her tastes and aptitudes; she can hope to exercise responsibilities at all levels of society and even, though more rarely, in Churches. In all these areas, men have become used to seeing women, no longer as their subordinate aids, but as their equals, their partners, and even sometimes, their rivals. Being seen and dealt with up close, women tend to lose the poetic halo that a certain romanticism set around them. A man's mistress has prosaically become only a "chum."

It may be, in fact, that people are now more alive to genuine feelings. As women have advanced in social, political, professional, and cultural fields, there have been similar changes in the family and the couple. In the traditional family, strictly defined roles are attributed to the husband and wife, to the father and mother, to the son and daughter. These roles shape their emotions as well, or at least, the ways these emotions are expressed. The man had authority and the right to make the big decisions; he had the responsibility to provide for the family and to maintain its "honor." The woman dealt with everything maternal, the care of the children, the sick; she had the oversight of the household and the responsibility for the daily chores. In the modern family, this differentiation of rights and duties is tending more and more to disappear in favor of a much less rigid and more balanced sharing of tasks and responsibilities.

Today, women who have a profession generally do not give it up when they get married, even if they want to have children, and most of them still do want to be mothers. They simply reduce the number of children to one or two, rarely more, and they space or "program" the births. It is at this point that increased knowledge and mastery of the fertilization process come in. As a result of such advances, mores have been unquestionably shaken, thus profoundly changing women's existence, the relationships of men and women as couples and also their relations to children.

For women, motherhood is no longer a fate, accepted with joy or endured with resignation. It is now a choice and desired, but at a time that is considered to be the most appropriate and in line with a decision arrived at by the two partners together, even though the dice are somewhat loaded in favor of the woman. The man thus feels more involved in the pregnancy and birth for which he is no longer just the biological progenitor. He wants the child, and he wants to be a father. The man thus develops a paternal, or parental, instinct that some thinkers claim is not naturally in him.[2] Think of Montaigne; he admitted not knowing the exact number of his children who died at a very early age! The "new father" feels more involved in the miraculous arrival of a new human being. He wants to be present at the birth and to live it as fully as does his companion. It is at this intense moment that their common parenthood is strengthened. The new father very naturally takes great pleasure in helping to care for the young children, a task that used to be reserved for the mother or the nanny. In order to lighten the mother's load, especially if she has a job, the father accepts to share with her the domestic chores.

> This is one of the discoveries of our time: the father becoming more sensitive to the needs of very young children and to the concrete need of the home . . . The opposition between the ancient roles of the husband and wife is breaking down. The new relation that we see taking shape includes more cooperation, more shared willingness, desire and joy.[3]

On the other hand, if this evolution is thus moving toward more freedom and equality and promoting more cooperation and more mutual interchange in men-women relations, it brings with it risks and uncertainties. In our society dominated as it is by technical and scientific pragmatism, does not this evolution involve the risk of transforming men and women into pawns that are interchangeable according to the whim of emotions, circumstances, and the vicissitudes of existence? This evolution also brings with it a heavy dose of anarchic individualism and makes the family extremely fragile. As a result of weakening the family structure, the whole fabric of society

---

[2] P. Evdokimov, *Sacrement de l'Amour* [The Sacrament of Love], Paris, 1962, p. 42.

[3] F. Quéré, "Un féminisme total" [A Total Feminism], *Esprit*, 458, June, 1976, p. 1076.

is weakened. Everywhere in the Western world, we see the instability of couples, and divorce rates are rising tremendously. Divorce nowadays is being sought more and more by the woman. She is tempted to reject her partner who has become an undesirable intruder on whom she no longer feels socially or economically dependent. The divorced or single woman thus becomes a hybrid creature, a "mother-father" and takes the "father's" place, he being himself nothing more than a solemn shadow, whose death some are pleased to announce.[4]

The divorce of parents often brings with it a bitter fight over the children who become rare and precious objects: Who is going to get custody? Being more maternal than before, the father demands an equal right to custody with the mother. At the end of these conflicts, often nothing remains but solitude for everyone, especially the woman. The children are torn apart or prematurely hardened so that they rarely are able to establish harmonious relationships with their parents. Because they lack adequate models to identify with, these children have a great deal of difficulty in fully assuming their sexual identity on the social and emotional level.

But some people ask, in a rather aggressive tone, if this sexual identity is not just a decoy. "Let's burn 'the women' in order to destroy 'the men.' We must get out of the structural couple which by eternally affirming the feminine, ties it to the masculine."[5] Is it possible that the liberation of women (and of men), at the cost of denying their otherness, may only be a screen for an ideological weapon based on biology, in the hands of an oppressive system?

---

[4] Y. Florenne, "La mort du père" [The Death of the Father], *Le Monde*, December 27, 1983.

[5] L. Giard, P. Meyer, M-C. Willcumier, "Note conjointe sur l'éminente relativité du concept de femme" [A Common Statement on the Eminent Relativity of the Concept of Woman], *Esprit*, 458, 1976, p. 1082.

The Sexual Differentiation as Seen by Science

Along with these questions born out of the questioning of a social structure whose basic element was the traditional family, we have problems raised by the scientific investigation of the bipolarity of human sexuality. Marc Oraison calls it "the human mystery of sexuality."[6]

Femininity and masculinity have an unquestionable organic base. Beyond the obvious anatomical differences, there are different hormonal functions that have an effect on the whole organism, including the brain. On the other hand, from the strictly organic point of view, as we have seen from biological and medical research, there is no absolute barrier between the masculine and the feminine. Each human being of both sexes has a certain quantity, of hormones of the opposite sex. This amount varies, however, according to the individual. The quantitative and qualitative balance between the two types of hormones is what biologically defines a sex. No person, however, can be reduced to hormones. The behavior of men and women is never the simple reflection of a hormonal situation. It is determined rather by external influences such as education, cultural models, and the symbolic value attributed to exterior sexual signs by any given civilization. There exists in every society a body language which is decodable through the use of variable interrelated grids. "Man is a historical idea," according to Merleau-Ponty. Man is also a thinking subject who can manipulate these grids, and finally he is a person capable of transcending them altogether. Throughout each person's history, always unique, personal, and formed out of many different experience, the subject is normally lead to accept and assume his sex. This process depends to a large extent on the person's psychic and spiritual balance. In each person, we can therefore detect several sexes, or better put, several

---

[6] M. Oraison, *Le Mystère humain de la Sexualité* [The Human Mystery of Sexuality], Paris, 1966.

levels of sex: an anatomical physiological sex, a social sex, and a psychological sex. These are the materials that each unique, mysterious person uses to build his personality as an original expression of his *being-in-the-world.*

In the view of the human sciences, the otherness of men and women, the *masculine fact* as well as the *feminine fact,*[7] shows itself as a complex and eminently "shapable" reality. Complexity and "shapability," however, leave a lot of leeway and thus allow human cultural intervention to have an influence on nature, not just to correct any eventual imperfections or to fill in gaps not covered by the instincts but also to give a *meaning* to nature, a significance and a direction that go beyond mere external sexual phenomenon. Because it transcends the male-female opposition of the animal world, the otherness of men and women belongs essentially to the realm of symbols. Now if our present-day civilization, through its inventive and fine-tuned techniques, is endlessly increasing our ability to intervene and influence the phenomenon of sexual differentiation, it seems to be failing to give that differentiation a properly human meaning. In the face of the collapse of ancient symbolisms, which both gave structure to life and introduced rigid boundaries, there sometimes seem to be space only for a negating nihilism that destroys traditional values and levels all differences.

Is the future going to be an atomized society, a mob of spiritually asexual individuals that move toward each other, bump into each other, and then move apart at the whim of circumstances, chance, or the necessities of a rational organization? Is the future going to be the test--tube baby, conceived *in vitro* and carried to term in an anonymous womb? This is fiction, agreed, but it is not too far from the mark!

Or will we be able to bring into reality, imperfectly of course, the vision of a *new human community* shown to us in the Gospel? According to the hope express by Fr.

---

[7] E. Sullerot, ed., *Le Fait féminin* [The Feminine Fact], Paris, 1978.

Teilhard de Chardin,[8] this community will be a place where "men and women, based on a collective and spiritual affinity, will be able to exercise their complementary gifts *in freedom* and in diverse and finely shaded relationships of association, contracts, and friendship."

As the Protestant theologian, Jacques Ellul, reminds us in an important book,[9] the problem of living the otherness and equality of men and women is a question of life and death. Today more than ever, we are faced with the mutilations and the risks of a disoriented and anarchic freedom which vainly provokes a sterile conservative reaction. We very much need to meditate on the words of Scripture, ". . . I have set before you life and death, blessing and curse; therefore choose life . . ." (Dt 30:19).

Many are asking, however: Where can we find this fullness of life that is not just fleshly but is the development of the human spirit in truth and love? As Christians, we answer in line with our faith: life is found in Him who said "I am the way the truth and the life" (Jn 14:6). It is in the Word of God who spoke in the Scriptures and whose Spirit does not cease to *make* this saying *real* in the Church and in each one of us if we open up to him. *To make real* the Word of God about men and women, in their mysterious unity-otherness, seems to me to be one of the important aspects of the common work, in the Church, which we are called to carry on today.

The Otherness of Men and Women in Christian Discourse

Christian discourse on the relationship of men and women is today accused of being anti-women, not without

---

[8] H. de Lubac, *L'Eternel féminin. Etude sur un texte du Père Teilhard de Chardin* [The Eternal Feminine: A Study of a Text of Fr. Teilhard de Chardin], Paris, 1968, p. 87.

[9] J. Ellul, "Les femmes et la liberté" [Women and Liberty] in *Les Combats de la liberté* [The Struggles of Liberty], Paris, 1984, p. 324 ff.

some basis. As the Catholic historian Kari Borresen has shown, Christian thinking on this question is quite ambivalent,[10] even though an Orthodox theologian, Paul Evdokimov, contests that conclusion in one of his first works called *Sacrement de l'Amour* [Sacrament of Love]. Evdokimov was surprised by the fact that in Church history, the spectacular development of the veneration of the Mother of God was accompanied by a growing and concomitant scorn for Mary's sisters who were condemned to silence and relegated to an inferior place in the ecclesial community.

Through the centuries, the Church has in reality always proclaimed the divine Word which sets out the fundamental equality of men and women before God. This proclamation is the honor of the Church while at the same time being her cross because she is judged by it. The proclamation also judges all Christians but especially the clergy who too often have obscured it by using subtle and warped interpretations whose purpose was to justify male domination. This deformation is less due, however, to the ill will of males, as individuals, as to a general mentality, to the influence of the *idols of the Forum*, in Bacon's words, which have not yet been sufficiently exorcised. Christian discourse is always set in a cultural context that leaves its mark, but the Word of God can still be heard. It is nonetheless only partially, progressively, and always imperfectly assimilated by people's minds.

Christians first and foremost search for the Word in the Holy Scriptures, transmitted in and by the Church, but they do not look for the "letter" that kills but for the spirit, in its dynamic intentionality which animates the letter and gives it life. This spirit, this intentionality, is what each person and each generation must *appropriate* so as to *become* flesh in the historic, personal, and ecclesial existence. Our reflection has its place in this effort of

---

[10] K. Borresen, *Equivalence et Subordination* [Equivalence and Subordination], Paris, 1975.

appropriation; it is in line with the "becoming flesh" in the history of the eternal Word about men and women. The point of departure for this reflection is a rereading of Scripture which naturally must be continuous and must go ever deeper. This rereading concerns especially the first three chapters of Genesis in which the Church, following Israel the people of the first Covenant, has always seen the basis of all Christian thought about men and women. Jesus himself referred to these fundamental texts when he opposed the way things were "in the beginning" (Mt 19:8) to the compromises and deformations due to men's "hardness of heart."

My commentary is not based primarily on scientific exegesis, on the historico-critical method, although I in no way reject the results of such a methodology. I in fact use certain results at some points, but my commentary is situated rather in the context of an ecclesial reading of the Scriptures, in continuity with the reading of the Scriptures carried out by the apostles and the Fathers. I hope that my commentary is also situated in the faith in the Holy Spirit who never ceases to work in the Church to make the Word real, to appropriate that Word to the circumstances of our personal and collective lives. My reflection will try to be existential. I want it to be in line with a "Christian theory" which always aims at being "practical", according to insistence of the father of neopatristic Orthodox theology, Vladimir Lossky.[11] Such a "Christian theory" does not seek purely intellectual knowledge about God but rather communion with Him.

The Creation Stories: Genesis 1:26-31 and 2:5-25

Genesis 1-2 contains two creation stories. It goes without saying that they are not historical documents. In symbolic language, they express deep spiritual truths about the

---

[11] V. Lossky, *Essai sur la théologie mystique de l'Eglise d'Orient* [in English: *The Mystical Theology of the Eastern Church*], Paris, 1944, p. 7.

relationship between humanity and God the Creator as well as the relationship between man and woman within this primordial relationship to God. We must never forget that the male-female relationship is always to be set in the larger context of the God-man relationship.

The two creation stories have different origins. The second story, historically called Yahwist, is older than the first by several centuries. Nonetheless, from the spiritual point of view, the biblical order of the stories has a meaning, and I will therefore respect it.

According to the first story, the creation of humankind is placed after the creation of all the other elements and living things and is the crowning event of God's six day work. As the founders of Christian anthropology and in line with the philosophers of antiquity, their contemporaries, the Cappadocian Fathers commented on this text in terms of "man-themicrocosm": man is composed of all the elements of the earth, he sums them all up in one integrated whole. At the same time, they forcefully affirm that man goes infinitely beyond the cosmos.[12] Like the cosmos itself, man is a creature that has his being and existence from God, and therein is his fragility. He was not made *for death* yet he is perishable. He lives solely by the will of the Creator receiving existence from an absolutely transcendent God.[13] Nonetheless, this God wants man to be "in his image and likeness." The Fathers read "likeness" in terms of "toward the likeness." They make a distinction between "the image" which is the inalienable gift and "the vocation" whose realization implies the intervention of the free will of man. Now right from the beginning, this humanity in the image of God is both one and dual: "So

---

[12] Gregory of Nyssa, *The Creation of Man*, chapters IV-VI.

[13] We have an Orthodox reflection on the notion of creation in J. Zizioulas, "Christologie et existence: la dialectique 'créé-incréé' " [Christology and Existence: the Dialectic "Created-Uncreated"], in *Contacts*, 126, 1984, pp. 154-172.

God created *man* in his own image, in the image of God he created *him*; male and female he created *them*" (Gn 1:27).

For the Judæo-Christian tradition, this is the essential revelation, the fiery sun whose light enlightens all reflection on man, and on males and females. At the same time, this mystery is also the source of many questions, even disturbing problems. What is the image of God in man? How are we to understand the unity and the duality-plurality of humankind? How do we conciliate the one with the other? The answers to these and other questions have varied throughout history. The emphases have also been different according to the preoccupations of different eras. Variety and legitimate differences: "Therefore every scribe who has been trained for the kingdom of heaven is like a householder who brings out of his treasure what is new and what is old" (Mt 13:52).

Among the various readings of Genesis 1:27, that of the Church Fathers remains for us a beacon, without of course excluding other readings. In its orientation and christological outlook, both universalist and personalist, the patristic reading of this passage is right in line with the whole New Testament. We do not find in the Fathers, however, a clear, precise, and common definition of the *imago Dei*. As the image of God, "man is a mystery," according to Gregory of Nyssa. He is a mystery, a depth that precisely excludes all definition: man is a created liberty, and as such, he cannot be captured in any concepts:

> We cannot know the nature of our mind, which is in the image of its Creator, because it possesses in itself the exact likeness with him who dominates it and because it carries the imprint of the nature which is ungraspable by the mystery in it.[14]

The Fathers did not apply to man the term *person*, or in Greek *hypostasis*, in the same sense that the word had in

[14] Gregory of Nyssa, *op. cit.*, chapter XI, 156a.

their trinitarian theology. In that theology, *person* meant a sign of the absolute and ineffable difference in the total communion of life and identity of nature of the Father, Son, and Holy Spirit. Nonetheless, their conception of the image of God in man is certainly, as V. Lossky remarked, the closest notion in ancient Christian thought to the modern idea of the human person.[15] Conceived as liberty, that is, royal sovereignty over oneself and the world, the *imago Dei* is also and especially "the ability that man has to transcend himself in order to participate in God."[16] The image of God is that which makes man a mysterious being, "open toward the On High," according to John Meyendorff's expression. Man is called to go beyond himself in communion with God. The image of God in man is not *something*, nor it is to be identified with one or another virtue. It rather indicates the dynamic orientation of humanity toward a transcendence where man receives his fullness. The Fathers expressly extend this vision to all humanity since it concerns the *one anthrôpos* created in the image of the Only-Begotten Son, himself being the substantial image of the "one God and Father of all, who is above all and through all and in all" (Ep 4:6), according to the verse the Fathers have never ceased to meditate on. All men and women are called to grow toward the likeness of God which is communion, through the Spirit, with the God-Man who by becoming man, assumed humanity in such a way that no human person is excluded. He opened to all the possibility of restoring in Himself the unity of all human persons.

In this spiritual and eschatological perspective, the accent is put on the unity, even the fundamental identity, of men and women. Gregory of Nazianzus summed up this

---

[15] V. Lossky, *A l'image et à la ressemblance de Dieu* [in English: *In the Image and Likeness of God*, St. Vladimir's Seminary Press, Crestwood, N.Y., 1974], Paris, 1967, p. 137.

[16] J. Meyendorff, *Initiation à la théologie byzantine* [in English, *Byzantine Theology: Historical Trends and Doctrinal Themes*, Fordham University Press, New York, 1974, p. 142], Paris, 1975, pp. 185-87.

conception when he cried out, "The same Creator for men and for women, for all the same clay, the same image, the same death, the same resurrection."[17] Here the differences seem secondary. For Gregory of Nyssa, they become quite secondary in relation to the creation of the one united humanity. In order to harmonize his vision of the unity of humankind, in the beginning as well as at the end, with the biblical affirmation of the creation of the human couple, he arrived at the hypothesis of a double creation. First of all and in a logical and non-temporal sense, there was the creation of *anthrôpos* in the image of God, in man's unity and wholeness. Afterwards, there was the creation of divided humanity, in two sexes, having in view a procreation made necessary by the introduction of death resulting from sin and the Fall. As the vehicle for transmitting life, sex appears at the same time tied to death and to the sinful condition of humanity after the Fall.

The double-creation hypothesis belongs to Gregory of Nyssa and has not been taken up generally by the patristic tradition. It seem to me, however, to be meaningful in relation to certain tendencies common to this tradition as well as to some problems that it has left unresolved. This hypothesis illustrates the difficulty of harmonizing the great affirmation of the unity of humanity with the concrete diversity of human beings and especially with the otherness of men and women. Is not this otherness fated to be overcome at the end of time, as certain texts of Maximus the Confessor seem to indicate, an end of time that has already been inaugurated in the life of the Church?

The double-creation hypothesis raises another question that concerns the nature of male-female otherness. Is this otherness to be reduced to biological differentiation, to the "little difference" with major social consequences, to use the language of certain contemporary feminists, both masculine and feminine? Does not Gregory's hypothesis

---

[17] Gregory of Nazianzus, *Discourse* 37, 6.

place the sexual differentiation outside of the *imago Dei*? Robbed of any real spiritual meaning, is not the otherness of men and women reduced to a functional difference in relation to procreation? This reductionist tendency also colors the interpretation of "Be fruitful and multiply . . ." (Gn 1:28) when it is seen only from the perspective of a numeric growth, a multiplication of human beings.

Does not such an interpretation unduly restrain the meaning of the biblical benediction which invites the man and the woman to have dominion over the whole earth? Are they not called to subdue everything to a properly human finality, to "cultivate" the earth according to the double meaning of the word which has been brought out by a recent translation of the Hebrew text? The man and the woman are called both to make the earth bear fruit and to offer those fruits *in worship*, as an offering to the Creator. Together they have the vocation of being the kings and priests of the creation, of being the celebrants of the cosmic liturgy.

On other points, the modern Christian reflection has the duty, it seems to me, to extend and complete, not to deny, the patristic meditation on the texts of Genesis. By emphasizing the unity of all human beings according to God's design as well as on the common vocation of all human persons, the Fathers affirm the spiritual equality of men and women. They have the tendency, however, of expressing this equality in terms of a moral and psychological unity that shapes the female according to the mold of the male.

Gregory of Nyssa, Basil the Great, and John Chrysostom unanimously celebrate the strong woman (do they mean she is *virile*?) who shows herself to be equal, and superior, to men in the battles for the faith. For them, however, femininity remains a synonym for weakness. Their thinking on this point only progressively and with difficulty detaches itself from the ideal of virile perfection they inherited from the wisdom of antiquity.

It was even more difficult for them to draw from men and women's spiritual equality the conclusions that seem to us to be required in today's society and families. Only Clement of Alexandria seems to have leaned in this direction when he affirmed that beings "that have the same life, grace, and salvation are called to the same manner of being."[18] His conclusion is nonetheless quite exceptional. For the Fathers, the subordination of the human female to the human male was in keeping with the law of nature, even though mutual love in the glow of divine charity tempers the rigor of this law. It is even possible that the spiritual order can reverse the law of nature and make the Christian woman her husband's guide. And finally, by opting for consecrated virginity, which means to jump ahead to the end of time and place herself in the *eschaton*, a woman can escape from the guardianship of father and husband. We are nevertheless left with a certain ambiguity or, at least, a double question: Why does the consecrated virgin escape from the law of nature? Is it because she represents an asexual humanity or because she has integrated her sex, her femininity, into the divine image? Why is it not the same for the married woman who assumes her sexuality in the context of her human and Christian vocation, a vocation that is integrated into the personal dimension of her life? The answers to these questions do not appear clearly in the thinking of the Fathers. We can even ask if such questions were ever really asked.

We need to note one last feature of the patristic meditation on the first creation story of man: its trinitarian context, a feature that marks all the Fathers' theology, ecclesiology and anthropology. By the fact of being trinitarian, patristic anthropology has been oriented in a direction that has found some interesting and fruitful development in the modern Orthodox reflection on men-women relations and on the vocation of womanhood in the Church. Discern-

[18] Clement of Alexandria, *Le Pédagogue* [The Instructor] 1, 4, quoted by O. Clement from *Sources Chrétiennes*, Paris, 1982, pp. 262-63.

ment, however, must be exercised in pursuing this line of thought.

Genesis 1:26 uses the plural saying "Let *us* make man in *our* image, after *our* likeness . . ." The Fathers were always very attentive to the plural of the divine decision and saw in it an allusion to the trinitarian Council: a spiritual reality whose most perfect iconic expression is no doubt the famous icon of the Holy Trinity of Andrei Rublev.[19] The God in whose image and likeness humankind was created is neither a solitary monarch, nor the Monad, the impersonal One of the pagan philosophies. He reveals himself as Trinity: Father, Son, and Holy Spirit. In the trinitarian perichoresis, that communion of life of the Three who are One, the opposition between unity and plurality is superseded. God's being is relation, personal love. According to the expression of a contemporary Orthodox spiritual master, God is "Love without limits."[20]

Man is not God, but he is in God's image and oriented toward his likeness. "What is given from all eternity in God, that is, Unity's unique mode of existence as Person in communion, man is called to bring into being in Christ, in the diverse flames of the Spirit." The idea of human vocation as a trinitarian life is but a germ in the patristic interpretation of Genesis 1:26, but it has been developed more extensively in modern Russian religious thinking as well as in some Orthodox thinkers who have been influenced by that school, such as the Frenchman Olivier Clement. In the *new* community whose womb is the Church, men and women are called upon to grow and develop together, being oriented towards each other, not against each other or in competition. Men and women are to have

---

[19] A Monk of the Eastern Church, "L'Icône de la Trinité de Roublev" [Rublev's Icon of the Trinity], *Irénikon* 26, 1983, pp. 133-40 and *Contacts* 116, 1981, pp. 351-57; Paul Evdokimov, *L'Art de l'icône*, Bruges, 1970, pp. 205-16.

[20] A Monk of the Eastern Church, *Amour sans limites* [Love without Limits], Chevetogne, 1971; *Jésus, Simples regards sur le Sauveur* [Jesus: Simply Looking at the Savior], Chevetogne, 1959, p. 144.

many-sided relationships of friendship, of conjugality, according to the criteria of reciprocal service and mutuality. Such relationships reflect the communion-in-distinction of the Son and the Spirit as they do the common work of actualizing the Father's will.

Can we go even farther? From Vladimir Soloviev to Paul Evdokimov, Russian religious thinkers have thought they could discern inside the divine sphere a bipolarity analogous to the tension between the masculine and the feminine inside humanity. For Russian sophiology, represented in France by Fr. Bulgakov,[21] the uncreated wisdom, *Sophia*, the archetype of the divine Wisdom, of the world and of humanity in God, is a feminine essence capable of being realized in a hypostasis, a person: it is a "hypostasibility." For Paul Evdokimov, who was more in the patristic line (than Bulgakov), the Holy Spirit is the divine archetype of a femininity defined as dynamism of life and sanctification, as hypostatic, personal, maternity. The Mother of God, the Theotokos, is the personification of this holy womanhood on the human level.[22] More recently, an American Orthodox theologian, Fr. Thomas Hopko, formulated and systematized these analogous speculations in which he found arguments against the ordination of women to the ministerial priesthood. According to Fr. Hopko, the priesthood is christic: "the priest represents Christ . . . while the key to the vocation of women is mystically and theologically found in the Person of the Holy Spirit."[23]

Fr. Hopko rejects any relation between his ideas and those of Soloviev and Bulgakov's sophiology, and they are rather different in form and substance, but they do have

---

[21] S. Bulgakov, The Wisdom of God, New York, London, 1937, in French *La Sagesse de Dieu*, Lausanne, 1983.

[22] Paul Evdokimov, "Le Saint Esprit et la Mère de Dieu" [The Holy Spirit and the Mother of God], *La Nouveauté de l'Esprit* [The Newness of the Spirit], pp. 253-78.

[23] Thomas Hopko, "On the Male Character of Christian Priesthood," in *Women and the Priesthood*, St. Vladimir's Seminary Press, 1983, pp. 97-134.

certain points in common. Firstly, both points of view derive from a noble and generous vision of femininity. Secondly, they ground the basis of the otherness of men and women in God, not just in his will but in a reality that belongs to his being, to his person, to his personal Uni--Trinity. Finally, the two lines of thought introduce a feminine symbolism into God-language which has largely been dominated by a masculine symbolism in the Judæo--Christian tradition, although scholars have shown that a feminine symbolism is not totally absent. This aspect must be rediscovered. Having said that, we are interested in the *theologoumena*, the personal opinions, of Paul Evdokimov and Fr. Hopko only in so far as they are in line with the interpretation, being enlightened by the trinitarian mystery, of the biblical affirmation of the creation of man in the image and likeness of God. This is in fact the way the Fathers of the Church interpreted things.

But aside from this common point of departure, the theologoumena of modern Orthodox theologians about the femininity of the Holy Spirit diverge from the spiritualist and personalist line which, as Vladimir Lossky stressed, is the foundation of the Greek Fathers' anthropology. For these Fathers, the sexual differentiation comes second to the creation of man as a unity and is in fact secondary. In the eyes of modern interpreters, sexual differentiation is essential and grounded in God's very being.

From Gregory of Nyssa to Maximus the Confessor, the Fathers accentuate the ontological unity of *anthropos* and the communion of persons, in a trinitarian perspective: unity of one humanity in its totality created in the image and toward the likeness of God, a transcendent God, One in Three Persons, an ineffable Spirit going far beyond all concepts borrowed from human experience. Beyond all the divisions coming out of that experience, especially beyond the "division male-female . . . added later and without any relation to the divine archetype," as Maximus the Confessor wrote,[24] each human person, and all together, are called upon to participate in the divine trinitarian life in order to form one single body and people. This is their ultimate destiny. In this eschatological perspective, sexual differentiation is not denied but is tied to this present age and is destined to be transcended, surpassed, in the Kingdom to come. By his baptism, the Christian has already received the firstfruits, the token, of this Kingdom where the male-female differences will be relativized.

This personalist spiritualism, however, carries within it a risk of deviation, that of an ascetical angelism which both despises and fears sexuality. Because women are for men the figures of sexual eros, they risk being swallowed up in this scorn and fear. Since the only legitimacy for sexual union is procreation, all spiritual meaning is drained away. The line of thought represented by Paul Evdokimov in France and Fr. Hopko in America, having its roots in the Russian religious thought of the early 20th century, reacts against these excesses. For this point of view, especially Paul Evdokimov, the bipolarity of human sexuality is grounded in God, and as a result, femininity is given a great value. The deep spiritual significance of human love, of male-female love even in its sexual expression, is very much highlighted. Fr. Hopko also affirms that sexual bipolarity is necessary for the realization of the human community: ". . . it is the present task to show clearly that human community, as the created epiphany of the uncreated Trinity, is made male and female so that it can realize and achieve the divine life given to it by its uncreated Archetype."[25]

These speculations, however, raise many problems. By grounding sexual bipolarity in a divine Person, are we not introducing sexuality into the very being of the transcen-

---

[24] Maximus the Confessor, *De Ambiguies*, PGT 91, col. 1305, quoted by V. Lossky, *Essai sur la théologie mystique de l'Eglise d'Orient* [in English: *The Mystical Theology of the Eastern Church*], Paris, 1944, p. 103.
[25] Thomas Hopko, *op. cit.*, p. 100.

dent God? Would this not be in contradiction with the biblical and patristic vision which opposed the pagan pantheons of masculine and feminine divinities? Would not the very notion of person be obscured by a speculation that tends to confuse the ineffable distinction of persons, in God as well as in humanity, with the difference between the sexes?

The consequences for the theology of redemption and soteriology seem equally ambiguous. Fr. Hopko affirms that ". . . the key to the vocation of women is mystically and theologically found in the Person of the Holy Spirit." This implies that the vocation of males is found in the Person of Christ. Are not Christ and the Spirit the two hands of the Father always acting together? Does that mean that there is a different salvation for men and for women? If this were so, it would be a dichotomy in complete contradiction with the great baptismal proclamations of Paul's letters (Ga 3:28 and 1 Co 12:13). Need we add that it would contradict the whole range of the Church's teaching on baptism?

Out of all these speculations, one that should be kept in mind is the need to understand first of all the spiritual significance of human sexual bipolarity and secondly the idea that something in God corresponds ineffably to what we call womanhood in our human language. From this idea-intuition comes the possibility of using feminine metaphors to talk about the absolutely transcendent God who himself, over the boundaries of his own transcendence, reveals himself to men. This possibility is seen in the Bible, in both the New and Old Testaments.[26] We find this feminine God-language applied to the Holy Spirit especially in the ancient Christian texts of the Syrian tradition. This fact may be partly explained by the feminine gender of the word *rouah* which in Semitic languages stands for both breath and spirit.

---

[26] See below section VII: The Symbolism of Masculine-Feminine Otherness in the New Covenant: Jesus and Mary.

An apocryphal gospel, the Gospel of the Hebrews, puts these words in Christ's mouth: "My mother the Holy Spirit." In the *Didascalia of the Apostles*, a document of Syrian origin from the late third century, we hear this recommendation which attests moreover to the existence of a feminine ministry: "Honor the deacon as having the place of Christ and the deaconess as having that of the Holy Spirit." The Syrian writer Aphraates recommended that we address the Holy Spirit as a "mother."[27]

In any case, these investigations reveal the diversity of interpretations suggested by the same biblical text along with the infinite richness of the Word of God. They bring us to the second story of human creation which, being older and perhaps more specifically Semitic, places greater emphasis on what distinguishes the creation of the woman from that of *adam*, the man taken from the earth (*adamah*) and into whom God, Yahweh, breaths his breath of life (Gn 2:7). Adam is not a proper name. The Hebrew word designates humankind in general. Yahweh notes that "it is not good for man to be alone." God therefore decides to find for man "a helper fit for him." Adam the man "gave names to all cattle, and to the birds of the air, and to every beast of the field; but for the man, there was not found a helper fit for him." Then follows the story of the creation or, more exactly the "making" of the woman from a rib (or from a "side," according to some translations). When Adam saw her, he cried out in wonder: "This at last is bone of my bones and flesh of my flesh; she shall be called Woman (*isha*) because she was taken out of Man (*ish*)" (Gn 2:18-24).

---

[27] According to R. Murray and other scholars, the origin of the Syrian tradition goes back to the biblical representation of the Spirit as "moving over the face of the waters" (Gn 1:2) like a maternal bird that flies above the nest of her young. See R. Murray, *Symbols of Church and Kingdom*, quoted by Bishop Seely and I. Beggiani, *Early Syrian Theology*, New York and London, 1983. We have a modern version of this tradition in A Monk of the Eastern Church, *La Colombe et l'Agneau* [The Dove and the Lamb], Chevtogne, 1979.

From this marvelous story containing a deep symbolism, both Jewish and Christian doctors have felt justified, alas, in deducing the idea of the inferiority of women and of their "natural" subordination to men. Created second after man, woman is thus secondary relative to the human male who alone is the complete and privileged human being before God in History. The aid that a woman can give to a man consists essentially in giving him children, but a masculine companion is to be preferred in all other areas. This opinion was crudely formulated by St. Augustine, even though it does not express the full range of his opinions on the subject, and taken up by St. Thomas Aquinas. This point of view, along with the misogynist interpretation of the second creation story with regards to women, has greatly weighed on Christian thinking. More than elsewhere, perhaps, the West has been marked by the overwhelming influence of the thinking of Augustine and Thomas Aquinas.

Nonetheless, nothing in the biblical story justifies these conclusions. The fact of having been created after Adam does not imply that the woman is to be subordinated to him. Is not man superior to the animals even though he was created after him? Some scholars have remarked that the verb *banah*, meaning "to edify, construct," is used to describe the divine creative act in reference to woman. Different verbs are used to describe the creation of matter and the animals (*bara*) and the creation of man, *adam* (*yatsar*). *Banah* introduces a notion of refinement, of perfecting, into the act of creation.[28] Taken from man (*ish*), the woman (*isha*) is not inferior to him but rather "interior" to him, as Adam's cry of wonderment expresses. In the woman, the man (*ish*) recognizes himself completely while at the same time recognizing that she is different from him. The difference is indicated by the letter *a* in the

[28] R. de Tryon-Montalembert, "Quelques pistes de réflexion sur l'homme et la femme dans la pensée juive" [Some Lines of Reflections on Man and Woman in Jewish Thought], *Contacts* 100, 1977.

word *isha*. She is the *other* who is yet similar to him. This is the *good distance, pure otherness*, without which there is no meeting between persons, as Emmanuel Levinas has written.[29] The woman is situated in dialogue with man. She is his "helper" standing before him, sometimes against him (*ezer ke-nequendo*). She is the one who brings to man another word, and he recognizes that he needs that other word. He felt his solitude even after having named and known the non-human creatures. He was still not satisfied.[30] It is in their dialogue that men and women are called to humanize themselves and the world. Man, with the help of woman, is called to this work of humanizing the earth, of submitting it to God's reign, to a reign oriented toward the coming of the Kingdom of God. Without this help, man could not rise to his vocation, but we must give to the word *help* (in Hebrew, *ezer*) the meaning that it has in the Old Testament where there is no sense of inferiority or subordination. Sometimes it even is used to refer to the help given by a superior. In many cases, it refers to Yahweh who comes to the aid of his people.

Here we have the man and the woman of the second creation which is a completion of the first. Man and woman are ineffably different but nonetheless "one single flesh" (Gn 2:24), one single humanity, called to dialogue, to work in a reciprocity of love and service so as to prepare the coming of the Kingdom of God thanks to their common obedience. The two creation stories have different intentions, but they carry the same revelation of one single order of creation: Alpha oriented "from the beginning" towards the Omega which will be its fulfillment. In the fullness of the grace of Christ, Savior of men and women, the initial orientation of the human couple reveals itself

---

[29] E. Levinas, *Le temps et l'autre* [Time and the Other], Paris 1983.

[30] R. de Tryon-Montalembert, *art. cit.*, and E. Levinas, "Le judaïsme et les femmes" [Judaism and Women], *Difficile liberté* [Difficult Liberty], Paris, 1984, p. 57.

fully; in that grace, it expands and is drawn towards its perfection.

The Story of the Fall: Genesis 3

The story of the Fall is told in a language rich in symbols, a language that is, however, difficult to understand. The existential meaning of its message, on the other hand, is quite simple: the empirical world we live in is not the harmonious creation that God intended. Ours is a dislocated and broken world. This disruption affects in particular the relationships between men and women, that is, their interior world. After the Fall, men and women collide in the very heart of the desire that brings them together. God said to the woman, ". . . your desire shall be for your husband, and he shall rule over you" (Gn 3:16). Hostility and mistrust comes between them and separates them. This internal catastrophe goes hand in hand with a cosmic catastrophe: the man and woman were expelled from Paradise. Sent out of Eden, the man has to cultivate the soil "in the sweat of your face," a soil that produces "thorns and thistles." For the woman, "I will greatly multiply your pain in childbearing." At the root of this disaster, we have sin described as disobedience to God, as a lack of confidence in him. The result is that the man and woman's hearts are opened to the suggestions of the Enemy, the Serpent. The rupture of communion between humanity (represented by the woman) and God is the source of disintegration and of death.

God is nonetheless faithful. Sin has disoriented humanity all through history in which men and women are literally lost. Even so God watches over humanity and "did not cease to do all things until you had brought us up to heaven," in the words of the opening lines of the Byzantine eucharistic prayer. The Fall inaugurates the *history of salvation*, and the feminine principle in humanity is called upon to work for the realization of that salvation just as that same feminine principle was associated with the first sin. The woman personifies an immanent energy in humanity which is opposed to the power of evil as personified in the serpent. There will be hostility between its descendants and those of the woman. The serpent will wound the woman's descendants in the heel, but the son born of the woman will crush its head.

It has often happened that exegetes, wanting to promote a misogynic interpretation of this story, only retain Eve's guilt and through her, that of all women. Deceived by the serpent, the woman is accused of being guilty of both stupidity and culpable weakness. Because she is the object of masculine concupiscence, the woman incarnates temptation: "Woman is temptation and temptation is woman. . . . Woman is the gate of hell," according to Tertullian who nonetheless loved his wife. Maybe he said that because he loved her too much. Tertullian is part of a choir of accusers whose members include such known names as those of St. John Chrysostom and St. Jerome. What seems strange though is that they too appreciated feminine friendship. Exiled far from Constantinople, the patriarch John Chrysostom wrote to the deaconess Olympia, and Jerome dedicated his works to Paula and Eustochia, two aristocratic Roman ladies who followed him to Palestine.

A misogynist discourse is certainly one of the common themes of moralistic rhetoric which characterizes the end of antiquity. But the interpretation of the Genesis story which places the full responsibility for a shared sin on the shoulders of Eve goes back much farther. Such an interpretation is evidence of the initial rupture that characterizes the fallen world. "The only milieu that unites is God," according to Fr. Teilhard de Chardin. Separated from God, men and women are tragically separated despite those fleeting "little eternities of orgasm," instants of psychosomatic fusion that Kierkegaard spoke about. The sought after dialogue is interrupted, and the search must always start all over again. The communion that makes itself felt in certain paradisiac moments never comes into full reality.

> The Creator himself is excluded from his creation, but he never ceases to give us the altogether good life that is mixed with death, not only in the physical sense but also in the global and everyday meaning of the word. Worry and hatred find a place in our very being, and the separation from God becomes a separation between men, and between men and women.[31]

Nonetheless, hope is still there, hope that is a theological virtue, that "little hope" which, according to Charles Péguy, God finds so surprising in man. Such hope echoes from between the lines of the story of the Fall. It was transmitted by Israel to the new people of God on pilgrimage, and woman is the carrier of the hope. Guilty and always thinking about the lost paradise, Eve announces Mary whose son carries the name *Emmanuel*, "God with us."

The Symbolism of the Otherness of Men and Women in the New Covenant: Jesus and Mary

The ecclesial tradition sees in Jesus (the Christ, "born of the Holy Spirit and the Virgin Mary," in the words of the Nicene Creed) the one in whom the promise of Genesis 3:15 is realized. He is the son of the woman, the strong man who crushes the head of the Serpent. He is the heavenly *Adam*, and as the pascal icon in the Orthodox Church proclaims, he descended into hell to deliver the earthly *Adam*. Moreover, this is the perspective, that of the light of the mystery of Christ, in which the Fathers interpreted the stories of creation and the Fall. They did not separate the order of creation from the order of salvation. The first is fulfilled in the second, but at the same time, salvation radically transcends creation.

---

[31] O. Clement, "La vie vivante" [The Living Life], *Contacts* 126, 1984, p. 182.

In line with this first approach to the theme of the otherness of men and women and taking into account the Christian interpretations of the stories of the Creation and the Fall in their unity and diversity, I would like to indicate certain other lines of research and set out some pointers along a road of exploration that needs to be pursued.

According to an outline that might appear arbitrary–but then every outline is somewhat arbitrary–I would like successively to draw attention to the following themes: 1) masculine-feminine symbolism in the persons of Jesus and Marie; 2) the attitude of Jesus as he spoke to men and to women; 3) man and woman in the teaching of St. Paul, as seen through his pastoral activity and his vision of the Church.

In relation to the first theme, we have the question of the meaning of Christ's masculinity and the conclusions to be drawn eventually from an elucidation of this meaning for the understanding of the otherness of men and women. This kind of questioning is relatively recent. It must be said first of all that the Fathers of the Church were not very interested in the fact that Jesus was *aner* or *andros*, that is, of the masculine sex. They were interested rather in the proclamation of his full humanity, that is, the fact that he was *anthrôpos*. Because of the poverty of certain languages, like French and English, however, these two categories, masculinity and humanity, are sometimes confused. This confusion is, however not without meaning.

The prologue of St. John's gospel proclaims that "the Word became flesh." As the commentary in the TOB translation of the Bible explains, the word "flesh" (*sarx*) designates the totality of man, the human condition in its wholeness as it is affected by that weakness which leads from birth to death. It was "by death" that Christ "trampled down death."

The whole christological debate of the first Christian centuries is situated in this context: the spiritual necessity of proclaiming the union, in the person of the Word, of the divine and the human in its totality so that humanity might be saved. According to the patristic saying, "What is not assumed [by the God-Man] is not saved."

Pilate said "Here is the man [*anthropos*]," in presenting Jesus crowned with thrones (Jn 19:5). The Son of God assumed, by self-renunciation–kenotically–the fullness of what is human in order to save it through his sacrificial love, even to death. In this total humanity which he mercifully assumed, Christ is the true neighbor of every man, whether Jew or Samaritan, as the patristic exegesis of the parable of the Good Samaritan underlines. And without fear of distorting the meaning of this exegesis, we can add the Christ is the neighbor of every man as well as every woman. In Romans, St. Paul says, ". . . the grace of God and the free gift in the grace of that one man [*anthropos*] Jesus Christ abounded for many" (Rm 5:15). In line with the contemporary Jewish interpretation, the whole of Romans 5 uses Adam as a name standing for the whole of humankind and not as a proper name applied to a masculine individual. Adam is the figure of "the one who was to come," Jesus who is designated as the "New Adam" and brings together in his person the new humanity, the new community of which he is both the firstfruits and the head. And that community is the Church where "there is neither male nor female," where all baptized people, all men and women who through baptism "have put on Christ," and "are all one in Christ Jesus" (Ga 3:28).

Jesus was nonetheless also man in the specific sense of *aner*. The sexual bipolarity is part of the human condition that he fully assumed. Jesus Christ "born of a woman, born under the Law" (Ga 4:4) was unquestionably a human being of the masculine sex. Beyond its general kenotic meaning in the framework of the Incarnation, does this masculinity have a theological meaning, a meaning that can enlighten the masculine-feminine symbolism in its application to concrete human persons? These are difficult questions which are being asked today in the highly charged emotional atmosphere surrounding the debate about the ordination of women to the ministerial priesthood. Without taking a position on the fundamentals of this problem which itself has many aspects and perhaps different solutions, I would like to put forward some suggestions.

First of all, Jesus' masculinity is a fact attested to by the Scriptures and by the Tradition of the Church. It seems difficult to deny to this masculinity all significance even if such significance was not clearly set out by patristic thinking. The divine Word became human in a young, masculine Jew. We can leave aside Jesus' Jewishness, which is also not without meaning, since it is not directly relevant to the subject at hand. We can, however, establish a link between Christ's masculinity and his relation to the heavenly Father for we know that according to the New Testament tradition, Jesus is and claimed to be the Son of God. In this perspective, does not sexuality become the sign of a *totally other* reality which infinitely goes beyond sex itself? In biblical language, as well as in Christian theological language, masculinity designates the transcendent God without attributing to him any real sexual or gender characteristics. In the trinitarian theology of the Fathers, the terms *Father, Son,* and *Holy Spirit* aim at the mystery of the relations of origin which precisely have no sexual connotations in the sense of genital sexuality. This is equally true for the Old Testament and the New Testament where Yahweh and Christ are called the Bridegroom of the people of Israel and of the Church, respectively. These metaphors evoke a relation of faithful and merciful love, and as they refer to Christ, they imply an intimate union, a communion in which Christ gives himself, communicates his life, to those men and women who believe in him. In the perspective of this communion, the predominance of a masculine symbolism for speaking about the transcendent God has a deep meaning, as Olivier Clement has noted in a meditation on the Our Father.[32]

---

[32] O. Clement, "Eglise et vie quotidienne" [The Church and Daily Life], *Contacts* 125, 1984, pp. 82-111.

In contrast to certain Eastern mystery religions which are dominated by a feminine symbolism, the masculine symbolism means that the Gospel of Christ, in line with the Old Testament, invites us to a meeting, to personal encounters. This vision does not imply a return to the uterine depths of the divinity or a depersonalized fusion in some totality but rather a meeting-communion. This meeting-communion, though it implies a distance, is between the human person and the personal God as well as between brothers and sisters in God. The predominance of masculine symbolism in the Bible, in which the experience of a patriarchal society has certainly played a role, does not however exclude from the Judæo-Christian tradition the application to God and to Christ of metaphors that are either feminine or have no reference to sexuality. The Bible speaks of Yahweh's "womb of mercy," *rahamim*, in the uterine meaning of the word, and witnesses to the Lord's maternal tenderness (Is 49:15). Jesus referred to himself as a hen who would like to gather her chicks together (Mt 23:23). He is the "good shepherd", "the door for the sheep." In his sacrifice, he identifies himself as the pascal lamb, "the Lamb slain before the foundation of the world," as Revelations calls him (Rv 13:8), but he is also the "sheep that before its shearers is dumb" (Is 53:7).

Thus, if it appears to be in line with the scriptural and ecclesial tradition to give a meaning to Christ's masculinity, which is a historical fact, this meaning is first of all theological, that is, it refers back to the transcendent relation between the heavenly Father and his only-begotten Son and then to soteriology: in Christ, Emmanuel, the transcendent God, one of the Holy Trinity is with us and saves us. This masculine language, used in speaking about the transcendent God who is also the incarnate God in the man (*aner*) Jesus, does not exclude the use of feminine metaphors. But is it not especially arbitrary and at least risky to apply this theological symbolism to the human sexual differentiation so as to conclude that men and women have radically different spiritual missions?

The solid grounding of this questioning seems to me confirmed by a reflection on the meaning of feminine symbolism applied to the Church as the extension of the role and ministry accorded to Mary for the realization of God's plan of salvation as it touches humanity.

It was from a woman, the Theotokos, that the divine Word took flesh, thus assuming humanity in its totality. By associating Mary with the work of salvation, the Lord did not however simply use her as a passive instrument. Likewise, she is not simply the personification of maternity as a biological function. The Orthodox tradition in particular has always insisted on the liberty of Mary's *fiat*, a liberty that is the inalienable image of God in humanity. It is this image of God, inalienable but darkened by sin, that, according to the grace of God and the divine pedagogy, shines anew in the Mother of God. This is why she is the seed and the image of the Church, of humanity saved in hope. She is not therefore just "the womb that bore" Jesus and "the breast that" he "sucked" (Lk 11:27). In the line of the righteous men and women of the Old Testament and at the same time in a radically new way, Mary is the one who heard the word of God and kept it (Lk 11:28) and who "kept all these things, pondering them in her heart" (Lk 2:19). Seen in this light, Mary is by no means the model only for women. She is the image neither of a submissive and obedient femininity, in conformity with a certain cultural stereotype, nor of an ideally beautiful human femininity, according to the æsthetic canon of a given age. She is not to be confused with the *Eternel Féminin* of the romantics even though she does correspond to a certain part of the truth that is contained in their intuition. Mary is both a woman and a human person as well as the inheritor of the women and prophetesses of the Old Testament, of Miriam, Deborah, Anne and Houlda who are associated with her in some ancient prayers for the consecration of deaconesses. She personifies human liberty restored, delivered from the ancient slavery, according to divine grace and looking forward to the Incarnation of the

Son of God. In her, because she welcomed the Word, "he has put down the mighty from their thrones, and exalted those of low degree" (the Magnificat, Lk 1:52). Mary is the figure of human hope already on the road to realization. She walks ahead of us all as the *typos* of a Christ-bearing (*christophoros*) humanity because she bears the Spirit (*pneumatophoros*): humanity *gratia plena*, purified, fruitful, sanctified by Christ and the Spirit. Her unique and personal maternity, whose dignity, however, falls on the most humble human maternity, receives by this fact a universal meaning. In her, the new humanity has the characteristics of a woman. Between Mary, the Church *in via*, and the eschatological Church, that "woman clothed with the sun" (Rv 12:1), spiritual intuition sees a mysterious link. But the feminine here becomes a sign, inscribed in the body of a woman, of the ultimate vocation of all humanity, of each man and woman: the new life of the Kingdom to which all men and women are called can only be received as a gift of God that each person can refuse or accept. Those who by the Word receive "power to become children of God," are born "not of blood nor of the will of the flesh nor of the will of man (*andros*) but of God" (Jn 1:13). They can only become children of God, however, by accepting the gift, and Mary is the sign of that acceptance. In their relation with God, all human beings are called to an attitude of free and humble receptivity, and according to biblical symbolism, the feminine symbolizes that receptivity. The humility of the Theotokos is not on the level of a feminine psychology, of a culturally conditioned way of acting. Mary is self-effacement before the God who speaks, the acquiescence of every part of her being to the Word of God. This is the ontological attitude that constitutes the very vocation of humanity and which also defines, par excellence, the true disciple of Christ, whether man or woman (Mk 3:33-35; Mt 12:47-50; Lk 11:27-28). In a sense that transcends sexual differentiation, both biological and social, the historic femininity of Mary is the fundamental axis of the human vocation.

Jesus' Dealing with Men and Women

The Christ of history was neither a political agitator nor a reformer of the traditional mores of the society in which he was born. Even though he showed himself free from many taboos and prejudices especially with regard to women, Jesus did not spend his time transgressing the customs of his time.[33] "The one thing necessary" for Jesus was the interior turning, conversion, the change of heart that opens the door of the Kingdom: "Repent, for the Kingdom of heaven is at hand." His preaching is summed up in these words, but this change of heart must be expressed in acts, whether it is expressed in ordinary or exceptional circumstances. Jesus did not encourage women to take on roles or life-styles that were considered masculine in the culture of the time. The women that Jesus associated with busied themselves with household chores and served at table. The number of such women is remarkable, and the gospels often give us their names. They were sometimes prostitutes. However, he did not send the courageous women who had been following him since Galilee back to their husbands and their pots and pans, and in fact, he praised Mary of Bethany who left domestic cares to her sister Martha. He did not separate his listeners into two categories with different vocations thereby necessitating two types of discourse. In the collection of his sayings, we find exhortations addressed to the rich, to Pharisees, and to the scribes. We find no advice given to women as women. Such advice was to appear later in the apostle Paul's writings since he was concerned about organizing the life of the communities that he founded while they were waiting for the Lord's return, a return that seemed overdue. For Jesus, the only thing that counted was the response given *here and now* to the invitation to the wedding feast of the Kingdom. This invitation was

---

[33] On this subject, see F. Quéré, *Les Femmes de l'Evangile* [The Woman of the Gospel], Paris, 1982.

addressed to everyone, men and women. Each person is called upon to assume the radical requirements of faith, love, sharing, renunciation of the egoistic self in order to enter the Kingdom of God which had arrived in the person of the Messiah, Christ the Anointed of the Lord. There is no essential difference between the confession of Martha before the resurrection of Lazarus (Jn 11:27) and Peter's later confession as related by the gospels.

Jesus fully assumed his historical condition as a masculine human being, but the values that he exalted, especially in the Sermon on the Mount, are those which according to cultural tradition, especially in the West, are supposed to be feminine: gentleness, humility (Mt 11:29), forgiveness of offenses, and nonviolence (see Mt 5). In opposition to the classical, virile, and unfeeling hero, Jesus did not attempt to put down his emotions. For instance, he wept at the tomb of his friend (Jn 11:34-35). His relations with women show no trace of domination or seduction; there is no sign either of an idealization of femininity. The exaltation of feminine purity was often hypocritical because it was a purity expected of women only and not of men. The ugly side of this exaltation was cruelty and scorn towards the prostitute and the adulterous woman. To this feminine purity, Jesus opposed the sober reminder of the common state of sin: "Let him who is without sin cast the first stone" (Jn 8:7). Jesus took care of the sick, of the physical and moral wounds of men as well as women. He healed them, put them back on their feet: the paralytic of Matthew 9:2 (Mk 2:3; Lk 5:18) just like the crippled and bent over woman of Luke 13:10-13.

Even more striking in the cultural context of the time is the fact that Jesus spoke with women. He asked them questions and allowed them to ask him questions, like the Samaritan woman at Jacob's well or the Syro-Phoenician woman of Matthew 15 and Mark 7. They were for him real persons, beings who could speak, and not merely sexual individuals; the dialogues with them were fruitful. Jesus confided the revolutionary secret about worship "in spirit and in truth" to the Samaritan woman, and the somewhat ironical conversation with the Canaanite woman ended up as a sort of preannouncement of the opening of the Gospel to the Gentiles.

Among Jesus' most intimate friends, we find women as well as men. Beside the "disciple that Jesus loved," Peter, James, and John, we have Martha, Mary of Bethany and Mary of Magdala who, on Easter morning, recognized the Master just by the tone of his voice when he pronounced her name.

This total equality of everyone, of men and women called to a personal meeting with the Bridegroom who opens to them the door of the Kingdom's bridal chamber, in no way implies a negation or a rejection of the otherness of men and women. In fact this otherness constitutes a modality of encounter. It permeates the encounter like a perfume, like a melody that is unique for each person.

The men and women in Jesus' entourage did not have stereotyped and uniform ways of behaving. The Lord respected their differences, partly linked to the sex of each person. With an infinite delicacy, he was inclined to what some would call manifestations of feminine sensitivity, even when these were disturbing. Others were scandalized by them or looked at them with an ironical eye. He did not rebuke the sinful woman when she let her tears fall on his feet, wiped them with her hair, and kissed them. She obviously put him in an embarrassing, even ridiculous, situation. He recognized the faith and the love of the woman, opposing them to the coldness of his host, Simon the Pharisee. Jesus said to the woman, "Your faith has saved you! Go in peace" (Lk 7:36-50).

Mary of Magdala in the garden on Easter morning, rightly or wrongly identified with the anonymous sinful woman at Simon's supper, "threw into the world an emotion that we still feel," according to the words of a contemporary Orthodox spiritual master. The waves of that emotion touch the hearts of men as well as women. We see the same love for Jesus break out in the masculine impetuosity of Simon Peter when he threw himself into the sea to go meet the resurrected Lord (Jn 21:7).

Jesus neither scorned nor feared sexuality. He performed his first miracle at the wedding at Cana, and his presence changed the earthly joy of conjugal union into the anticipated joy of the messianic Kingdom. Likewise, the woman who is joyful after the suffering of childbirth is mentioned in the farewell address as a sign of the glory of the age to come, a glory that must first endure the afflictions of the present time (Jn 16:21).

All the richness that has its origin in human sexual bipolarity is found in the gospels, but it is transfigured by Jesus' glance. In that bipolarity, he sees the signs of the Kingdom. We are very far, however, from a rigid and structural opposition of the masculine and the feminine. Just as the call to enter into the Kingdom through Jesus the door is for all men and women, so is the promise of the Spirit.

"All these with one accord devoted themselves to prayer, together with the women and Mary the mother of Jesus, and with his brothers" (Ac 1:14). This is the first Christian community, the embryonic Church, as we hear about it in the Acts of the Apostles. In this little group, the prophecy of Joel is fulfilled, a prophecy that Peter recalls on the day of Pentecost:

> And in the last days it shall be, God declares, that I will pour out my Spirit upon all flesh, and your sons and your daughters shall prophesy, and your young men shall see visions, and your old men shall dream dreams; yea, and on my menservants and my maidservants in those days I will pour out my Spirit; and they shall prophesy (Ac 2:17-18).

The Teaching of the Apostle Paul

The apostle Paul has been the principal target of those who accuse the Christian Churches of having taught the subordination of women to men and of having thereby sort of canonized this subordination. The accusation is based on certain passages in Paul's letters which are set apart and isolated from the context of Paul's vision of the Church: a vision of *koinônia*, communion of all men and women who, by the Spirit, have in baptism been immersed into the death of Christ in order to participate also in his resurrection.

The targeted texts are mainly the following: 1) Ephesians 5:21-32 which establishes an analogy between the union of husband and wife in marriage with the union between Christ and the Church; 2) 1 Corinthians 11:3-15 which seems to establish a descending hierarchy from God to man and from man to woman; 3) 1 Corinthians 14:34 with the famous injunction "the women should keep silent in the churches," an injunction that is taken up again in 1 Timothy 2:11-15. A detailed exegesis of these texts would go beyond the limits of this study. The Catholic scholar, Annie Jaubert, has in any case already done this, and her conclusions have been taken up and developed by Professor Veselin Kesich, of St. Vladimir's Orthodox Seminary, Crestwood, New York. I shall make full use of the works of these two New Testament scholars.[34]

We must first of all note the specific character of these texts. They are pastoral exhortations addressed to a precise milieu that the apostle intends to evangelize. These men and women have been baptized into Christ, but they have still to learn, over and over again, to live according to the Spirit of Christ in the concrete conditions of their existence, to harmonize their lives with the appeal that they have received, "with all lowliness and meekness, with patience, forbearing one another in love" (Ep 4:1-3). This naturally concerns in particular the very important realm of marriage and conjugal life. Just like every other part of Christian existence, interwoven as it is with diverse

[34] A. Jaubert, *Les Femmes dans l'Ecriture* [Women in the Scriptures], Paris, 1974, p. 44; V. Kesich, "Saint Paul Anti-feminist or Liberator?" in *St. Vladimir's Theological Quarterly* 3, 1977, pp. 123-47.

personal relations, marriage must be set in the context of the mystery of Christ. Therefore, instruction concerning marriage is preceded by a general exhortation in which the following statements must be understood: "be filled with the Spirit . . . singing and making melody to the Lord with all your heart . . . Be subject to one another out of reverence for Christ" (Ep 5:19-21). By omitting this prologue, we run the risk of misinterpreting all of St. Paul's teaching on marriage. In a climate of joy and community praise, in the Holy Spirit who fills and assembles all members of the community, the apostle calls upon the Christian community, a *eucharistic* community, to give thanks together; the members are to practice a mutual submission in the respect of Christ which implies also reciprocal respect. It is true that for St. Paul, this reciprocal respect does not imply totally symmetrical relations between man and woman, but must we not take into account the historical milieu in which those Christians found themselves? In a Jewish and hellenistic milieu, the submission of the wife to the husband went without question as the foundation of the family order, and in turn, of the order of society. No doubt, the preaching of the Gospel introduced into this milieu a radically new spirit. At the same time, that Gospel had to be *inculturated* without betraying it. This is a problem that all missionaries encounter. Paul had to take into account the tradition, mentalities, and particular historical conditions of his hearers. The first Christians were in fact accused, and not without reason, of disturbing the social order. Paul himself feared the excesses of an extravagant and anarchical charismatic spirit. His preoccupation was to show that the God of love "is not a God of confusion but of peace" (1 Co 14:33). Now in the mentality of the men and women to whom Paul addressed his teaching, the notion of order always and necessarily implied a hierarchy. We thus have the recommendation, "Wives, be subject to your husbands as to the Lord." The notion of submission referred to established and accepted ideas, but the analogy with the mystery of Christ introduces a new dynamic: "In marriage, Paul celebrated the figure of the reestablished unity between God and his people. In regards to man, he expressed requirements that were as inconceivable to the Jews as to the Greeks."[35] The husband must imitate Christ who gave himself for the Church. Being the superior according to the ideas of ancient culture, the husband must give himself up totally for his wife. Far from being oppressive or alienating, his function must be liberating like Christ's function is to liberate. "Cut to the quick in his masculine egoism as the *first sex*, the husband is finally, like Christ, in the position of a servant." The analogy with Christ does not in any way imply, however, that Paul felt that the husband must be "the savior" of his wife. The apostle hastened to add, "This is a great mystery, and I take it to mean Christ and the church." There is only one single Savior for husbands as for wives.

We have in 1 Corinthians 11:3-15 an obscure text, rather difficult to interpret in detail, but its main purpose is clear: in a given area, the social conventions must be respected. These required that women wear a veil in order to safeguard the honor of the husband. This social convention was justified by a laborious reasoning which has given rise to different interpretations and which seems to imply a hierarchy: the man (*aner*) is "the image and the glory of God," and this seems to mean that he is called to manifest humanly divine grandeur and holiness. "The wife is the glory of man." means that the wife's vocation is to radiate this same divine glory, but the husband is for her a sort of mediator. Nonetheless, in order to counterbalance and correct this hierarchical conception which reflects the ideas of the times, the apostle added right away: "Nevertheless, in the Lord woman is not independent of man nor man of woman; for as woman was made from man [reference to Gn 2], so man is now born of woman. And all things are from God." We thus have the proclamation of the mutuality of

[35] A. Jaubert, *op. cit.*, p. 44.

the husband and the wife, their reciprocity in difference, according to a circular movement which excludes any idea of ontological subordination.

1 Corinthians 14:34 is considered by some exegetes to be a latter addition to Paul's original text. However that may be, this passage does not aim at condemning women to silence in worship services of the Church. Such an interpretation has been held by many for a long time, but it is in contradiction with chapter 11 of the same letter. How could Paul, on the one hand, invite women to dress decently when they prophesy in the Church assembly and on the other, forbid them to speak? The famous *mulieri taceant*, as understood by John Chrysostom, was aimed only at the disorderly chatter of certain women or perhaps the excessively exuberant manifestations of their piety that risked creating disorder.

All these pastoral recommendations must be set back into the context of Paul's great vision of the Church. According to that vision the Church is, on the one hand, the *Body of Christ* whose members having equal dignity maintain solidarity among themselves, and on the other, the communion, *koinônia*, of persons united by the gift of the Spirit that each one has received individually. That spirit thus unites them to Christ and to each other. All the persons are distinct yet complementary, corresponding to the "economy of the Son and the economy of the Spirit," as the Orthodoxy theologian Vladimir Lossky has pointed out.[36] These two definitions of the Church flow into a unique trinitarian vision. They are intertwined in the letter to the Ephesians, an ecclesiological letter par excellence, where the two definitions find their perfect expression in the great *catholic* proclamation: "There is one body and one Spirit, just as you were called to the one hope that belongs to your call, one Lord, one faith, one baptism, one God and

---

[36] V. Lossky, "Deux aspects de l'Eglise" [Two Aspects of the Church] *Essai sur la théologie mystique de l'Eglise d'Orient* [in Englisht: *The Mystical Theology of the Eastern Church*], Paris, 1944, pp. 171-92.

Father of us all, who is above all and through all and in all. But grace was given to each of us according to the measure of Christ's gift" (Ep 4:4-7). This is the true *catholicity* (in the etymological sense of the word) of the Church: unity in Christ by the Spirit in the diversity of persons and personal vocations. It is proper also to read the baptismal hymn from Galatians in the same personalist and trinitarian perspective: "For as many of you as were baptized into Christ have put on Christ. There is neither Jew nor Greek, there is neither slave nor free, there is neither male nor female; for you are all one in Christ Jesus" (Ga 3:27-28).

In Christ, by the Spirit, all the differences that exist between humans cease to be separations that generate hatred and division. This idea will be powerfully developed later on by Maximus the Confessor.[37] Christ is "our peace" (Ep 2:14), and he totally unites those who have communion in his life in and by the Spirit. In the Church, the dislocation of humanity, the result of being separated from God, is overcome. Vivified by the energies of the Spirit, the Church is the new community where Jews and Greeks, masters and slaves, women and men are once again able to communicate by the Spirit who gives to each one the ability to speak and understand the language of the other. Nevertheless, the Church has only received the firstfruits of the Spirit and therefore is this new community only in hope: the return of the Lord is taking longer than presupposed, and "we know that the whole creation has been groaning in travail together until now and not only the creation, but we ourselves, who have the firstfruits of the Spirit, groan inwardly as we wait for adoption as sons, the redemption of our bodies" (Rm 8:22-23). The apostle knew well by his own experience what this groaning is, as

[37] Maximus the Confessor, *Mystagogia* 1. "Men, women, children are profoundly diverse in what touches race, nation, language, work, science, dignity, fortune. . . . The Church recreates them all in the Spirit. Everyone receives from the Church a unique nature which cannot be broken. . . . Thereby, everyone is united in a truly catholic manner."

he admitted painfully: "For I delight in the law of God, in my inmost self, but I see in my members another law at war with the law of my mind . . ." (Rm 7:22-23). In a world torn between the old and the new, we are to build the Church as a community where new values, a new world must be established. We must build a community where the social status of the old world becomes secondary and ultimately of no importance at all. Interpersonal relations must be reconstructed in the Spirit of Christ. Each person must recognize the other as "co-man" whether the relations are between husband and wife or master and slave. Paul is neither a conservative nor a revolutionary in the political or social sense. He calls Christian men and women to the freedom in Christ which is in the heart of an eschatological community, a community that lives in the tension of the *already* and the *not yet* but that also has the vocation to be the here-and-now sign of the final reality.

It is at this point, however, that a very serious question must be raised: to the extent that the values of the Kingdom of God transform the interpersonal relations in the Church where those values dominate the Christian consciousness, should not those changes be reflected in the social structure? Can the Good News remain without influence on the behavior and the laws of the social structure that regulate human relations? Paul, being convinced of the approaching end of the world, never seemed to have asked that question. He was not interested in the legal status of women or of slaves for that matter, which seems even more shocking. The two cannot be entirely dissociated.

Vladimir Lossky rightly insisted on the personalist aspect of Paul's vision of the Church: the Spirit assembles the baptized into one single Body and is given to *each member* "according to the measure of the gift of Christ." Each member, according to a spiritual growth that is intimately personal, is called to grow toward Christ and to attain "to mature manhood, to the measure of the stature of the fullness of Christ" (Ep 4:13). The difference is on the level of the person and not of his sex, and all together are called to the same fullness.

Likewise, the charisms that structure the Church and define its various ministries are given by the Spirit to persons and not to social or biological categories. The distribution of these spiritual gifts is not guided by the criteria that govern the distribution of ranks and tasks in the present age: race, nation, fortune, sex. There is no mention in Paul's letter of *feminine charisms* which would be different from those given to men. This idea of *feminine charisms* is very dear to certain modern defenders of femininity, especially male ones, but the use of this idea runs the risk of being a mystification. In any case, the idea cannot be based on the conception of charisms as we find it in Paul's writings. "The Spirit blows where it wills," as John also proclaims in his gospel. For Paul, men and women have received diverse personal charisms in the Church: prophecy, teaching, aid, and direction. He exhorts all, "Do not quench the Spirit but test everything." At the same time, Paul recognizes that he has the right, as apostle, to regulate the exercise of these gifts "for the common good" (1 Co 12:7). This call to order, however, concerns all the charismatics, masculine as well as feminine.

A great number of women are named in Paul's letters and in Acts as being his co-workers. Although it is sometimes difficult to know just exactly what their ministry, *diakonia*, consisted of, these women played an important role in the building up and in the life of the Pauline communities.[38] The couple Prisca and Aquilas, the wife always being named first, is the typical example of this collaboration.

One last remark: in 1 Timothy, Paul or one of his disciples acting in his name, takes up the problem of

---

[38] A. Jaubert, *op. cit.*, p. 52-53; "Le rôle des femmes dans le peuple de Dieu" [The Role of Women in the People of God] in *Ecriture et Pratique chrétienne* [Scripture and Christian Practice], Lectio Divina 96, Paris, 1978, pp. 53-68.

women's dress in the liturgical assembly which was apparently agitating some people and provoking criticisms and discussions. Repeating the injunction of 1 Corinthians 14:34 and justifying it by a rabbinic exegesis of the second creation story and of Eve's culpability, the author adds, "Yet the woman will be saved through bearing children, if she continues in faith and love and holiness, with modesty" (1 Tm 2:15). He is obviously not trying to make biological maternity women's sole vocation but rather to honor her in the function that is hers alone: bringing children into the world. The point is directed against certain heretical gnostics who disparaged sex, marriage, and procreation. In contrast, Paul associates maternity with the life of faith for the Christian woman. In and by this integration, maternity finds its true dimension and receives its salvific meaning. Nothing in this text permits us to affirm that for Paul maternity is the "totality of a woman's being" even though maternity has profoundly marked her being.

Conclusion

The Scriptures are a collection of texts from various sources and reflect all the rich variety of human situations. It is therefore not possible to find in them a simple and uniform model for the relationship between man and woman in their identity/otherness. Even less are we asked to follow *literally* the Old Testament regulations in this area, regulations that were the expression of the Word of God for a milieu that is no longer ours. We are called upon rather to grasp the spirit of these texts underneath the letter and to uncover the dynamic purpose which constitutes their unity and which also applies to our own situation. In trying to make the Scriptures a living reality for today, we do not mean to make it say simply what we want to hear. We must humbly listen to the divine Word that rings throughout its pages in order to discern the will of God for today. According to the Lord's promise (Jn 16:13), this attempt at making the Scriptures a living reality is the work of the Spirit in the Church, till the end of time.

Having confidence in the Spirit's assistance calls us to, and in no way excludes, a process of critical thinking, and one of the forms of that process is the modern scientific exegesis of the Scriptures. By analyzing the relationship between the Scriptures and the cultural milieu of a given historical period, precisely the task of historical exegesis, we are accepting and using the tools that allow us to grasp the divine intention as it took form in the language of a given culture. By discerning the divine intention through the use of new tools, we are letting ourselves be guided by that intention in a world where "we have no lasting city but we seek the city which is to come" (Heb 13:14). One of the forms of this "seeking" particularly important today is the search for new forms of men-women relationships.

Grounded on the bedrock of the Scriptures and washed of all the disfiguring historical deposits, the ecclesial tradition proclaims the unity of humanity and the equality of man and woman as *persons* in the image of the personal God, of the God who is One in three persons. By its bisexual organization, humanity is linked to the animal and plant kingdoms. Nevertheless, humanity greatly transcends these levels and integrates sexuality, being neither denied nor depreciated, into the life of the person, that is, the image of God in the truly human man. In sexual polarity, the multiple and diverse relationships between men and women receive their true dignity in the transfiguring light of the trinitarian Mystery. These relationships are human only to the degree that a respectful and loving meeting of persons takes place in and through them, a meeting of persons who recognize each other as equals in dignity: "Here is flesh of my flesh and bone of my bone!" Adam's cry of wonderment at the sight of Eve proclaims the identity of nature of man and woman. The identity of nature, understood as well as a unity of destiny and dignity, also implies, not the negation, but the subordination of life and of sexual differentiations to personal relationships that are "equality itself."[39]

If we set aside certain fundamentalist groups, the question of the inferiority of woman and her *natural* subordination to the masculine human being is hardly even debatable in Christian circles. Nonetheless, we quite willingly talk of *otherness*, of difference: a difference that designates man and woman for different and complementary social roles and spiritual missions. Under the cover of what seems obvious and despite the affirmed intention of valorizing the so-called "feminine charisms," this thesis of otherness is full of ambiguity. In practice, does it not often come round to perpetuate, under a sublimated form, the traditional subordination of women and their relegation to secondary roles under masculine control? "Woman's charism is to be the prophet of holiness," one masculine theologian affirms in weighty tones. He goes on to add, "It is only through the ministry of man that woman keeps pure her availability to the Lord, by submitting her prophetic graces to the discernment of the pastor."[40] It is of course taken for granted that the pastor is masculine.

Such a dichotomy between masculine and feminine charisms is alienating not only for woman but for man too. Is he not also called to be "the prophet of holiness"? This dichotomous conception is based on a notion of mechanistic and "organismic" complementarity according to which two forms fit together to form a whole or inside the same organism, each of two biological functions completes each other. However, such analogies cannot be applied without discernment to man-woman otherness. Human per-sons in the image of the one God in three persons, men and women do not complete each other like the parts of a whole, the parts of a mechanism, or the members of a body. This last image, already used by the apostle Paul to

---

[39] E. Levinas, *Difficile Liberté* [Difficult Liberty], p. 58.

[40] J.-M. Garrigues, postface to a work by G. Blaquière, *La Grâce d'être femme* [The Grace of Being Woman], Paris, 1981, pp. 196-205.

suggest the solidarity in the Church of the baptized in Christ, must itself be completed and set in the perspective of Christian personalism as the Orthodox theologian, Vladimir Lossky, saw so clearly. In this perspective, each human person, man or woman, constitutes a unique wholeness, the possibility of a unique and total relation with God, a unique point from which to look at the universe. Their complementarity is that of two mysterious totalities. Their otherness, therefore, cannot be defined essentially in quantifiable psychological terms: the absence or presence in various degrees of certain aptitudes or certain types of behavior in which the fullness of one fills up the emptiness of the other, and vice versa. Woman is not *necessarily* more intuitive or more interiorized than man, supposedly more reasoning and more active. Experience invalidates this type of stereotypes.

Does not the otherness of men and women designate rather the mysterious distance, which cannot be caught in concepts, "the good distance," in the words of Emmanuel Levinas, which makes dialogue between persons possible? Created in and by the *Logos*, men and women are by essence creatures of the word. They speak with and to God as well as with and to each other. As such, they are called to cooperate and to mutually grow to full development in this double dialogue that sometimes culminates, during moments of grace—"when the heart speaks to the heart"—in the silence of ineffable communion. This communion is neither the putting together of parts made to be assembled nor the fusion into an indistinguishable mass, but rather the reciprocal gift, the total welcoming of the different other: "Lord-Love, I thank you for the feminine principal that you introduced into your universe and that you intimately associated with the salvation of the world."[41]

From Eve to Mary, from the women of the Old Testament to those of the Gospel and beyond to the women martyrs

[41] A Monk of the Eastern Church, *Amour sans limites* [Love Without Limits], p. 95.

and saints of the universal Church, well-known and unknown, women have had active roles to play at important and critical moments of salvation history. These roles have been different in different ages, in various circumstances, and according to the call of God inscribed in the signs of the times.

Today, faced with the catastrophes that threaten all of humanity, perceptive spirits such as Teilhard de Chardin, Paul Evdokimov, and closer to us the woman theologian France Quéré, are calling on the energies of women to oppose the forces of dissolution and destruction. "A deep, confused, multiform, wild, or sublimated instinct attaches woman to life, to children, to nature."[42] When woman denies this instinct, she denies herself. It matters little whether her otherness is basically innate or acquired under the influence of culture and education, is openness to *the other* as well as distance. Is not her vocation, *here and now*, to try to break the circle of solitude in which Western man has enclosed himself?

Western man is "master and possessor of nature" but is also a being closed in on himself, closed in a world where the heavens no longer sing the glory of God. He seems today like the unhappy Prometheus of a civilization dominated by the hard values of virility: self-affirmation, the spirit of domination and conquest. Is it not women's role to work for a more humane civilization which gives priority to life, dialogue, and love: to the love-gift of self so that the other might exist? God is in fact the source of that kind of love; he is the "lover of man," *philanthrôpos*. Women's service, instead of being in the background, could here become prophetic, but in order to accomplish this task, women must wage a two-front war: prove their strength so as to be recognized as the equals of males and at the same time affirm their specificity which is not psychological but essentially ethical and spiritual. In fact,

---

[42] F. Quéré, *La Femme Avenir* [Femininity As the Future of Humanity], Paris, 1978, p. 121.

they must call for a profound change of heart, a conversion from the inhuman to the God-Man and to values which he incarnates. Women must call for conversion, *metanoia*, for all men and women, and an authentic Christian feminism, an "integral feminism," in the words of France Quéré, can lead the way.

Most notably among an elite of intellectuals in contemporary Russia, we discover the signs of such a feminism as it avoids the temptation to use violence, supposedly virile.[43] In a remarkable way, this feminism is linked to a renaissance of Marian veneration whose roots go deep into popular religion. It also has subtle links with the intuitions of Russian sophiology from the beginning of the 20th century, intuitions which see the world and humanity in God, and Mary, the Mother of the incarnate Word, *Theotokos*, is the revelation of those intuitions.

According to the symbolism that runs through the Holy Scriptures, the chosen people of the first Covenant and the regenerated humanity of the new Covenant, the Church, are represented by feminine figures. Mary the mother of Jesus, proclaimed *Théotokos*, and the "Woman clothed with the sun" from Revelations (12:1) are united by a mysterious link. Mary represents the first-fruits, and the "Woman clothed with the sun," represents the fulfillment of saved, sanctified, Christ-bearing, and Spirit-bearing humanity. In Byzantium as well as in Russia, the veneration for *Hagia Sophia*, Holy Wisdom, has been manifested by the numerous churches of inspiring beauty which are dedicated to it. This veneration ties the devotion to Mary to the envisioned transfiguration of the cosmos, a cosmos whose center is saved humanity. From this perspective which must be more deeply meditated on, Mary's *fiat* takes on a meaning that goes beyond her feminine individuality and whose sign is precisely her femininity. Mary brings to God the willing agreement of all humanity. She personifies

---

[43] T. Goritcheva, "Délivrée des larmes d'Eve, réjouis-toi" [Delivered from the Tears of Eve, Rejoice], *Femmes et Russie* [Women and Russia], Paris, 1980.

the human liberty restored through grace and following the divine plan of love.

During the vespers of Christmas, the Orthodox Church sings the following hymn, "Every creature made by you offers you thanks. The angels offer a hymn; the heavens a star; the Magi, gifts; the shepherds, their wonder; the earth, its cave; the wilderness, the manger: and we offer you a Virgin Mother." "We," meaning humanity, bring to God his mother, that is the place where he can become flesh. Mary is not the passive instrument of the Incarnation. She represents the people of God of the Old and the New Testaments. She accepted the Word of God, the divine Word who saves humanity by becoming fully human. Mary thus does not appear at all as the model just for women, as the archetype of feminine humility. Her humility is ontological and not psychological; it is the humility of an obedient humanity standing before God. This is how we must understand her holiness.

The Orthodox venerate the icon of the Virgin of the Sign, and this popular devotion contains a profound meaning. In her person, the *Theotokos* is the sign of the Kingdom of God come with power through the union of God with humanity, and in that humanity he took flesh. Mary is the mother, the beginning of the new humanity made fruitful by the grace of the Holy Spirit: *gratia plena*. Her full femininity is inscribed in her entire and integral humanity.

That holy humanity carries the characteristics of a woman and is a mystery on which the ecclesial community must meditate. Existentially, this mystery signifies that in relation to God, every human soul is called upon to have an attitude of humble and free acceptance of grace, and the femininity of "the humble conceiver"[44] is its symbol. But, in her body, each woman also carries the sign of this humble and free acceptance. Through Mary, through the Unique Woman, "full of grace," we all receive the call to

---

[44] Lev Gillet (A Monk of the Eastern Church), "Marie, mère de Jésus" [Mary the Mother of Jesus], *Contacts* 108, 1979, p. 364.

welcome the Word. Thus in the person of the Theotokos, the otherness of men and women is recognized, expressed in its spiritual meaning, and transcended. Following Mary, men and women are called upon, in the Church, to become those in whom and by whom Christ-Emmanuel, "God with us" comes into the world.

CHAPTER TWO

"Woman is Also Made in the Image of God"*

Although the idea of man's being created in the image of God is based on Genesis 1:26-27, it does not have in the Hebrew Bible the central place that it will acquire in patristic anthropology in relation to christology. The idea of man's creation in the image of God is like a single erratic rock at the beginning of the first covenant, an idea which was not to be developed or gone into deeply until the time of Philo of Alexandria when Jewish thought encountered Greek philosophy. To the extent that it was based on Platonism, ancient Greek thought frequently used the concept of the image to express the relation of the world to the Divine. The Fathers of the fourth century, especially Basil of Cæsarea and Gregory of Nyssa, wanting to speak as philosophers in order to "convert" philosophy to Christ found in the two verses of Genesis 1 the scriptural basis for a synthesis of biblical anthropology and the "germs of truth" (*logoi spermatikoi*) scattered throughout pagan wisdom. The Fathers meditated long and deeply on these verses, commenting on them over and over again. Philo and Origen had already begun to go this way, but the fourth century Fathers parted from these earlier writers by

* St. Basil of Cæsarea.

their concern to eliminate any traces of gnostic speculation. They rooted their anthropology in the radically new revelation of Christ.

In Greek philosophy, especially in Platonism and Neo-Platonism, the word *image* is used to designate the relation of the Divine to the world, of God the Absolute to contingent beings. It implies a likeness of nature, an ontological relation, as wells as a degradation which is determined by the degree to which being moves away from the impersonal One and descends toward the multiplicity of individual empirical beings. Nonetheless, these beings *naturally* continue to participate in the Divine to one degree or another. For those who are wise, salvation implies turning back and climbing up the ladder of beings so as to once again find the One and to allow oneself be absorbed into it. This conception influenced certain Christian mystics during the patristic era, especially Evagrius Ponticus. But from the point of view of the founders of Christian anthropology (Iræneus of Lyons and especially Basil of Cæsarea and Gregory of Nyssa), the expressions *image of God* and *being in the image of God* pointed to a radically different relationship when applied to the human being (*anthrôpos*).

According to the biblical revelation, the distance between the transcendent and personal God and his creature is infinite. This infinite distance excludes any *natural* kinship, and this is the whole point of the affirmation about the creation *ex nihilo*. God, and he alone, transcends so to speak his own transcendence by the overabundance and the sovereign freedom of his love. He alone can thus bridge the gulf that separates the creature from his Creator. What Christian theology calls grace is precisely this relationship of absolutely free love, a relationship established by the personal God who calls into existence a creature endowed with freedom. From this point of view, grace is freely given and is therefore opposed to any notion of a *natural* relationship. From another point of view—and this is precisely what is meant by the biblical affirmation about the creation of man in the image of God—grace corresponds to the fundamentally dynamic orientation of human nature as it was intended and created by God.

The Anthropology of the Fathers

Patristic anthropology is not a monolithic block. A systematic examination of the different ways of conceiving the image of God, even if limited to Basil the Great and Gregory of Nyssa, would greatly exceed the limits of this study. Although they had a common theological framework and shared both a mystical and eschatological perspective, the Fathers differed on certain points. Their thought sometimes held back and attempted to find its own way especially when confronted with Greek dualism and biblical personalism. Nonetheless, as Vladimir Lossky,[1] and Fr. John Meyendorff[2] after him, have noted, beyond these differences and hesitations, the Fathers had a fundamentally unified, theocentric, and dynamic vision of man (*anthrôpos*). In this vision, humanity in its profound nature is not, or rather does not *become* itself, except to the degree that it exists "in God" or "in grace." Man is an "existing being" open toward God and is called upon to "grow in the divine life" according to the mysterious synergy of his created freedom and of the divine Breath. This Breath in man does not come from him but is nonetheless more intimate to man that he is to himself; it is the source of all the life that is in him. Gregory of Nazianzus wrote the following commentary on the creation of man in Genesis 2:7:

---

[1] Vladimir Lossky, "La théologie de l'Image," *A l'image et à la ressemblance de Dieu*, Aubier Montaigne, Paris, 1967, pp. 123-37. In English: "The Theology of the Image," *In the Image and Likeness of God*, St. Vladimir's Seminary Press, Crestwood, N.Y., 1974, pp. 125-40.

[2] John Meyendorff, *Initiation à la théologie byzantine*, Paris 1975, pp. 185-87. In English: *Byzantine Theology*, Fordham University Press, New York, 1974, pp. 138-50.

> The Word of God took a lump of newly created earth and gave us our form with his immortal hands and gave life to that lump, for the spirit that he breathed into it is a blast of the invisible Divinity. Man was thus created from dust and breath; he is the image of the Immortal One because the spiritual nature reigns in the one as in the other.[3]

The image of God is not a *thing* or a part of man. It relates to the dynamic and global orientation of an existing being who is endlessly called upon to go beyond himself and to transcend his nature. As such, the image of God is both a gift and a task: the task of *becoming* "the likeness of God."

Anthrôpos is radically different from all other created beings by his ability to transcend himself. Gregory of Nyssa thus ridiculed the philosophers who thought they were glorifying man by saying that he was a microcosm. From the biblical perspective, man infinitely surpasses the world by the spirit of life, that divine spark, that God breathed into him. Man (*anthrôpos*) was created after all the other creatures but in line with God's eternal project, a project which sin can disturb but not totally destroy. In this divine plan, man is destined to reign over the world, explore it, and delight in the beauty of the cosmos.[4] Such a royal dignity implies a profound solidarity. In the words of Gregory of Nyssa, humanity is a "free mirror" which by turning toward God the Sun, receives and communicates light. If humanity separates itself from God and wanders away from him, man and the world are plunged into darkness.[5]

The Cappadocian Fathers did not apply the word *person*, or *hypostasis*, to man with the precise meaning that it was

---

[3] Gregory of Nazianzus, *Poëmata Dogmatica* VIII, v. 70-75, PG t. 37, col. 452.

[4] Gregory of Nyssa, *op. cit.*, chaps. II-VI.

[5] *Ibid.*, chap. XII, 164a. p. 132.

to receive in their trinitarian theology. In that theology, the word *hypostasis* meant a sign of the absolute difference within the absolute communion which is designated by the identity of nature between the Father, the Son, and the Holy Spirit. Nonetheless, the Cappadocian Fathers' conception of the image of God in man, while being somewhat different in each author, is certainly very close to the modern idea of the human person, an idea, by the way, which developed out of Christian trinitarian theology. The image is the *noûs* seen as "the properly and uniquely human ability of man to transcend himself, to participate in God."[6] It is this freedom that Gregory of Nyssa especially, insists on, that is, a sovereignty over himself and the world. The image is what makes man an mysterious being, going beyond, like God himself, every concept in which thinkers have tried to enclose him.[7] The divine Uni-Trinity is the fullness of the communion of different persons, the archetype of the restored human communion of which the Church is both the prophetic sign and seed. It is also the firstfruits of a community, a community in which every person is called to grow and develop to his or her full potential. Each person is called to this self-realization according to his own uniqueness, in communion with all other persons, while at the same time participating in the divine life.

The Fathers extend this vision quite explicitly to all humanity, and it concerns man (*anthrôpos*) created as *one* in the image of the only-begotten Son who is the substantial image of the Father. This word *Father*, after being purified of any gross anthropomorphism, must be understood as designating the transcendent and transpersonal Source of all existence. The Word, by becoming flesh,

---

[6] J. Meyendorff, *op. cit.*, p. 214.

[7] Gregory of Nyssa, *op. cit.*, chap. XI, 156a: "We are not able to know the nature of our spirit which is in the image of its Creator. This is because our spirit possesses in itself the exact likeness of Him who dominates it and because it carries the imprint of the ungraspable nature by the mystery that is in it."

"assumed humanity in a manner that does not exclude any human person but rather opens to all the possibility of restoring in Him the unity of all.[8]

A Double Creation?

It is in the perspective of the unity of humanity that we must understand Gregory of Nyssa's hypothesis about a double creation. Firstly, or rather primarily, God created man in a non-temporal logical sense; he created the total and universal man in the image of God. Then secondly and in anticipation of the Fall which was to result in death, God created a composite humanity as a multitude of sexed individuals for the purpose of procreation.

Gregory of Nyssa insisted on this unity in the following excerpt from his writings:

> When the Scriptures say that "God created man," they mean all humanity by the use of this indeterminate formula. In fact, in this creation, Adam is not even named . . . The name given to the created man is not "so-and-so" or "so-and-so" but rather the name of the universal man. For it is not in a part of human nature that the image is to be found, anymore than beauty resides in a particular quality, but it is on the whole race that the characteristic of the image is extended equally.[9]

This universal man preexists in God's thought but is not simply an ideal type. He is the concrete totality of humanity gathered together in Christ, *totus Christus*, the fullness, *pleroma*, that the Spirit will progressively bring to its full stature by working in and through human history.

According to the double creation hypothesis and in a perspective that remains marked by a certain dualism, the division of humanity into two sexes is part of God's good

---

[8] J. Meyendorff, *op. cit.*, p. 214.

[9] Gregory of Nyssa, *op. cit.*, 185b, pp. 159-60.

plan but only with an eye to the Fall. The male-female duality has no part in the divine image. Sexuality represents a sort of fall into the animal realm, a fall that precedes the fall into sin. It therefore seems like an overprint on the purely spiritual, divine image and does not seem to be penetrated by its radiance. Although sexuality is used for a transcendent purpose, that is, the ultimate deification of humanity, it is not itself transfigured. From this point of view, woman is not disparaged since she is part of humanity, but for the monk, who anticipates the end-time by his vow of virginity and his renunciation of perpetuating himself by fathering descendants, is not woman the incarnation of temptation? It may be that in his own life, Gregory of Nyssa lived the contradictions and ambivalence that his anthropology reflects. After all, he did grow up in the radiance of two women, his mother and his older sister, Macrina, and was married but had to give up married life when he became a bishop.

For Gregory, as for the vast majority of his contemporaries, regardless of their other beliefs, femininity was a synonym for weakness. We must not forget either that for the Christian elite, to which he belonged, an elite powerfully influenced by the monastic movement, virginity preserved for the Lord was objectively superior to the state of married men and women. From this point of view, it is not difficult to slide into a kind of angelism. Men and women, but especially women, best fulfill their vocation of being and becoming the image and likeness of God by transcending their sexual nature; for women, this means ceasing to be female. In the following passage, Gregory of Nyssa calls up the image and life of his sister Macrina who was for him a spiritual mother and master (*didaskalos*):

> A woman is the object of our story, if we can still call her woman. For I do not know if we can designate her

according to her nature since she was raised above nature.[10]

Basil of Cæsarea

Basil the Great's approach to this problem seems more scriptural and pastoral and less influenced by philosophical speculation. The basic personalism of the Gospel breaks through a language that remains dualistic. St. Basil responds to an imaginary woman questioner who interprets the word *man* (*anthrôpos*) in the story of Genesis 1 to mean the "husband." St. Basil rectifies the error in the following way:

> Oh no! So that no one, through ignorance, takes the word *man* to mean only the masculine sex, the Scriptures add "man and woman he created them." The wife also, like the husband, has the privilege of being created in the image of God. Their two natures are equally honorable; equal are their virtues; equal are their rewards; and alike are their condemnations. Let no woman say, "I am weak." Strength is in the soul. Since assuredly the image of God [everywhere] carries the same honor, let the virtue and good works of both the husband and the wife be equally honorable. There is no recourse for those who want to use the weakness of the body as an excuse: but, by compassion, it [the body] is capable of enduring privations and of standing firm during vigils. Are males capable of rivaling females who go through life with privations? Can males imitate the endurance of females in fasting, in their ardent prayer, in the abundance of their tears, in their zeal for good works? . . . The virtuous woman possesses what belongs to the image. Woman, you have obtained the likeness of God by goodness, patience, attentive listening, by loving others and your

---

[10] Quoted from Ruth Albrecht, *Das Leben der heiligen Makrina auf Grund der Thekla-Traditionen* [The Life of St. Macrina Based on the Thecla Tradition], Göttingen, 1986, pp. 187-88.

> brothers, by detesting evil and by dominating the passions of sin in order that the power to command might belong to you.[11]

It is remarkable that in this portrait of a woman "in the image of God," Basil seems, almost on purpose, to pile up both feminine and masculine traits: strength of soul and gentleness, patience, boldness and physical endurance. Personal holiness transcends sexuality without denying it. It is the shining forth of the "soul" or the "interior man" through the veil of the "exterior man," that is the "body." The soul and the body are not alien to each other. The person constitutes their unity: "My most inner being says to the interior man: what is exterior is not me but mine . . . The body is thus the instrument of the soul."[12]

For St. Basil, the male as well as the female are, above all, persons called to "bring themselves to their fullness," to self-realization, looking toward the glorious body which lives in the intimacy of God, in Christ: "Acquire compassion and good will so as to put on Christ. Intimacy with Him will make you intimate with God."[13]

In thus praising women and calling upon them to go beyond themselves, St. Basil knew what he was talking about. He knew Christian women who were equal or superior to many men. Like his brother Gregory of Nyssa, St. Basil recognized in his older sister, Macrina, the woman who was teacher and guide to both of them in their spiritual life.

The memory of women confessors and martyrs during the last persecutions that fell on the Christians was still fresh in their minds. In one of his sermons, St. Basil referred to Julitta, early fourth century; he puts in her mouth this exhortation in which she proclaims the com-

---

[11] Basil of Cæsarea, *Sur l'origine de l'homme, Homélie* I, 18 [On the Origin of Man, Homily], *Sources Chrétiennes*, pp. 213-15.
[12] *Ibid.*, 7, p. 183.
[13] *Ibid.*, 17, p. 211.

plete spiritual equality of the two sexes, and also implies their equal responsibility:

> We women are taken from the same matter as men. We were created in the image of God like them. Like the masculine sex, the feminine sex is capable of virtue, and this by the will of the Creator. Eve was not only taken from the flesh of Adam but also from his bone. Like men, we are called by the Creator to witness with strength, firmness and endurance.[14]

In the anthropology of the Fathers, we can see that the revolutionary idea of the equal dignity and responsibility of human persons, males and females, was opening a path through the language of a culture that saw the male as the paradigm of humanity. This change was taking place in relation not only to the biblical story of the creation but also to Galatians 3:28, as a recent study shows.[15]

Following the rabbinical exegesis, the Fathers often attributed the responsibility of the Fall firstly to Eve. Adam gave in when his turn for testing came. First in the Creation, Adam was second in sin. Did not Satan attack Eve first because woman represents God's crowning achievement? Moreover, the Fathers often draw special attention to the global infidelity of humanity, and this without stopping to compare the respective responsibility of man and woman. Thus, unfaithful Eve, seeking to make reparations, full of nostalgia for the lost paradise, whose posterity, according to the divine promise, will crush the head of the serpent, this Eve becomes for the Fathers "the symbol of humanity in its tragic quest for God," this humanity with its undying hope for redemption. It is the fulfillment of this hope that Mary sings about in the Magnificat.

---

[14] R. Albrecht, *op. cit.*, pp. 203-204.
[15] *Ibid.*, pp. 191-97.

Deification: Our Common Vocation

This sketchy outline of the theological anthropology of the Fathers concerning the *imago Dei* in woman, is only the beginning of a study that must be continued elsewhere. We have not at all dealt with the mariology of the Fathers which would also require a special study.

I have deliberately not considered the verbal excesses against human beings of the feminine sex in which the Fathers sometimes indulged. Such excesses were dictated by pastoral concern that sought to castigate a weakening of the moral fabric of society that they rightly or wrongly laid at the doorstep of women. This aggressiveness may also be the expression of unresolved personal psychological problems. Nonetheless, this kind of rhetoric, along with its excesses remains alien to their global theological and theocentric vision of humanity. Their conviction about the fundamental equality of man and woman and their common vocation of deification was in no way shaken by this sort of language. Gregory of Nazianzus expressed his conviction in a powerful statement: "The same Creator for man and woman, for both of them the same clay, the same image, the same law, the same death, and the same resurrection."[16]

Such is the thinking the Fathers have transmitted to us, a talent that Christians have often hidden in the ground and that others, not of the Church (or at least not considering themselves of the Church) have sometimes better developed and made more fruitful than Christians themselves although falling sometimes themselves into other excesses.

Even though the Fathers profoundly believed in the equal dignity of men and women as the bearers of the same image and as having been equally called to deification, that is, to an assimilation to God by grace, they did not draw the conclusion that men and women ought to

[16] Gregory of Nazianzus, *Discours*, 37, 6.

occupy identical places and functions in society, or at least in the Church. How can we explain what seems to be a lack of consistency? The reasons are certainly complex. Some are of a cultural and historical order, and today they seem in large part completely outdated; others are of a theological order founded on Scripture and Tradition and deserve a serious study. Their presentation is, however, often sketchy and unsatisfactory. Do these reasons only serve to justify, to "rationalize"—in the psychoanalytical meaning of that word—the drive of masculine power? This explanation, put forward today by certain feminists, seems to be over simplistic. With regard to the reluctance to ordain women, at least to the presbyterial ministry,[17] and beyond the alleged reasons, we certainly have the feeling that something is left unsaid, something has been left unexpressed. This may be the result of what seemed obvious in concrete living experience, that is, the intuition of a symbolism of the masculine and the feminine in their reciprocity, a symbolism whose meaning is revealed in the body as well as in a book.[18] This symbolism runs all through the Scriptures, but it has also been infected in practice by archaic taboos, by traces of Greek dualism and the fear of sex. The time seems to have come for a clarification, for a serious theological study of this complex set up, for a study to be carried out in the spirit of the Fathers that is a spirit not of petrified traditionalism but of creative faithfulness in the dynamism of the authentic Tradition.

---

[17] The ordination of women to a diaconal ministry in certain Eastern Churches cannot be historically doubted. See R. Gryzon, *Le Ministère des femmes dans l'Eglise ancienne* [The Ministry of Women in the Ancient Church], 1972; Evangelos Theodorou, "Das Diakonat der Frau in der Griechisch-orthodoxen Kirche" [The Female Diaconate in the Greek Orthodox Church], *Diaconia* 2-3, 1986.

[18] S. Herzel, "The Body is the Book in Peter Moore," *Men, Women, Priesthood*, London, 1978.

CHAPTER THREE

"Toward a New Community"*

"Looking toward the building of a new community, what *resources* can you draw from the tradition of your Church?" I would prefer to say "what *inspirations* . . . ?"

I was asked to answer this question in the name of the Orthodox that participated in the Sheffield study, but only on the eve of my departure. The speaker originally slated for the job was not able to make his presentation. I imprudently accepted the challenge, and I hope you will excuse the improvised nature of my answers. It is more of a spontaneous reaction than a text carefully prepared and meditated on.

Tradition

Thinking over the question, my attention was first of all drawn to the word *tradition* itself and to the meaning which we can ascribe to it. What is the Tradition of the Church? It is clear that we must make a distinction between the many traditions and the Tradition of the Church. This distinction is unfortunately forgotten in some quarters. It is not always easy, however, to discern where the line is to

* A paper presented at the international conference of the World Council of Churches on the subject of "The Community of Women and Men in the Church" in Sheffield, England, July 10-19, 1981.

be drawn between the two. There are popular, family, and religious traditions that are linked with various cultures, and they should in no way be despised. In non-Christian cultures, these traditions often were, and still are, the seed of the Gospel, the "word-seeds" (*logoi spermatikoi*) which look forward to the coming of the unique Word. Among the peoples that the Church has evangelized, though always imperfectly, popular traditions carry elements of the authentic ecclesial Tradition. At the same time, however, Tradition and traditions are not to be confused.

An Orthodox Christian would never describe Tradition, as some have done, in terms of "a collection of experiences and hopes that belong to the past." For him, Tradition is the very life of the Church in its continuity as well as in its ever-flowing newness. Both continuity and creative newness in Tradition are the work of the Holy Spirit. Tradition is certainly expressed in the beliefs, doctrines, and rites: it is also expressed, though to a limited extent only, in the popular traditions that I just mentioned. At the same time, Tradition transcends them all. It is essentially a dynamism of faith, hope, love. Tradition has its origin in the Pentecost event and even before that in the meeting on Easter morning of some women with the risen Lord; it is a shock wave that is reverberating around the world and throughout the centuries. Tradition carries an energy, a yeast that never stops causing the heavy dough of institutions to rise. From it springs an eternally new event, an ever new, and ever to be renewed, meeting of each believer, in communion with all the rest, with the Lord of the Church. This is what we call "the communion of the saints."

We must not confuse faithfulness to Tradition with a sacralization of the past, of Church history. Tradition is not a kind of sacred and unshakable monument, nor is it a prison in which we are to be locked up. It is a river of life, penetrated and fertilized by the energies of the Holy Spirit. This river necessarily carries along with it historical and therefore transitory elements as well as impurities and other pollutants. Sometimes Tradition even seems frozen under a great ice shell, but below this frozen and rigid surface flow ever fresh springtime waters. It is up to us, with the help of God's grace, to break the ice that is above all the ice of our hearts become cold. When our hearts will once again burn in our breast, like they did for the disciples of Emmaus, we will recognize the Lord, and he will himself explain "in all the scriptures the things concerning himself" (Lk 24:27). For us and in us, Tradition will become a spring of living water. From the ancient spring, we will drink water that will give us new force so as to answer the questions of today.

This renewal of Tradition also concerns the aspiration that has assembled us here at Sheffield, an aspiration toward a "new community" from which will be banished all forms of domination, servitude, and exploitation of one person or group by any others. The Church has a vocation to enlighten this aspiration by the light of the Gospel and thus become, in human history, the sign and seed of such a community.

This aspiration seems to be one of the "signs of our time." Is it, however, absolutely new? Is it not rather a new awareness of the ancient baptismal faith? The Spirit that is at work in the Church is opening us today to a deeper understanding of the existential and ethical implications of baptism seen as a participation in the death and resurrection of Christ and an accession in him to the new Life. According to the mysterious plan of the one God in three Persons, this is a grace that is poured out on all humanity. "Go and make disciples of all nations baptizing them in the name of the Father, of the Son, and of the Holy Spirit" (Mt 28:19). This is the dismissal given to the apostles. The new life is offered to everyone; it unites together those who open themselves to it into the one Body. Each individual, regardless of race, culture, sex, or social condition, becomes a necessary and precious stone in "the house that God built" (1 Co 3:9).

"For as many of you as were baptized into Christ have put on Christ. There is neither Jew nor Greek, there is neither slave nor free, there is neither male nor female; for you are all one in Christ Jesus" (Ga 3:27-28). This proclamation of St. Paul, which does not abolishes the difference but rather the scorn and hostility, has echoed throughout the centuries. In the Orthodox Church, we sing this verse with great solemnity at each baptism and at the great baptismal feast such as Easter and Pentecost. But what is the empirical reality inside our so-called Christian peoples and societies? With all other Christians, we Orthodox must confess our collective and individual unfaithfulness to the "heavenly vision." This is the tragedy of our historical existence, not yet transfigured by the Light that emanates from Christ, even though we have already received the "down payment" of the Spirit. Martin Luther said that the Christian is *semper justus, semper peccator*, and this is a saying that the Orthodox ascetics and saints would not reject.

We must be very careful, however, not to give way to an unhealthy masochism and to caricature the teaching and practice of the Church in the past as though it is nothing more than a sad story of the oppression of the weak by the strong and of women by men. A certain form of criticism expressing itself, even here at the conference, as a global and unilateral condemnation of the historic Church shocks me deeply. I can say this without in the slightest way ignoring the imperfections, the ignorance and the sins of past generations of Christians. I am shocked not only in regards to my own community, in whose depths I perceive the fullness of the catholic (*kat'holon*) Church, but also in reference to other ecclesial communities in which the Spirit has not ceased to raise up apostles and saints.

The patriarchal model has certainly influenced the institutional structures of the different Christian Churches, and it has penetrated into our collective models. Would it not be a good idea, however, to be more precise, from a scientific point of view, about the exact meaning of *patriarchal*? The Church already anticipates the Kingdom of Heaven but is also a historical reality *in* this world. As such it cannot escape from this influence. Nonetheless, the ideal of the patriarchal family and society contains some positive aspects. It does not necessarily imply the absence of respect for women. Especially, the Church has been able to say some radically new things from inside these structures and while using a language that may seem practical.

Some people attack St. Paul for having exhorted women to be submissive to their husbands, but these same people often neglect the fact that this recommendation is found in the context and following a much more general exhortation to goodwill and mutual service. The chapter begins like this: "Be subject to *one to another* out of reverence for Christ" (Ep 5:21). It is quite true that doctors of morality have often forgotten the beginning of this chapter. In the same way, Paul's preaching raises the union of man and woman, including its carnal aspect, to the dignity of a sign of the mystery of the mutual love of Christ and his Church. It is thus a sign of supreme love, a love so deep that each partner gives himself totally to the other; it is a love in which there is no longer any place for dominator and dominated.

In the patristic era, St. John Chrysostom, who was very severe against coquettish and gossipy women of his time, declared nonetheless that the woman could be the "head" of the man, his guide, and the person responsible for his salvation when she went beyond him in courage and spiritual force. St. John equally encouraged husbands not to try to rule over their wives as over a slave. From his wife, the mother of his children, the husband should seek not the submission of a slave but the love of a *free* woman. To recognize that the light of Christ has been able to transfigure the mores of a patriarchal society is not the same thing as to impose on the Church the duty of perpetuating those structures in her own organization. It is in fact the fermentation of the Gospel that is exploding today the worn out, oppressive, and outmoded framework. I recognize the authentic Tradition of the Church in a women's movement in which women express their will to be respected as free and responsible persons. It is in the dynamic of the authentic Tradition, and not in ephemeral ideologies, that we will find the source of eternal life, the source of our own true liberation. In line with and in the dynamic of this Tradition, we will invent life-styles of community life in the family, society, and Churches. We will follow the example of the scribe in the gospel story who "brings out of his treasure what is new and what is old" (*nova et vetera*, Mt 13:52).

Being blown along by the wind of the Spirit which fills the sails of the ship-Church, we must let ourselves be carried by the great river of life and grace which is the authentic Tradition. We must sail with faith, hope, and love toward new continents that God will give us to discover. We will use the human sciences with discernment: psychology, sociology, even psychoanalysis and Marxist analysis. These are interpretive arts rather than exact sciences, and they will succeed in showing us, to a certain degree, the mechanism that govern the conduct of the old sinful man, the determining factors that weigh down our humanity tangled up in its anxieties and contradictory desires. The true faith, that concerns the *Totally Other God* and the good news of the radical newness that He has given to man, has nothing to fear from these sciences. Besides, they appear powerless to create the future or to raise man out of the cavern in which, according to Plato's profound myth, he finds himself chained up facing the wall. The believer receives this ability to transcend in his free acceptance by his faith of the word of God, of the divine vision given to the Church. The faithful receives it in the communion of the saints and the righteous of all the peoples throughout all time, in solidarity with the a humanity still plunged in chaos. But the Spirit hovers over this humanity like the gentle maternal dove of the first chapter of Genesis (Gn 1:2).

What is this vision of faith about the new human community that must emerge from the framework of the historical tradition of the Orthodox Church? Better perhaps that an abstract theological discourse are two icons that can give us an understanding of the vision, or at least can suggest its essential qualities.

Two Icons

Icons are images that an Orthodox believer prays in front of because, through the face of Christ and the saints, they carry mysterious presence of Him who is beyond every image. Humanity, men and women, has nonetheless been created in His image. A Father of the Church recorded this saying from a pagan: "Show me your man, and I will know who is you God." From the perspective of the Fathers of the Eastern Church, this sentence could easily be inverted: "Show me your God, and I will tell you what kind of man, what kind of human being, you are called to become." And in fact they have always said, "God became man so that man might become God." In the image of this God, men and women were created, and in his likeness they are both called to grow, according to Genesis. This God is neither the impersonal One, the faceless Absolute of the philosophers, nor is he the solitary monarch of a certain kind of theism. He is the one God in three Persons as expressed in the ancient creeds of the Christian faith, the "Lord Love" as he is called by an Orthodox spiritual master that I have already mentioned.[1] Such is the mystery of communion, of the fullness of a completely shared personal life, communicated and received. A Russian monk at the turn of the 14th and 15th centuries tried to express this fullness by creatively renewing an ancient iconographic theme. Andrei Rublev took his inspiration from the Old Testament story of the hospitality of Abraham at Mamre (Gn 18:1-8). He based his icon on a traditional allegorical exegesis of the story and represented the Persons of the Trinity in the form of three marvelously young and beautiful angels seated around a table. They lean toward each other in a

---

[1] A monk of the Eastern Church, *op . cit .*, p. 12.

grace-filled movement that expresses both the absence of all constraints and the total giving of self one to the others. They do not touch each other, but their image is inscribed in a circular movement, in a sort of dance. One single life circulates between the three. They are distinct yet one. Each one is himself precisely in the unique inclination of his face toward the other and their individual gesture by which their hands converge. There is a cup in the center of the table that represents the sacrifice of the Lamb "slain before the foundations of the world," the Cross of the Son with the Father and the Son are in sympathy to the highest degree. Around the three who take up the center space of the icon, we can barely see trees, cupolas and roofs. They represent the physical universe and the historical world of men. They also appear to be animated by the same circular movement as the angels. Led by its head who is Christ, reconciled humanity, along with it the world, enter into the divine dance. Enlightened by the light that emanates from the center, they are not swallowed up but participate at their own creaturely level in the trinitarian Life. In the ecclesial vision of which the iconographer becomes the interpreter, all authentically human communities take root in and are drawn toward this trinitarian Life. The icon transmits this call. It invites us to enter into the mystery of communion without confusion, without annihilating the human person. It is a mystery of abnegation without servitude, of love and of mutual giving in full freedom.

And finally, I would like to rapidly call your attention to another iconographic theme: the icon of the Deisis, that is *supplication.* This icon is traditionally found in Orthodox churches above the royal doors of the iconostase. The Deisis icon and that of the Trinity constitute one of the major expression of Orthodox spirituality. Christ is majesty occupies the center of the Deisis icon. The Virgin Theotokos in the orant position and John the Baptist are on either side of Christ and lead two corteges toward him, one of men and the other of women thus representing the men and women saints of all time. The two corteges converge toward Christ as toward their goal and fulfillment, a fulfillment of humanity in God where masculinity and femininity are not denied but where their opposition is overcome. It is overcome by conversion to the Lord in reciprocal relations but also in each one's depth.

Meditating on the meaning of this icon, I see a message that we need to appropriate and make a reality. In his infinite respect and love for his creature, God wanted to associate man and woman, or more deeply the masculine and feminine principle, with his work of salvation. These principles are represented in the icon first by John the Baptist "the violent one" whose violence when turned inward shows itself in the struggle against the possessive and egotistical self. Mary, the humble servant who welcomes the Spirit as a husband, represents the second principle and becomes the Theotokos, the mother of the God-Man. As an archetype of the Law in its rigor and of bitter and fertile repentance, John the Baptist prepares the way and makes level the paths. But a woman, whose femininity is the sign of welcoming the other, and the supremely Other, is the beginning of the new humanity in which God takes flesh. "among those born of women none is greater than John; yet he who is least in the kingdom of God is greater than he" (Lk 7:28). A woman represents the "least" and "poor" to whom the Kingdom belongs (Mt 5:3). This is to say that the humble acceptance of faith in the divine Word and wonder-filled humility before the Mystery of the love of God manifested in Jesus Christ are the gospel values par excellence. And according to the wedding symbolism of the Scriptures, femininity is their symbol. In this sense, the Church made up of women and men is essentially feminine. Nonetheless, each one of those who belong to the Church is called to assume in Christ his part as well as the part of the "other" that is also in him.

The Heavenly Vision

What is the relation between this "mysterious" vision and our daily struggle to create a true community between men and women, between all human beings whatever their race, culture, or economic level? I believe that this struggle can find a powerful inspiration in the heavenly vision which will keep the earthly community from dissolving into a utopian and immanentist humanism or from getting lost in the sands of feminist or political militancy which by its aggressive violence sometimes denies the reconciled community which we are moving toward. I use the word *inspiration* and not a *solution* to specific problems that such and such a situation sets before us. The "heavenly vision" must inspire action, but it cannot lift from our shoulders the obligation to act, nor the necessary effort of thinking about and analyzing the problems of present-day situations. For the West, the temptation is to neglect or forget the vision; for the Orthodox, it is the temptation to become enchanted by the vision and sometimes find in it an excuse for laziness, a justification for a rigid conservatism claiming not to know about the questions that modern non-believers are asking. In their time, the apostles and the Fathers did not, however, refuse to answer such questions. They answered them through the spiritual exploit of a "crucified intelligence," to use an expression of one of the masters of contemporary Orthodox theology, Fr. George Florovsky. They used an intelligence that dared to invent new words and inspire new attitudes while remaining faithful tot he evangelical and apostolic core of the ecclesial faith. We must move forward *here and now* in the same faithfulness, in the spirit of the Fathers.

CHAPTER FOUR

Women in the Orthodox Church: Heavenly Vision and Historical Realities*

This study is the fruit of a group meditation undertaken during the "Consultation of Orthodox Women" at Agapia in September, 1976.[1] To be precise, it is a meditation that began in a quiet way a long time ago, Agapia being the occasion that brought it out into the open. It does not propose to set out any finalized and closed certainties nor to formulate any aggressive demands. It rather aims at helping to define certain problems about women in the Church, to formulate some questions and to open a dialogue.

Breaking the Silence

We are today faced with cultural changes that affect the entire planet. One of the significant phenomena of this mutation is the fact that women are now speaking out; they, along with a number of men, are concerned to promote specifically feminine values. Despite the efforts and intuitions of some avant-garde theologians, like Paul

* This article was first published in *Contacts* 100, 1977.

1 See the Introduction, note 1.

Evdokimov in particular, the historical Orthodox Churches have up to now paid little attention to this. Could it be that women have no problems in Orthodoxy? It would seem to me quite thoughtless to make such a categorical statement. Could it be that in view of political and cultural conditions of East European societies[2] as well as those of the Middle East where the historical Orthodox Churches have their roots, such problems have *not yet* begun to arise? Or, without underestimating the role played by cultural factors, are the real reasons for this attitude, for the Orthodox "difference," to be found in a global vision that is theological, anthropological and spiritual all at the same time? We are, in fact, only now becoming aware of this vision. But must not this luminous and dynamic vision be freed from the thick layer of dust and deposits that has dimmed it over the centuries? Do we not have to rediscover the living inspiration of Tradition under the crippling shell of prejudices?

From the beginning, woman's place has been assigned to her by *nature* and by *Tradition*. And in fact, women have felt quite comfortable there, not feeling in the least oppressed or frustrated. At any rate, this is what we often hear from ecclesiastic circles and it is partly true, but only partly so. Besides, do not those who usually speak on this question, mostly men, most often forget to ask women for their opinions?

A few years ago, the Orthodox episcopate of a certain region of Europe organized a consultation on the problems of contraception and abortion. Priests, theologians, male doctors were invited, but as far as I know, no woman was invited. Therefore, obviously, no woman was able to

---

[2] Marxism denounces feminism as a bourgeois ideology that distracts women from the only important battle, the class struggle. Women's problems, however, are also surfacing in socialist societies as we see in a beautiful Soviet film which perhaps had a secret Christian inspiration. It is called *I Ask to Speak* by Panfilov and was shown some years ago in the West. See also the almanac, *Femmes et Russie* [Women and Russia], Paris, 1980.

express an opinion on these questions. Is such an attitude really outdated today? It did not indeed result from any canonical rule but rather reflected a mentality: the thinking Church is made up of men as though women by nature were not capable of participating in a debate, in the light of the Word of God and under the guidance of the Spirit, about an existential problem that is of immediate concern to them. In fact, the concepts of *tradition* and *nature* which are used to justify this exclusion are quite ambiguous. Are these concepts petrified mental habits, holdovers from paganism, or do they come from the transmission of the fire of divine revelation? And really, what *nature* are we talking about? Is it the broken and torn nature of Adam and Eve in their fallen condition or the nature of the new creature reunified and reconciled in Christ? Must we recall what the Church solemnly proclaims at each baptism and celebration of Pentecost: "For as many of you as were baptized into Christ have put on Christ. There is neither Jew nor Greek, there is neither slave nor free, there is neither male nor female; for you are all one in Christ Jesus" (Ga 3:27-28).

Attentive to the apostolic word and trying to read the signs of the times in its light, I believe that Orthodox women must be called out of their silence. I am not referring to the blessed and fruitful silence of prayer from which flow strong and inspired words, but rather to the sterile silence of resignation and indifference, a silence that does not exclude but rather produces futile chatter. It was probably that useless noise that St. Paul had in mind when he issued his famous injunction which people never fail to bring up.[3] Yes, it is time that Orthodox women dare to speak out: not in a spirit of surly confrontation, bitterly demanding certain rights. Orthodox women should rather speak out in order to undertake a reflection together with

---

[3] 1 Co 14:34: ". . . the women should keep silence in the churches." The meaning of this verse is obscure, all the more so because it appears to contradict 1 Co 11:5. Certain exegetes see 1 Co 14:34 as a later addition.

their fathers, brothers and husbands on the tasks that confront us today, we who are all the members of the royal and priestly people of God.

The women's cause infinitely transcends feminist demands for equality although we should not, of course, ignore them. As a leading Protestant woman theologian, France Quéré,[4] has suggested, women are intimately related to the Gospel. We would say that they are related to the realization of human accomplishment in God, to the *theosis* of the Fathers. *Here and now*, could not there be an authentic dialogue between men and women that would bring about the renewal of the aborted dialogue in the West between humanism and faith? In place of a Cartesian humanism of the male, "master and possessor of the earth," we must substitute a new humanism pervaded with respect for *the other*, with tenderness and compassion for mankind and the whole of God's creation. Would not a genuinely feminine presence in all domains of culture, including the concrete life of our ecclesial communities contribute to such a humanism?

The Women's Movement: a Sign of Our Times

The problem concerning the place of the feminine principle in the plan of salvation and in the life of the Church has an anthropological dimension. It concerns the divine plan for humanity and its revelation in Christ by the Holy Spirit in the Church. From this point of view, we can and must see it *sub specie æternitatis*. The problem, nonetheless, has its historical side and we must deal with it today in the context of the cultural mutation of the last quarter of the 20th century. The women's movement and the aspiration for the "promotion of women" are certainly important aspects of the problem.

---

[4] See F. Quéré, "Un féminisme total" [A Total Feminism], *Esprit*, 458, June, 1976.

Some Orthodox think that this mutation does not concern the Church but only "the changing face of this passing world." Such an attitude certainly reflects one of the aims of Christian life: to keep the agitation of the world a salutary distance away. The Church is thus preserved from becoming infatuated with ephemeral fashions, from "kneeling down before the world," in the words of the "peasant from the Garonne," Jacques Maritain. Even though the disciples of Christ are anchored in the *eschaton* and look forward to the *omega*, they are not for all that relieved of the duty of reading the "signs of the times." In fact, their master specifically imposed that duty upon them (Mt 16:3). Jesus' kingdom "is not of this world" if we understand "world" to mean the kingdom of Satan, the reign of the powers that are arrayed against God. Jesus' kingdom, however, is not a stranger to historical development. The Gospel parables compare this kingdom to a seed thrown into the earth of men; in this earth it sprouts, grows and becomes "a tree and the birds of the air" make "nests in its branches" (Mt 13:32 and Lk 13:19). The contemporary women's movement (rather than the "feminist" movement) is, in spite of its weaknesses, a sign of that secret and irresistible force of the Spirit that is lifting humanity toward the Kingdom of the life-giving Trinity. This movement is certainly an ambiguous and sometimes irritating sign, written in clumsy letters and spoken of in consciously provocative terms, a sign of "a Christian idea gone haywire" in our Far West that finds itself submerged by a nihilistic tidal wave. We live in a time of violence that often takes on atrocious or absurd forms. This blind violence carries along with it, however, a tremendous hope for the liberation of mankind, for the respect of dignity, for the *right to be different*, whether on the ethnic, cultural, or sexual level. The women's movement participates both in the violence and in the noble hope that is the divine image in man. Despite its excesses, violence and distorting simplification, the women's movement asks serious questions of the Churches. Let us pray that the Churches do not pass by on the other side as the Levite in the parable. Through the sound and fury, let us hope that they discern the murmuring of the Spirit.

> Today, at the end of a long period of patriarchy, women are seeking to affirm themselves as full human persons, as free and responsible subjects. It is the Gospel fermentation acting to liberate us finally from old pagan structures.[5]

Without knowing it, the human sciences, like psychology, sociology and ethnology, have been fertilized by the Gospel revolution and have themselves become liberating forces provided we know how to make good use of them. They have helped women to become conscious of the social and cultural mechanisms that have enslaved them, mechanisms that have deepened mere differences so as to transform them into inequalities. In general, we note that "collectivities have only tolerated differences by transforming them into hierarchies and hierarchies have been set up by profoundly deepening the differences."[6] Differentiation is nearly always tied up with inequality whether we are dealing with differences of race, skin color, culture, or sex. It does not obviously stand to reason that the recognition of women's specific difference is compatible with the recognition of their equality. Realizing this bitter truth, we can only appeal, from the fallen world in which we are bound, to the revelation hidden from the wise and intelligent ones of this world, to the revelation of the one God in three Persons. The Trinity is a sign of supreme distinction in supreme communion and equal dignity, a sign of love's total reciprocity. But the ability to receive such a mystery, which secretly orientates all human nostalgia for

---

[5] O. Clement, *Questions sur l'homme* [Questions About Man], Paris, 1975, pp. 114-15.
[6] P. Thibaud, "La part des femmes" [Women's Part], *Esprit*, June, 1976, p. 1051.

fulfillment, requires a conversion and a leap of faith. If women do not go beyond the empirical knowledge of fallen humanity and this is the only knowledge open to "the human sciences," they may be tempted today to reject as a mystification any idealization of womanhood which stresses their specific differences in order to limit their freedom. "The soul" or "feminine charisms" are exalted but only to keep women from real responsibilities in a society run by men. Women are thus assigned to the home and to motherhood. But is this not just a way of covering over with vain words the emptiness of the lives of many women in the conditions of modern life: the nuclear family reduced to the couple with one or two children who rather quickly attain psychological and moral independence; a growing number of single women who do not feel a calling to monastic life just because they are single. Very often these women are the most demanding and have very rich inner lives, but they feel the need to go beyond the narrow framework and the self-centeredness of contemporary family life made up of two or three.

The women's movement is thus against a conception of woman that has in part been rendered obsolete by the scientific and industrial revolution. We must add that it is also a revolt against a "primitive freudianism" that is widespread in our permissive societies.

> Women protest against a pleasure-oriented society in which they are made into erotic objects and where female nudity is a publicity tool. Our society is finally just a vast bordello of the imagination. Women want a real reciprocity with men, a participation in society where for a long time now they have demonstrated their ability.[7]

Women's demands have their origins in New Testament preaching, in the revolutionary proclamation of the equal dignity in Christ of men and women. This proclamation

---

[7] O. Clement, *op. cit.*, p. 115.

was revolutionary in the rabbinical context of the time, but women are not always aware of the origins of their demands. However, the women's movement, being cut off from its spiritual roots and being secularized and made profane, has become "feminist" and in the process has caused a deep and widely spread identity crisis. In societies dominated by perverted masculine values, by sin, by a spirit of competition and domination and an appetite for power and pleasure, women end up denying their own most profound being, open as it is to the inspirations from On High. Sexual differentiation is reduced to a biological accident and femininity becomes the product of social pressures, or rather of social oppressions. After so many interpretations that lower and debase the symbolism of the feminine body, this very symbolism has become meaningless. Its language is no longer heard except in its most trivial meaning. According to the expression of a contemporary psychoanalyst, men and women are indistinctly nothing more than "desiring machines." Aggressively claiming equality, militant feminists end up by internalizing the hated image of the dominating male and by manifesting his negative traits. These women become "little dictators."[8]

> Violence creates a type of homosexual and dominating Amazon and ignorance of the disciplines of metamorphosis—once the old dikes have been broken—merely frees instincts and very ancient magical forces.[9]

We have here a tragic shipwreck in which there is the risk of losing an essential dimension of what is human. Without this dimension humanity will be forever mutilated and deprived of its wings. "Who am I?" "Who are we?" "Where do we find our fulfillment?" Many women and their

---

[8] L. Giard, "La fabrique des filles" [Manufacturing Girls], *Esprit*, June, 1976, pp. 1108-23.
[9] O. Clement, *op. cit.*, p. 115.

male companions are asking these questions today. The human sciences can only take to pieces the mechanisms of fallen empirical reality. They are powerless, however, to orient human hope and we must therefore turn once more to the experience of faith and to the divine message transmitted by the Church.

In line with the conclusions of many contemporary thinkers, we agree that one of the important tasks of a reflective and living faith is to find theoretical and practical answers to the "questions about man," about men and women. These answers are implicit in the doctrine of the Church and we are called to uncover its existential meaning and to incarnate it in a spiritual art of living.

Signposts Leading to a Theo-anthropology about Men and Women

Biblical and patristic anthropology is really a theo-anthropology. Man is never thought of as being self-sufficient but always in an immediate relationship with God. Created in the image of God, humanity can only grow toward and be fulfilled in Him, in the radiance of the trinitarian light. When man turns away from his prototype, he falls to the animal level and even lower, as such great modern Russian thinkers as Boukharev, Dostoevsky and Berdiaev have affirmed, in line with patristic thinking. Mankind's vocation is therefore to strive for the likeness of God, or to use the language of the Fathers, to strive for *theosis*, that is, holiness. Man, in holiness and faithulness to his divine vocation, is called to reign over the earth (Gn 1:28-30), humanize it and submit it to the divine will of love. Now mankind was created in the image of God and destined to grow in and toward the divine likeness through his freely offered obedience of faith; he was also created from the beginning as masculine and feminine: "So God created man in his own image, in the image of God he created him; male and female he created them" (Gn 1:27).

The use of the singular and the plural personal pronouns "him" and "them" reflects the Hebrew text and is of great importance. We thus have the scriptural affirmation of two truths: at the same time, human nature is *united*, that is, the totality of mankind is made in the image of God, as well as being *diversified*. Man from the beginning carries the ontological image of God. He is called to advance endlessly toward God. He is not to do this, however, as a solitary individual or as a non-sexual being like the angels, but rather in the masculine-feminine bipolarity. In the words of a Father of the Church, man is essentially a "conjugal" being. The *condominium* of the earth and the task of cultivating it has been given to *two* who were drawn from the same clay and destined to become one single flesh, without confusion of persons and to form one single humanity. Far from being the consequence of original sin, human bisexuality is a blessing, from the fundamentally optimistic biblical point of view: "And God blessed them and God said to them, 'Be fruitful and multiply and fill the earth and subdue it . . . And God saw everything that he had made and behold it was very good" (Gn 1:28-31). Even though the Church has never ceased to read this biblical passage, Christians have not become fully conscious of all its anthropological, or rather theo-anthropological, implications. Too many prejudices, too many ancestral taboos have darkened our minds. A fruitful dialectical relationship between theology and anthropology, mutually enriching each other, can make possible today a new reading of these verses in a new light. What is more, this rereading is proposed as a task which Orthodox thinkers cannot escape. As an American Orthodox theologian has written, the time has come to elucidate the spiritual meaning of human bisexuality:

> If it has not been specifically explicated and articulated in the past, it is the present task to show clearly that human community, as the created epiphany of the uncreated Trinity, is made male and female so that it can

realize and achieve the divine life given to it by its uncreated Archetype.[10]

To answer today's questions about man and woman, we are invited to look beyond the horizon of fallen empirical reality toward the divine Mystery which is the foundation of all that is authentically human. Every human person is transfigured in the radiance of this mystery: the Mystery of one God in three distinct Persons, united in a sacred order without subordination, equal in dignity; each Person set with and not against the others, in supreme difference and in supreme communion; each One communicating himself to the others in an eternal movement, in an eternal dance of love. Mankind has the vocation of becoming like this God who is the archetype, the model of the fullness of personal life in the fullness of communion. Man, both one and multiple, was created in the image of this divine Tri-Unity, according to the diversity of sexual persons who are called to reflect "the trinitarian life and love" in their reciprocal relationships. They are to work out these relations on the level of the creature but are also to be drawn up On High by the weight of grace.

Sin, which essentially is separation, breaks up the paradisiac unity of humanity, but this unity is restored in Christ the God-Man and we participate in it in the Church, his Body (Ga 3:27-28). This eschatological unity, whose firstfruits we have already received, is not brought about by suppressing all distinctions. What is abolished is not the *difference* between men and women but rather the *quarrel* (when they "differ") the hostility between a bad masculinity and a bad femininity both of which have been perverted by sin. The Son and the Spirit are united for the joint accomplishment of the Father's will, each One according to his proper modality and mission. In the same way, men and women in the Church are called to work

[10] T. Hopko *Women and the Priesthood*, St. Vladimir's Seminary Press, Crestwood, N. Y., 1983, p. 100.

together for their salvation and the world's; they are to fulfill themselves with and by each other in their striving toward the Third: God, who is the foundation of their unity. For, as Fr. Teilhard de Chardin so profoundly said, "Only one *milieu* brings together: God."[11] The Lord calls by name those who advance together toward Him and in Him: Simon, John, Andrew, but also Martha and Mary. The catholic unity of the Church is a dynamic unity in Christ, not of angels, but of human persons differentiated by sex, sanctified, "pneumatized" in the fullness of humanity.

Women in the New Testament

There is no theoretical development in the gospels of the condition on women unless we count the affirmation about the indissolubility of marriage. In relation to the Jewish custom of repudiation, this affirmation is an immense progress in women's favor. Women are, nonetheless, present in the earthly life of the Son of God from the beginning to the very end, from Matthew's genealogy, where women are specially named and the Annunciation till Calvary and the first announcement of the Resurrection given to the Myrrh-bearing women. Women had profound personal relationships with Jesus of Nazareth: Martha and Mary, Lazarus' sisters, the Samaritan woman at Jacob's well, with whom the Lord had a "theological" conversation, Mary of Magdala of the "Easter garden" story. Jesus allowed women to touch him, in both the physical and spiritual meaning of the word. He was not afraid of being in contact with them even when one was a prostitute. He had compassion for their suffering and was moved by their

[11] "Two magnets can stay indefinitely attached to each other: in their coming together, they slowly pass each other by . . . Only one milieu brings things together: God." P. Teilhard de Chardin, quoted in H. de Lubac, *L'Eternel Féminin: Etude sur un texte du Père Teilhard de Chardin* [The Eternal Feminine: A Study on a Text of Fr. Teilhard de Chardin], Paris, 1968, note 1, p. 69.

woman (Mk 7:28). His disciples were surprised by this attitude which contrasted so sharply with rabbinical principles (Jn 4:27 and Lk 7:39). Such an attitude indicates a spiritual direction: any notion of women's ritual impurity is for ever abolished.

We must take note, though only in passing, of the Virgin Mary's place in the Scriptures and afterwards in Orthodox piety. The Church proclaims that God took flesh from a woman and the Church gives Mary the title of *Theotokos*, Mother of God. God did not use Mary like a passive instrument. He had the divine audacity to let the realization of his loving plan hang on her *fiat*, on the free acceptance of her faith. Mary participated in the work of the world's salvation not just in her body. She participated in her body because of her personal faith and obedience that opened her integrally and nuptially to the "Spirit of the Most High" who overshadowed her with his shadow. The crowd cried out when Jesus went by, "Blessed is the womb that bore you and the breasts that you sucked." He answered, not to lessen the role of his mother but to underline the personal and spiritual dimension of her motherhood: "Blessed rather are those who hear the word of God and keep it" (Lk 11:28). They were to keep it like Mary kept it (Lk 2:19). In the Virgin, "more venerable than the cherubim and more glorious beyond compare than the seraphim," all women can feel honored. In the conscience of the Church, her image is not one of a fragile and passive femininity. She is the new Eve, the mother of the true Life, the archetype of the fulfilled humanity, *gratia plena*, overflowing with the life-giving grace of the Spirit. Between Mary, between "the woman clothed in light"–*amicta sole*–of Revelations and the Holy Spirit, spiritual intuition senses a mysterious correspondence that contemporary Orthodox theology has tried to make explicit.

Figures of Woman: Distorted Images of Woman through History

The radiant image of the Virgin Mother has taken root and grown in the consciousness of the faithful throughout the centuries and has for women enlightened the darkest ages of so-called Christian societies. Paradoxically, however, the light of the Unique One has left her humiliated sisters in the shadows.

> Between the summit of humanity, the Virgin Mary "more glorious than the seraphim" whose veneration has risen very rapidly and an incomplete and demonic feminine human being, there does not seem to exist a middle position. A striking alienation has set itself up in history as a normal situation.[12]

In fact, in the East as well as the West, Church practice as it concerns women is often a compromise between the Gospel affirmation of the equal dignity in Christ of men and women and a persistent pagan mentality that says that women are inferior, incomplete (even going so far as to deny that they have an immortal soul) and demonic beings. Because of the desire they stir up, women are seen as upsetting the well-ordered society established by males who objectivize and condemn in them their own concupiscence. The Gospel yeast nonetheless continues to raise the heavy dough of historical Christianity. All through the centuries, Christian women have been baptized, chrismated and invested with the fullness of the royal priesthood; they have confessed their faith in Christ, endured martyrdom, evangelized, prophesied and attained the

---

[12] P. Evdokimov, *Sacrement de l'Amour* [The Sacrament of Love], Paris, 1962, p. 19. Among the recent works that deal with Church antifeminism, we can cite the following: J.-M. Aubert, *La Femme, antiféminisme et christianisme* [Woman: Antifeminism and Christianity] and "Les femmes dans l'Eglise" [Women in the Church], *Concilium*, 111, 1976.

heights of holiness in the life of consecrated virginity as well as in married life.[13]

Women played an unquestioned and important role in the diffusion of Jesus' message in the apostolic age. Despite the injunction of silence we hear in 1 Corinthians 14:36, whose meaning in the text is obscure as we have seen, Paul's letters show that women prayed and "prophesied" in the first Christian assemblies (1 Co 11:4). The apostle evoked examples of evangelists such as Aquila and his wife Priscilla, deaconesses like Phoebe and Junia (Rm 16:1, 3 and 7) whose zeal he recognized and praised. These allusions are not clear enough to allow us to determine exactly what the deaconesses did at a time when the organization of the Church was still in the developmental stage. The ministry of the deaconess was to survive and develop into the patristic age, but we will come back to that later on.

The Fathers of the Church were influenced by the cultural stereotypes of their time and reacted strongly against the depraved mores of a society that was only superficially evangelized. They were also marked by the rabbinical exegesis that laid on woman the prime responsibility for original sin. As a result, the Fathers have frequently shown themselves very stern towards the feminine sex. It is not difficult and it has already been done, to gather together a long list of anti-feminist patristic

[13] Among the canonized saints of the Orthodox Church, and they represent only the visible part of the iceberg of holiness, married women are relatively rare. Usually the married saints are empresses such as Helen the mother of the emperor Constantine or princesses such as the grand duchess Olga. We must not forget, however, the popular veneration in Russia for Juliana Lazarevskaya (+1604). She was a mother of numerous children who for the love of others renounced the monastic life that she was attracted to. See also E. Behr-Sigel, *Prière et Sainteté dans l'Eglise russe* [Prayer and Holiness in the Russian Church], Bellefontaine, 1972, pp. 109-13.

statements.[14] But this severity is above all inspired by a pastoral concern and by the elevated spiritual ideal that makes monasticism appear to be the way par excellence of Christian perfection. The anti-feminist excesses are often the result of more or less heretical tendencies that have been influenced by gnostic dualism. It is characteristic that the Fathers who represent a balanced theology and an authentically catholic thinking, like John Chrysostom, loudly proclaim the equality of woman and man, even women's superiority in the order of holiness. This vision of equality did not prevent him, however, from railing against so-called feminine faults. St. Jerome is often very hard on women, but while acknowledging their intellectual gifts, he advised them to be modest so as not to run directly up against the sense of superiority that is natural to males. He wrote the following:

> It is accepted that women remain at home while men take care of the affairs of the city. But in the various battles and trials that must be endured for the Church, the women and not men, easily take the prize for courage when it comes to doing battle and sustaining long and tiresome efforts.[15]

In ascetic effort as well as in martyrdom, women of Christian antiquity proved that they were equal and sometimes superior to men when it came to the firmness of their faith. John Chrysostom recognized that grace "reverses the order of the law as formulated by the apostle Paul," and he advised husbands to follow the advice and

---

[14] "Woman is the gate to hell" (Tertullian). "Every woman ought to be weighed down with shame at the thought that she is a woman" (Clement of Alexandria). These passages are quoted by P. Evdokimov, *Sacrement de l'Amour* [The Sacrament of Love], p. 19. St. John Chrysostom saw in women's beauty a terrible trap set by Satan, and he sharply criticized women's taste for makeup and clothes.

[15] *Letter* 170, quoted by F. Quéré, *op. cit.*, p. 61.

example of their wives when they spiritually out run their husbands.

Unlike Thomas Aquinas and the medieval scholastic theology influenced by Aristotelian theories, the Fathers of the Eastern Church never attempted to supply rational grounds for the inferiority of women. They never question that inferiority, however, as an accepted fact in the social structures of their time.

The official doctrine of the Orthodox Church has never wavered on this question.[16] This is true despite the latent temptation in certain monastic circles toward a gnostic dualism in which woman is the figure of sin par excellence and of course that means sins of the flesh. Although gnosticism has been condemned as a doctrine, it has nonetheless left traces in people's way of thinking. Paul Evdokimov wrote that "we sometimes get the impression that salvation is an affair only of males and that those who wish to be saved must above all be saved from women."[17]

Between the angel and the beast, between being a nun and a purely sexual object, it would appear that there are no other alternatives for women. Things are not as simple as that, however. By calling women to consecrated virginity, monasticism has also powerfully contributed to their affirmation as persons and to their liberation from social constraints. A nun escapes from the patriarchal guardianship of the family. She freely disposes of her body. The obedience to a call from On High frees her from biological and social determinism.

It is true that certain exhortations from Christian antiquity that exalt the monastic life also belittle the servitudes of married life and maternity. In this, they seem to foretell the most extreme demands of contemporary

---

[16] A. Jensen, "Wie patriarchalisch ist die Ostkirche?" *Una Sancta* 1985/2, pp. 131-32.
[17] P. Evdokimov, *Sacrement de l'Amour* [The Sacrament of Love], p. 17.

feminism, especially the refusal to have children.[18] In both cases, we see the danger of denying womanhood: on the one hand, there is an egalitarianism that levels all differences; on the other, there is a hidden pseudo-angelism that generates neuroses. We must repeat, however, that these tendencies are exaggerations of extremists who have fallen away from the measured and balanced approach that characterizes the ascetic art of the Fathers, an approach that does not aim at abolishing the multi-faceted richness of humanity but rather aims at integrating this richness in the divine sphere. By becoming a "spiritual mother," the nun does not kill but sublimates by the Spirit her maternal vocation.[19]

If monasticism has greatly contributed to the recognition of women's status as free persons, the Church has also exalted married women as such, not only as mothers but also as wives. We often hear of the apostle Paul's misogyny, but he is also the one who pointed to conjugal unity as a mystery, an epiphany of the reciprocal love that unites Christ and the Church-humanity (Ep 5:21-32). Marriage participates in this mystery and is called upon to reflect it. The wife is for the husband the icon of the Church that he must love as his own body. If women are urged to be submissive to their husbands, it is in the general framework of the law of love, sacrificial love that orders all Christian living. "You who fear Christ, submit yourselves to one another" (Ep 5:21). This is the commandment that reveals the meaning of the entire passage. The accent is

---

[18] "In truth, does a servant of God have the duty to have children? Are we so sure of our salvation that we can allow ourselves to be invaded by children? Are we going to accept those burdens odious to so many pagans who get rid of them by killing them in the womb?" (Tertullian, *Traité contre les secondes noces*, 2,1 [Essay Against Second Marriages]) Even St. John Chrysostom saw in the sorrows and worries that children bring a reason for opting for monastic celibacy (*Traité de la virginité*, 57 [Essay on Virginity]).

[19] A. Frachebond, *Les Mères du désert et la maternité spirituelle* [The Mothers of the Desert and Spiritual Motherhood], *Collectanes Cisterciensia* 48, 1986.

not so much on the submissiveness of the women, that went without saying in Jewish and Greek societies, but on the *reciprocity* of respect and love that characterizes the new relationships in the Kingdom of God. We must also add the exaltation by Paul of Christ the Servant (Ph 2:5-8). The Spirit of Christ urges the believer to follow his example. The submission each to the other in conjugal relations here receives a radically new meaning. A submission of the husband to the wife is also implied: "For this reason a man shall leave his father and mother and be *joined* to his wife . . ." (Ep 5:31). "The husband does not rule over his own body, but the wife does. Do not refuse one another except perhaps by agreement for a season . . ." (1 Co 7:4-5).

And last but not least, Paul taught the husband as well as the wife to discern in each other, beyond the weak and sinful creature, the divine image which marks them both and which shines through their infirmities: "Wives, be subject to your husbands, *as to the Lord*. . . . Husbands, love your wives, *as Christ loved the church* and gave himself up for her" (Ep 5:22, 25). On the basis of Paul's statement, the Church promoted a new image of woman. The Church conferred on women, as well as on men, the dignity of being shining icons of a presence that goes beyond each woman but which manifests itself in her, in her person.

Unfortunately, the practice of Christians has not always measured up to the greatness of this vision, but the Church proposes an ideal from which she has not deviated in spite of heresies such as encratism,[20] a deviation the Church condemned. Even though it has been darkened by personal sin and by a paganism that lingers on in the collective awareness of societies, this ideal has always been

[20] The Encratites condemned all sexual relations, even in marriage. It is very significant that they even substituted water for wine in the eucharist. For this reason, they were often called "Aquarians." The Orthodox service of marriage recalls the miracle of the wedding at Cana, and the new couple is presented with a single cup of wine and invited to drink from it.

proclaimed and transmitted by the profound and wonderful mystical poem that is the Orthodox rite of marriage. It has no parallel in Western Christian confessions. The Church's pedagogy aims at forming women who, without weakness or affected delicacy, assume their condition of wife and mother while transcending such conditions in the radiant brilliance of the mystery of Christ and the Church. The traditional Orthodox ideal, being enlivened by an intense current of Marian piety, has been the inspiration of holy and fulfilled women, both courageous and humble. Orthodox hagiography as well as secular literature, especially the Russian novel from Dostoevsky through Tolstoy to Pasternak, stand witness to this fact. The "feminine" is present in the Orthodox Church and permeates the atmosphere of the liturgy itself as well as the liturgical assembly. As one contemporary Orthodox writer says,

> In our churches, women feel not only tolerated but honored. They are at home in the house of the heavenly Father. They come with their children carrying their babies in their arms. Their children bring to church their noise, their toys and sometimes their disorder.[21]

In this apparent disorder, that sometimes shocks strangers, the richness of life circulates, a life whose guardian is woman. In the words of Paul Evdokimov, human beings receive from their experience of the "maternal and feminine" "the indestructible nostalgia of the heavenly Kingdom well before meeting the priest or the bishop."

Without calling into question the hierarchical structure of the Church, Orthodox men and women feel this structure to be essentially a communion of prayer and love, not a pyramid of powers. For Orthodox believers, the Church is not a society with a patriarchal structure thought up by

[21] M. Zernov, "Women's Ministry in Church," *Eastern Churches Review*, 1 1975, p. 38.

men and governed by and for them, a structure that is denounced by certain Western feminists.[22] Despite a sometimes parasitical clericalism, "the Church of the Holy Spirit," as Fr. Nicholas Afanassieff called it, is filled and permeated by a mysterious feminine presence whose sign and personal archetype is the Theotokos.

Is this to say that the Orthodox have nothing to receive from the Western women's movement, that we can ignore and neglect the questions that are being asked of the Churches today? Does this mean that we can answer them by referring to archaic cultural models, that we can be content to repeat the sayings of the Fathers without having their creative spirit? Should we not be attentive, as they were, to the "signs of the times" and to what the Spirit is saying to the Churches in each generation? Does not authentic faithfulness to the Fathers consist in building on the foundations that they laid, in exploring new roads that are but the extension of ancient roads paved by our patristic ancestors?

Modern Orthodox Thinking about Women

In this study, we can only superficially touch on a subject that is vast and multifaceted. A whole continent emerges especially in Russian religious thought and it must be explored. At the present, we can only indicate its presence.

Alexander Boukharev (1822-1871),[23] a great but little known Russian theologian, began a reflection on women and the Church, in the second half of the 19th century. He carried out his reflection in the perspective of a living and inventive appropriation of the ecclesial Tradition.

---

[22] B. de la Bouillerie, "Religieuses, femmes libérées" [Nuns as Liberated Women], *Spiritus* 61, 1975, quoted in 6, 1976, p. 1079.

[23] E. Behr-Sigel, *Alexandre Boukharev: Un théologien de l'Eglise orthodoxe russe en dialogue avec le monde contemporain* [Alexander Boukharev: A Theologian of the Russian Orthodox Church in Dialogue with the Contemporary World], Paris, 1977.

Boukharev was both anchored in the soil of the Church's faith and open to contacts with the acids of modern Western culture. As such he was the first modern Orthodox theologian to dare to address the problems of human sexuality and marriage with boldness, depth and delicacy. He integrated sexuality and marriage into a vision of womanhood as a complementary spiritual principle of manhood in the work of salvation. After Boukharev, Russian religious thinking moved away from the solid terrain of the biblical revelation where he had always set himself and took the more adventuresome road that led to the sacralization of sexual eros, with Rozanov, or to the speculation about the eternal feminine in God with the sophiology of Vladimir Soloviev (1853-1900) and his disciples Paul Florensky (1882-1943) and Serge Bulgakov (1871-1944). Theirs was of course an audacious adventure, not without its ambiguities and risks. Nonetheless, the serious study of this current of opinion remains to be undertaken after some too hasty and global condemnations.[24]

The merit of Paul Evdokimov (1901-1970), being heir to the dynamism of Russian religious thinking, is to have put the intuitions of these thinkers back into the context of the Fathers' christocentric and trinitarian anthropology and theology. In the domain of a theology about women, marriage and sexuality, Paul Evdokimov was especially responsible for opening "windows and letting in some air where the atmosphere was sometimes hardly breathable. He gave new life to subjects that for too long people had been too silent or reticent about."[25] As a married lay theologian, Evdokimov indignantly rejected a conception of womanhood that contained the clumsy definition of the

[24] The wish that such a study might finally be carried out was expressed by Fr. Alexander Schmemann, former rector of St. Vladimir's Seminary in New York. See A. Schmemann, "Trois images" [Three Images], *Messager Orthodoxe* 57, 1, 1972, dedicated to Fr. Bulgakov.

[25] L. Gillet, *Contacts*, 73-74, p. 8.

goal of the marital union, a definition, moreover, that hangs on in the manuals of moral theology. According to this conception, going back through Thomas Aquinas to Augustine, women's function is reduced to nothing more than an organ of biological reproduction. In the words of the Scholastic saying taken in its literal meaning: *Tota mulier in utero.* Males need women only to assure physical descendants. Thomas Aquinas affirmed that "for all other works, a man is better off being helped by another man than by a woman."[26]

Paul Evdokimov noted that if we start from this position, it is only a small step to affirm that "woman, except for a nun, is by nature inferior to man" and to contest her direct relation with God, a relation that only a man is supposed to have. Evdokimov opposed this crude and degrading notion with the intuition of "the mystery of woman." Throughout history, societies have formed or deformed feminine types. Nonetheless, women have kept in their inner depths the mystery and charisms of womanhood which St. Paul designated by the symbol of the "veil" (1 Co 11). This mystery must be "unveiled" and explained in order to understand its destiny, a destiny that is coupled with man's. Having deciphered the Genesis stories, Evdokimov saw in them the original model of a consubstantiality between the complementary masculine and feminine principles. Eve is the flesh of Adam's flesh, the other who is just like him. Man and woman are thus called to be a single flesh in the diversity of persons. Sin broke up this unity by opposing a bad masculinity and a bad femininity; the tension thus created resulted in discord and hopeless struggle. But divine grace, in Christ, reconstituted the initial cell. "The conjugal community stands as a prophetic figure of the Kingdom of God, a community of the masculine and of the feminine in their totality in God. The biological level becomes the sign of a spiritual level

---

[26] Quoted by P. Evdokimov, *Sacrement de l'Amour* [The Sacrament of Love], p. 27.

that transcends the biological. Humanity in its plenitude, whose womb is the Church, is only brought to fullness by joining the feminine and masculine principles." Going even farther, Evdokimov suggested a mysterious relationship, an analogy, on the one hand between the masculine principle and the Word who expresses, orders and structures and on the other between the feminine principle and the Spirit who incarnates, inspires and consoles. In Semitic languages, in particular in Hebrew, the word *spirit, rouah,* has two genders. It is sometimes used in the feminine. There is certainly no question of introducing a sexual differentiation into the Trinity and apophaticism, that is silent respect in the face of the divine mystery, must constantly correct the analogy. Nonetheless, a spiritual intuition based on the scriptural revelation discerns what might correspond in God to the feminine aspect of the image of God in man.[27]

In a text written just before his death, Paul Evdokimov spoke about "the hypostatic maternity" or "generating function of the Holy Spirit."[28] He based his statements on the fundamentally triadic character of the eastern Fathers' theology in which each Person of the Trinity is contemplated simultaneously in his relation to the two others. Evdokimov felt justified in saying that "the Father begets the Son with the participation or the presence of the Spirit." In other words, the Son is born *ex Patre Spirituque.* According to Evdokimov, the presence of the Spirit in the eternal nativity of the Word conditions his function in the economy of salvation. In the creed, Christ is "born of the Holy Spirit and of the Virgin Mary." In the words of Fr. Bulgakov, taken up by Paul Evdokimov, the Spirit is "the breath of birth-giving and hypostatic maternity." The

[27] P. Evdokimov, *La Nouveauté de l'Esprit* [The Newness of the Spirit], Bellefontaine, 1977, p. 251.

[28] P. Evdokimov, "Panagion et Panagia" [Panagion and Panagia], *Bulletin de la Société Française d'Etudes Mariales,* 1970, reprinted in *La Nouveauté de l'Esprit* [The Newness of the Spirit], pp. 259-62.

virginal maternity of the Mother of God is in a correlative sense "a figure of the Holy Spirit."

From these speculations, we may retain one intuition especially. We can see it better through the veil of symbols than we can in human conceptions. It is the intuition of a mysterious and ineffable correlation between the feminine as a way of being, as an ontological and constituent structure of humanity and something or rather someone in the superessential Divinity. God is not only Being but also openness and interpersonal tension.

> The Shekinah. The glory, the life, the Breath, which come forth from a God who is so full that he might crush man but from a God incarnate and crucified; they spring out from his voluntary emptying, his self-hollowing so that the other might be what constitutes the ultimate form of love.[29]

This love expresses itself in the most perfect way in creaturely existence through maternal love.

Pervaded in her whole being, even in her flesh, by the Spirit "the Giver of Life" to whom Mary opened herself, she became the new and true Eve, the "Mother of all the living" because she is the mother of Him who is Life itself. Veiled and yet unveiled in the archetypal figure of the Mother of God, the divine mystery enlightens both the ultimate vocation of the Eternal Feminine, even in its most humble creaturely expression and the God-bearing destiny of all humanity according to the eternal divine plan. Poets too sometimes sense this mystery of faith: Louis Aragon wrote that "woman is the future of man."

"Woman is closer to the sources of life than is man the technician and builder." In a moment of spiritual enlightenment, Paul Evdokimov adopted and deepened this

---

[29] O. Clement, *Le Christ, terre des vivants* [Christ: the Land of the Living], *Spiritualité Orientale*, Bellefontaine, 1976, pp. 37-38.

statement of Nicholas Berdiaev.[30] Carrying on Evdokimov's thinking, we may say that the distinctiveness of women belongs to two areas at the same time: the transmission and preservation of life and the relation with the other, with concrete others who are loved and accepted in their otherness. To be a woman means to aspire to fulfill oneself by welcoming the other, by bringing into the world "an other" life that has been allowed to grow inside oneself and which must be lovingly cared for. This is at the opposite end from solipsism which is the masculine temptation par excellence. The openness of being a woman is not without its ambiguities, however, since by it Eve was opened to the Serpent's suggestions. By her very openness, though, she was predisposed to become, in the words of Evdokimov, "the spiritual organ of human nature," to receive the divine Word and allow it to bear fruit within herself. In the name of the divine law, of the law from On High, the "little Antigone," as the symbol of feminine force and passion, has never ceased through all the centuries to defy and disturb the order, or the "established disorder," of the Creons who are the prudent and skeptical administrators of the earthly city. The immense reservoir of cosmic and spiritual energies that men sense in women make them fear a throw back to the primitive chaos, concerned above all as they are, by order and hierarchy. This fear is not always baseless, but the Spirit of God, the "chaste and luminous energy," according to Teilhard de Chardin, never ceases to hover over the original watery depths until the "woman robed in light" is formed in them, in the solar brilliance of the Christ-Bridegroom. As the carrier of the future, womanhood, obscurely or consciously, is striving toward "Him who is coming."

Holy womanhood is not a matter of empirical data in the fallen world, but faith and hope sense this holiness in Mary of Nazareth, the unique woman, the "Mother of God," from whom

---

[30] N. Berdiaev, *Un nouveau Moyen Age* [A New Middle Ages], pp. 163-64.

> . . . the Lamb of God condescended to take flesh and who, more intimately united to her Son than the seraphim, shares his love for the sinners even to the point of feeling co-responsible with Him for their salvation.[31]

Along with the image of Christ, every woman carries potentially within her, with the image of Christ, the image of his mother.[32] Purified and transformed by the fire of the Spirit, the deep, though sometimes wild and stifling, instinct that attaches women to life and to their children, changes into "universal motherhood,"[33] at once interiorized, spiritualized and open. This motherhood makes her compassionate toward all those who suffer, are hungry, in need, lost, are sinners. The masculine mind is at home in the world of ideas, though individual women also participate in this world; it runs the risk, however, of getting lost in the infinity of abstractions and in the desert of ideologies. The charism that is proper to women, without excluding an aptitude for intellectual activity, is to give life and to care for it. A monk of the Eastern Church has written, "Blessed are you who are receptive and welcome, you whose gift is not profits and production, . . . but a keen feeling and devoted care for what is living.[34]

---

[31] "Lettres de l'archimandrite Théodore (A. M. Boukharev) à l'archiprêtre V. Laverski et à son épouse, Alexandra Ivanovna" [Letters of Archimandrite Théodore (A. M. Boukharev) to Archpriest V. Laverski and His Wife, Alexandra Ivanovna], *Messager Théologique*, April-May, 1917 (in Russian). A French translation is provided in *Alexandre Boukharev, op. cit.*, p. 104.

[32] "In the presence of a woman . . . may your eyes rise toward the Lord whose image is imprinted in her according to her human nature and redemptive grace. . . . Then will be revealed to you in this woman, in this human person, at the same time as in the icon of the Lord, the image—though still troubled and tarnished—of her from whom the Lamb of God condescended to take flesh," *Alexandre Boukharev, op. cit.*, p. 104.

[33] P. Evdokimov, *Sacrement de l'Amour* [The Sacrament of Love], p. 41.

[34] A Monk of the Eastern Church, *Amour sans limites* [Love Without Limits], p. 96.

Today's Questions

These views touch an essential reality which is experientially felt by many women. They are, however, angrily denied by a certain kind of feminism which itself may already be outdated. Rethought and brought up to date, the Orthodox theo-anthropology could help the women's movement to keep from getting bogged down in an aggressive and wounding militancy instead of becoming conscious of the meaning of women's authentic human vocation. But once again we must not allow the heavenly vision to be an excuse for promoting a sort of sublimated sexism. It sometimes seems that the only purpose of a certain exaltation of "feminine charisms" in relation to Mariology is to justify the exclusion of women from real responsibilities in the Church and society. It seems to me that Evdokimov himself gave way to this temptation when he set the properly masculine gift of creation in the cultural area over against women's charism of birth-giving:

> If it is intrinsic to men to act, it is intrinsic to women to be and this is the religious state par excellence. Men create science, philosophy, art . . . Women are at the other end of all objectification, for women's strength is not in creation but in birth-giving.[35]

Do we not have here a very distinguished way of expressing the ancestral and naïve conviction of the intellectual superiority of the masculine sex? It seems to me that the error in this way of thinking comes from an "inclination toward cerebral abstractions" which Evdokimov himself justly denounced as the masculine bent par excellence. In the place of concrete human persons, men and women, with their varied and rich talents and their subtle differences, we substitute concepts, even cultural stereotypes. We confuse the "feminine," or the idea that we

---

[35] P. Evdokimov, *Sacrement de l'Amour* [The Sacrament of Love], p. 41.

have of it even though such an idea may be partly true, with persons in their concrete uni-complexity. From the biological, psychological, but also spiritual, point of view, every human person is in reality a composite being having either a masculine or feminine dominance which has been more or less accentuated, formed or deformed by education and cultural influences. Olivier Clement has written that "every human being, whether man or woman, is called to a certain virility in relation to his nature—we think of the "strong women" of the Bible—but also to a certain femininity in relation to God." We would add: and to his fellow creature. The distinction between cultural creation and birth-giving, though partially well grounded, cannot be hardened into a radical opposition unless we intend to reduce birth-giving to a purely biological phenomenon and cultural creation to a simple fabrication or arrangement of objects. Is not the first, birth-giving, extended into education that is a creation? And the second, cultural creation, when authentic, does it not always come close to birth-giving in which the creator gives himself to the object he has created?

It is quite obvious that men and women have different ways of being in the world. They function according to very different styles: a difference composed of harmonies and subtle assonances. What we have here is a qualitative difference with no necessary and permanent relations to any particular domain; nothing is reserved to one or the other and these domains vary across cultures and eras. To limit more or less arbitrarily "the charisms of women" to the home or to what are called today "feminine" occupations, which generally mean carrying out the decisions made by others, is an anachronistic point of view and contradicted by the facts. The richness of women is "a sometimes embarrassing plethora of resources,"[36] which at times compels them to make crucifying decisions, but this richness makes it possible for them to give birth and

[36] F. Quéré, *La Femme Avenir* [The Future as Woman], p. 122.

to create. Women can be writers or artists but also engineers, scientific researchers, company presidents, or political leaders: they do not carry on these professions any better or worse than men when we take into account the possibility of making mistakes which is part and parcel of human frailty. In carrying out these professions, women do not necessarily lose their femininity. They must not be excluded from this or that profession but rather from the temptation "to play the man," that is, to imitate the worst aspects of masculinity: self-centeredness, hardness, dominating spirit. Women's strength, though it seems close to the weakness that makes them vulnerable, is to get deeply and personally involved in whatever they undertake, but they are also capable of unlimited devotion. Instead of playing dangerous and sterile games of competition, instead of mutually ignoring and denigrating each other, men and women should learn today how to collaborate in all cultural domains! Let women bring what can be considered to be their proper gifts: intuition, sympathy, attention to the other, a natural propensity to love and protect life. It would be unfair and vain to try to limit their choices in an authoritarian manner whereas the real question for us, men and women alike, is that we must become more and more aware of the ultimate choice: "I have set before you life and death, blessing and curse; therefore choose life, that you and your descendants may live . . ." (Dt 20:19).

The over-evaluation of women's work outside the home is often a hoax; that is a fact. Far from letting women grow and develop, their entry into the production cycle, under present-day conditions, opens them to the risk of being reduced to a double servitude. Nonetheless, for many women, working "outside the home" is a hard economic necessity or a way of acquiring a minimum of material and moral independence. For some it is an act of social solidarity, a specific vocation in which they develop and grow. But, unless one has a special calling or unless living conditions are too inhuman, for most women (and sisters, I call on you to bear witness) nothing surpasses "the joy," "that a child is born into the world," a joy which is a foretaste of eternal beatitude (Jn 16:21). It is a joy that is extended in the celebration of infancy, of the awakening to self-awareness that the mother has the vocation of watching over and caring for. The home, "domestic chores" whose noble gratuity makes them similar to the service of the supreme Servant, the education of children, truly a work of creation, all of these will remain for us privileged moments of growth and fulfillment that some men are beginning to envy.

The high point of aggressive feminism, wounding for women and humanity, seems today to be on the decline. It is perhaps the role of Christian women to contribute and promote "a total feminism," a feminism that does not cut anything off but which "respects the likenesses and the differences."[37] The ecclesial vision of the divine Tri-Unity, far from being an abstraction without any relation to real life, as some think, must be the guiding image of a new humanism or rather of a divino-humanism in which men and women mutually recognize and respect each other in their common divine vocation and in their differences. Let us hope that women can help men against themselves, against their deformed masculinity, which women carry in themselves too and stop humanity at the edge of the abyss and stop the destruction of History. Perhaps the time has come, as such Christian thinkers as Soloviev, Berdiaev, Teilhard de Chardin felt, when, in the secret radiance of the transcendent mystery, men and women will be able to exercise in freedom "their complementary characters, in their finely shaded and diverse relationships of association, friendship and conjugal love. What history up till now has not seen, except in certain rare cases, could come about in the future through a collective refining for which women, the feminine as a spiritual virtue, would be the main workers."[38]

---

[37] *Ibid.*, p. 123.
[38] H. de Lubac, *op. cit.*, p. 87.

There is no question, certainly, of making men effeminate any more than of turning women into viragos, but it may just be that we want to feminize human beings, in the most noble meaning of the word, to preserve and awaken in them a feminine attitude of effacement and of acceptance when confronted by mystery, the Mystery of God and the mystery of the neighbor, the mystery of the other that I cannot come to know except by opening myself to Him. For those who look at love through the archetypal image of the Mother of God, woman is the figure of love and her mission is to remind humanity that the law of love, of every kind of love, is to open oneself to the universal. Love is fulfilled by accepting and welcoming the Third One: the child, the poor, the stranger, all images of Him who is himself, in person, the "Lord Love."[39]

In this way, a new art of living could bloom, even if it were only on a few islands, like the first Christian communities or medieval monasteries. These communities would be places where being would have priority over having, where inner fulfillment would be more important that competing for power and where science and technology would serve life, not death.

Women in Today's Ecclesial Community

Can the utopia that we have just sketched out inspire an effort not "to reform" the Church but to bring our Christian communities more in line with their spiritual principle so that they may reveal what the Church *is* in its hidden depths? Western culture now finds itself in a crisis despite the fact that it is becoming the planetary culture. Can we not ask therefore if one of the tasks of the Christian churches is not to invent, on the basis of revealed Truth, a new style and new models of collaboration between men and women? At the empirical and historical level, we are

---

[39] A monk of the Eastern Church, *Amour sans limites* [Love Without Limits], p. 18.

indeed faced with the need to innovate not by following ephemeral fashions but by applying the divine Word about men and women, in its eternal newness, to our situation and to our present-day problems.

As Fr. Nicholas Afanassieff and Paul Evdokimov have shown in their convergent studies,[40] Fr. Afanassieff being more historical and Evdokimov more doctrinal, the Orthodox Church has preserved in the depths of its consciousness the sense of the royal priesthood of the laity, of the whole people of God (*laos tou Theou*). This is true despite the fact that this consciousness has been obscured by a parasitical clericalism. Baptized, chrismated and admitted to the communion of the body and blood of Christ, Orthodox women are conscious of participating in this priesthood. They know that they are called to holiness, to *deification* not only in the life of the world to come but also here and now. They are called to the confession of their faith in Christ in words and deeds, deeds that must be carried out in the midst of this world as prophetic signs of the coming reign in us and among us of the life-giving Trinity. This doctrine has never wavered. Millions of women, known and unknown, nuns and laywomen living in the world, single or married, all have incarnated this doctrine in their lives, sometimes sealed by their sacrificial deaths: from the Christian martyrs of the first centuries of our era to Byzantine deaconesses and on to contemporary Russian Christian women; from St. Blandine of Lyons to Olympias, friend and inspirer of St. John Chrysostom, to St. Macrina, sister of Basil the Great; from Juliana

[40] We will quote from the first, especially his great work, though debatable on certain points, N. Afanassieff, *L'Eglise du Saint-Esprit* [The Church of the Holy Spirit], Paris, 1975. Chapters I, II, and III are dedicated to the royal priesthood of the Christian people. The second, P. Evdokimov, sets out his views in numerous works, especially in *L'Orthodoxie* [Orthodoxy], Neuchâtel-Paris, 1959, pp. 238-284.

Lazarevskaya[41] in 17th century Russia to Mother Maria Skobtsov who died in 1945 in the Ravensbruck camp.[42] No one can doubt that it was this heroic faithfulness of women believers, of mothers and grandmothers, that in our own time has allowed the Russian Orthodox Church to survive the persecutions of Stalin and Khrushchev.[43] Even today in the Soviet Union, women are most often responsible for the administration of the parishes as well as for maintaining the delicate relations with the civil authorities.

Elsewhere in traditionally Orthodox countries and in the Diaspora in Western Europe and North America and Africa, women are members and often presidents of parish councils, Sunday school teachers, choir directors, editors of Orthodox publications, etc. The status of the *Church woman*, as the Anglo-Saxons say, is obviously not the same as what we might find in Mediterranean countries, or the Near East, in the Soviet Union or in the United States. Nonetheless, everywhere we feel a more and more effective participation of women in Church life and responsibilities to which all Orthodox lay people have access. Where it is possible, a greater and greater number of women aspire to theological studies both to a deepen their own personal spiritual life and to serve the Church better.[44]

---

[41] The exceptional personality of Juliana Lazarevskaya (+1604), whose heroic life was recorded in a biography written by her own son, is today the object of historical research in the USSR. An English student of Slavic studies is now doing a doctoral thesis on her.

[42] *Contacts*, 51, 1965.

[43] The icon of these Christians who heroically confessed their faith has been set out by A. Soljenitsyne in a story, "*La Procession de Pâques*" [The Pascal Procession]. See also *Zacharie l'Escarcelle* [Zachary Money-bags], coll. 10/18, 122. See also the testimony of a Communist, E. S. Guinsburg, *Le Vertige* [Dizziness], Paris, 1967, pp. 389-90 and Wladimir Zielinski, "Une Nouvelle Génération de Croyants" [A New Generation of Believers], *Les Quatre Fleuves* [The Four Rivers], 14.

[44] The Moscow Theological Academy has a section for the formation of choir directors which for several years has been open to women who are now also admitted to the theological faculty of the University of Athens. In the

This relative openness, sometime encouraged, sometimes limited by political conditions, an openness that no canon of the Church seems to impede is in contrast to the seemingly eternal customs, rites and interdictions that we have inherited from paganism through the Old Testament. These seem to point out women as dangerous beings and ritually impure; for example, the Orthodox Christian woman must not, in principle, go into the sanctuary. This interdiction is even extended to newly baptized baby girls but a dispensation is often given to women to do cleaning in the altar! Ritual practice requires women to be "purified" after giving birth and finally it is the custom in certain local churches that women cannot come to communion during certain periods of their monthly menstrual cycle. Very often a woman or a young girl is in fact a reader in the church, but they cannot be acolytes at the liturgy or receive the minor orders of acolyte, reader, or sub-deacon. In practice, these rules are often relaxed or they fall away by themselves into disuse. The fact that they are officially maintained is nonetheless a cause of sadness and trouble for some women. The Orthodox women at the Agapia conference hoped that these rules would be abolished.

Too often, we have the tendency of giving women tasks that are considered inferior: material jobs, tasks of carrying out the orders of others, or Sunday school teachers—a task that in reality is very difficult and carries a great deal of responsibility. Teaching theology and, in general, any theological discourse seem too often to be a domain limited to men. Any woman who attempts to move into this area causes raised eyebrows and suspicion even though the same woman could be a doctor or lawyer without anyone thinking twice about it. Accepted with humor and humility, as much as that is possible, this situation is not really tragic, but at the same time, does it not deprive the

---

Diaspora, St. Sergius' Institute in Paris and St. Vladimir's Seminary in New York are equally open to women without any restrictions. Women can also teach there.

ecclesial community of riches and talents from which it could greatly benefit?

A century ago, Alexander Boukharev wrote that "the Church must be a fire lighted in the middle of the city." If our parishes were taken in hand by the priest and fraternal groups of men and women with different charisms who were encouraged to exercise their gifts, this action would transform our simple cultic assemblies into centers that radiate spiritual life, into places that welcome the lonely, the shipwrecked as well as seekers and creators.

From the doctrinal point of view, nothing stands in the way of a multiplication of diverse charismatic ministries in our communities, within the context of the radiant eucharistic mystery of which the priest is the celebrant. The Spirit blows where he wills, on women as well as on men.

Within an ecumenical context, there remains of course the thorny problem of women's ordination to the presbyteral priesthood and, sooner or later, to the episcopate.[45] It is necessary today to carry out a theological reflection on this subject and Orthodox women have the right and the duty to participate in it.

We are morally obligated to think seriously about a problem that is being put to all the Churches as a question of conscience. This was the general feeling of Orthodox women at the Agapia consultation as it was expressed in the final resolution:

> The problem of the ordination of women to the priesthood has been considered as though it is not a question for Orthodox women. (The first draft of the text said "is not a question for Orthodox women *right now.*") Nonetheless, we recommend that this problem be studied in the light

---

[45] The problem of women's ordination has now eclipsed even the *filioque* clause and is today at the center of the dialogue crisis between Anglicans and Orthodox. Up to the present, that dialogue has been particularly fruitful. See *Church Times*, London, July 29, 1977. In a general way, this problem opposes Churches of the *catholic* tradition to the various Protestant denominations.

of Orthodox Tradition in the hope of making a clearer statement of the Orthodox position in the ecumenical dialogue.

For some time now, individual Orthodox theologians, as well as assemblies of bishops, have issued many warnings about this new obstacle to the continued ecumenical dialogue. In the view of the majority of Orthodox believers, the unilateral decision of certain church groups to accept *de jure* the ordination of women to the presbyteral priesthood and to proceed *de facto* to such ordinations, for example, the Episcopal Church in the United States and the Anglican Church of Canada as well as the Reformed and Lutheran Churches. The Orthodox position cannot, however, simply be reduced to a refusal to discuss the question, to an invocation of the argument of Tradition without any explanation of that Tradition. To those who ask us for the bread of understanding, we cannot be satisfied with offering only the stones of certitude hardened in negation. Moreover, we Orthodox do indeed find regrettable the haste, so uncharacteristic of a conciliar spirit, with which the Church members of the World Council have decided to ordain women without any real concern for the opposition of Churches of the *catholic* tradition, that is, not only the Roman Catholic Church but also the Chalcedonian Orthodox and the Non-Chalcedonian Churches. The sense of continuity in the life of the Church is one of the characteristics of the Orthodox mentality. There can therefore be no question of sweeping away, in an inconsiderate manner, the 2000-year-old tradition of a masculine presbyterate and episcopate. Again, we must attempt to uncover the intelligible principles behind the tradition and to set out the authentic meaning to be found under the *customs* that have been conditioned by history and culture.

At this point we must carry out a necessary reflection on the meaning of the specific sacerdotal ministry in the Orthodox Church. Other more competent studies have been carried out, but we would, nonetheless, like to try to set out certain main points. For the Orthodox faith, Jesus is the only High Priest, the only mediator between God and men, the unique source of grace in the communion of the Father and the Holy Spirit. All priesthood in the Church derives from the priesthood of Christ and is a participation in his unique priesthood.

By the fact that all members of the Body of Christ are intimately united to the head of the Body, Jesus, they participate in the priestly life and the sacrificial death of the Redeemer. According to the spirit of the *Philocalia*, an anthology of the most significant texts about Orthodox monastic spirituality, every believer can celebrate an interior and invisible liturgy by associating himself with the eternal offering of Christ, by purifying his heart and by offering to the Lord the spiritual eucharist of his thoughts, feelings and acts. This can be done with regards to the most humble work or to creations of art and science done in the name of Christ and in Christ. The royal priesthood consists in this offering, and all the members of the Body of Christ, clerics or laymen, men and women, are called to it.

The liturgy celebrated by the eucharistic assembly is a *public* act of worship offered to God by all together. The ordained minister together with the faithful celebrates in Christ by the Holy Spirit and in communion with the whole catholic Church of the saints of all times, with the invisible bodiless powers and with the living and the dead. The consciousness of the royal priesthood of the people of God in no way, however, implies a negation of the special priesthood whose charism is authenticated by the sacrament of order. It rather situates this priesthood in its proper place: *not above but within the Christian community*. In the whole Church, united and given life by the Holy Spirit, the bishops and the priests delegated by them have received the charism of being the witnesses of the apostolic faith and of carrying out sacred acts, of dispensing the sacraments. Their priesthood is not different from the priesthood of believers, but they have received a special mission. They are called by God and the sacrament of order is the efficacious sign of this call, *to express and exercise the universal priesthood.* They are the instruments of this priestly and invisible grace of which the total Church, laymen and clerics, men and women, is the depository. The laying on of hands links them to the apostolic tradition, that is, connects them to the long chain of witnesses who, from the first apostles on, have attested to the reality of God's gift. Ordination thus confers a special grace linked to the public exercise of the universal priesthood and it designates the bishop, or his envoy the priest, as the one who is "to preside in the Lord" in the eucharistic assembly. "The bishop and priest only apply the eternal mediation of Jesus at a certain point in time and space."[46] They re-present, make present, the unique mediation and the unique mediator for the assembly of the faithful. But those who attend the liturgy are not present as though at a show. They participate in it intimately and intensely. They can and must show their participation by singing and saying the prayers together. The participation of the faithful is particularly expressed by the triple *amen* after the epiclesis which is said today out loud by the faithful in most Orthodox communities of the Diaspora. Even if their participation is silent, the faithful do participate: in principle, it is always the whole community that implores the grace of being united by the Spirit to him who "offers and is offered" for the salvation of men. The celebrant says, "Your own of your own, *we* offer to you on behalf of all and for all." Clericalism, ignorance and human sin can, however, dim this vision which nonetheless remains present in the intimate consciousness of the Church and inspires her doctrine. And this doctrine establishes a happy balance between the royal priesthood of the Christian people and the special priesthood conferred by ordination. Both priesthoods come from and

[46] Un Moine de l'Eglise d'Orient (L. Gillet), *L'offrande liturgique*, Paris,, 1988, p. 73.

participate in the unique priesthood of Christ. It is the delicate balance between them that explains the serenity of Orthodox women. Even though they are not called to the special liturgical priesthood, they do not feel frustrated; they rather feel called in a positive way to a personal prayerful communion which is intensified all the more in the divine mysteries.

It remains true, however, that the arguments against women priests are not all of equal value. Some of them seem weak and even opposed to the spirit of the Gospel. We would like to hear a clear statement that ritual impurity has nothing to do with excluding women from the altar of Him who was born of woman and who allowed himself to be touched by the sinful woman.

Some women who feel called to the priesthood are accused of being ambitious or of having an "inferiority complex" for which they are trying to compensate. These arguments seem rather frivolous. They are in fact *ad hominem* arguments and could they not just as easily be turned against many male candidates?

It is a historical fact that women priests have never existed in the Orthodox Church up till now, but can we deduce an unchanging rule from a fact? As an earthly institution, the Church is not totally set apart from history and cultures. What was unthinkable in cultural conditions of one given period can become a moral and spiritual necessity for the Christian whose conscience has acquired a greater degree of maturity. As we noted before, the liberation of slaves, as inscribed in the dynamism of the Gospel, only became a necessary duty during the 19th century. The question therefore must be asked: Is there a requirement of conscience based on the Scriptures to change the 2000-year-old tradition of a masculine presbyterate? Or on the other hand, is it just a demand of abstract equality without spiritual roots and whose consequences, if carried out, would scandalize simple souls and divide the Church? "All things are lawful for me, but all things are not helpful" (1 Co 6:12).

What do the Scriptures say? According to the New Testament, Jesus indeed only chose apostles of the masculine sex. Nonetheless, St. Paul's letters show that in the primitive Church, there were women's ministries of teaching, prophecy, communication of the faith that were far reaching indeed. A Roman biblical commission made up of specialists when asked about this question concluded that there is nothing in the Bible either for or against women priests.

This lack of certainty in biblical science brings us back to theology or more exactly to Orthodox theo-anthropology in its relations with the Orthodox doctrine of ministries. This is an immense problem that we can only touch on here. It certainly has to deal with religious symbolism and especially with the liturgical symbolism in the Church.

As we said at the beginning of this study, the Orthodox reflection on man insists, as part of the scriptural revelation, on the specificity of womanhood. Orthodox anthropology sees femininity not as inferior but as a value that has its basis in the Being of God himself. Woman and man, as human persons, both carry the indestructible image of Him who is the substantial image of the Father, though this image has been darkened by sin. However, women in their own way of being human also prefigure the "new creature" that is completely penetrated and filled with the Holy Spirit and therefore able to engender sons of God. The recognition of women's significant difference implies the recognition of their eminent dignity according to faith and hope. Men and women are equal and different in the image of the Son and the Spirit in the trinitarian life and in the economy of salvation. They are called to work together in the world, each one according to its own modality.

Does this theological vision of humanity imply that women cannot be priests or bishops? More than a formal exclusion imposed from the outside, we can see it as a call to an inner deepening that would allow women to discover themselves and to perceive their most authentic vocation: a vocation of personal charisms, of inspiration and of prophesy rather than of the objective and cultic expression of the divine mystery.[47]

At this point, we begin to see the Orthodox conception of the liturgy and of the liturgical function of the bishop and of the priest, his delegate.

For the Orthodox believer, the liturgy is the sacramental and iconic expression of the mystery of redemption. It proclaims this mystery with the aid of the symbolic language of rites and gestures that accompany the word and make its meaning clear. The whole liturgy, with the celebrants, is a spoken and acted out icon, a sacred poem that points to the ineffable through the veil of symbols. Liturgical symbolism is not arbitrary. It obeys the rules of a grammar that is the work of the Church inspired by the Spirit. Signs have been chosen for their appropriateness and because they can be read by the greatest number. They have not been chosen because of someone's individual inspiration. In the liturgical drama, the priest represents Christ not in the crude naturalistic sense or as a juridical representation. He represents Christ like an icon in which we sense a spiritual reality that goes beyond the icon itself. At the same time, the icon is the ecclesial sign of that reality. By withdrawing into the background and in a way emptying himself of himself, the priest-bishop in the eucharist as the central liturgical act, designates the unique High Priest, the incarnate Word who assumed the fullness of humanity. Christ, however, clothed himself with that humanity in its masculine modality and this was not simply an accidental happening.

Masculinity, obviously, does not make the priest, but it appears as an appropriate sign for designating the Bridegroom of the Church, He who loves the Church with a passionate love in which the conjugal love of husband for wife mystically participates on the level of the creation.

---

[47] See the Introduction at the beginning of this book concerning a certain evolution in my thinking on this matter.

However, the eucharist is not only the actualization of the Lord's eternal Pascha. It is also the renewal of Pentecost, a new outflowing of the Spirit in which all, men and women, participate: "They were all together in one place," says the Acts of the Apostles of Pentecost when the prophecy of Joel was fulfilled: "I will pour out my Spirit upon all flesh and your sons and your daughters shall prophesy" (Ac 2:1, 17).

Toward the Restoration of Deaconesses in the Orthodox Church?

We have already seen in St. Paul's letters that deaconesses existed inside the first Christian communities. We do not have a lot of information, however, on what they did or how they acted. Progressively taking on an institutional form, this women's ministry developed throughout the patristic period and continued in Byzantium until the twelfth century. Before the 1917 Revolution, the Russian Church had already been thinking of restoring the female diaconate. Today, the double awareness of feminine values and the social implications of the Good News makes this project once again quite timely. On the basis of his historical investigations, a theology professor at the University of Athens, E. Theodorou,[48] has become an ardent supporter of the women's diaconate.

According to a Syrian document of the first half of the third century, the *Didascalia of the Apostles*, the ministry of deaconesses is linked to that of the Holy Spirit. It says that "the deacon has the place of Christ and you should love him; you should honor the deaconess in the place of the Holy Spirit."[49]

---

[48] E. Theodorou, *La cheirotonia ou cheirothesis des diaconesses* [Cheirotonia or Cheirothesis of Deaconesses], Athens 1954 (in Greek). The author sums up his thesis in a document published by the World Council of Churches in 1967 under the title *Deaconesses*.
[49] *The Didascalia* 2, 26 (F. X. Funk, ed. Padesborn, 1905).

Canon 19 of the council of Nicæa (325) mentions the ordination of deaconesses by the imposition of hands. The prayers that accompanied this ordination are found in the *Apostolic Constitutions*. The canons of the council of Chalcedon speak of this ordination and sometimes use the word *cheirothesis*, sometimes *cheirotonia*. Among the famous deaconesses of the patristic period, we must note Olympias, the friend and collaborator of St. John Chrysostom; St. Macrina, older sister of Basil the Great and Gregory of Nyssa who both revered her greatly; Theosevia the wife of Gregory of Nyssa. She was consecrated deaconess when Gregory became a bishop and she continued to live with him. These women were both pious and cultivated, capable of understanding and discussing theological problems. In the following centuries, the women's diaconate went through a great development in Byzantium. The Byzantine deaconess was nominated by the bishop and consecrated by the laying on of hands, a *cheirotonia* and not just a *cheirothesis*, as is reserved for minor orders. The deaconess received an *orarion* as a distinctive sign of the diaconate as well as a eucharistic chalice that she put on the altar after the communion of the clergy. The *Novellæ* of the emperor Justinian counted the deaconesses among the members of the clergy.

The deaconesses were usually chosen from among the virgins and widows, but we know of some married deaconesses. Like deacons, deaconesses could not marry after being ordained or consecrated. They exercised their ministry in the liturgy as well as in education, but they were especially active in charitable work. E. Theodorou wrote that "they were the servants of the crucified and resurrected Lord at the side of the sick, the poor, the children and all those who needed their help." In the liturgy, deaconesses had the function of undressing women at baptism, anointing them and submerging them in the baptismal font and bringing them dressed in white to the bishop.

From the ninth to the tenth centuries, the feminine diaconate lost its real functions and became only honorary. This degeneration may explain why it disappeared in the twelfth century.

It goes without saying that the restoration of a purely formal woman's diaconate as it existed in Byzantium would seem today anachronistic and meaningless. Perhaps we should give women who feel called to the diaconate the task of exploring this ancient path so as to adapt it to new situations in the spirit of the Gospel and the Tradition of the Church? Such an experiment is actually being carried out in the Coptic Orthodox Church which is living through a period of great spiritual fervor which in no way excludes a lucid analysis of social problems. Universities in particular are interested in the matter.

We need to reconsider the diaconate, under the guidance of the Holy Spirit, but not only the diaconate of women. We need to rethink it in terms of a new and original ministry. In no way should it be thought of as a substitute for the presbyterial ministry. Blessed and authenticated by the Church, linked to the priesthood of the altar, as a complementary ministry, yet distinct from it, an authentic and reinvented diaconate could become a sign. It could be a sign of the presence of the comforting Spirit at the side of the Bride who is looking for the Bridegroom "in the streets and squares of the city," as the Song of Songs says. It could be a sign of the presence in the Church of her "in whom everything is grace,"[50] who extends over the world her gold-woven veil and who teaches us every day what tenderness is.

---

[50] A Monk of the Eastern Church, *Amour sans limites*, p. 95.

CHAPTER FIVE

The Place of Women in the Church

What is the point of asking questions about the place of women in the Church? A woman author rather slyly remarked that "men would probably be very surprised if anyone had the idea of writing about the place of men and masculine ministries."[1] If the question is not asked about men, does it not mean that their place appears to be securely established? In a society in which the feminine difference is seen as an inferiority, men have their place at various levels but unquestionably always at the top of the pyramid of powers and responsibilities which the institutional Church represents, in the eyes of many. As for women, their place is at the base of the pyramid, not outside the Church but at the bottom. In any case, they are below the place occupied by men.

Patriarchy and Communion

This conception of the Church is pyramidal and patriarchal; it follows the pattern structures which in antiquity were intended to insure peace in the family and society. For a very long time, this notion has infected Christian thinking. It coexists, nonetheless, with another vision and

---

[1] Quoted from P. Michalon, "La femme dans l'Eglise" [Women in the Church], *Unité chrétienne* [Christian Unity] 53-54, Feb.-March, 1979, p. 5.

experience of the Church that have their roots in the New Testament: the Church as *koinonia*, communion of persons and of local Churches in Christ through the Holy Spirit. It is a communion of men and women in the radiance of the divine Uni-Trinity. As human persons, they are irreducibly different but equal in dignity. In this communion, the Spirit does not abolish the differences of sex and culture but rather transcends them and sovereignly distributes his diverse gifts for the edification of the common "spiritual house" (1 Pt 2:5).

The question of the place of women in the Church has its origins in the tension between these two conceptions of the Christian community. This question is being asked in a society that has already been influenced by the fermenting action of the Christian Gospel. The yeast of the Gospel is raising the heavy dough of human nature, not without some resistance however. We must also set the ambivalence of ecclesiastical statements about women in the perspective of this dialectical tension, an ambivalence that is rightly denounced today by the historians of Christian antifeminism. A Catholic woman theologian, Kari Borresen, has written a doctoral thesis whose title *Equivalence et Subordination* [Equivalence and Subordination][2] clearly shows the internal contradictions.

On the one hand and in line with Jesus, churchly discourse affirms the spiritual equality of men and women. On the other, however, women's participation in the ministries of the Church, in its apostolate especially when it is public, is governed by all sorts of restrictive and limiting rules that vary according to times and cultures. In order to justify these rules, the authority of Scripture, and especially the rabbinical exegesis of the second creation story (Gn 2:18-24), are cited. Being created after and from Adam, Eve is *naturally* subordinated to him; her being is

---

[2] K. Borresen, *Equivalence et Subordination* [Equivalence and Subordination], Paris, 1976. See also J.-M. Aubert, *La Femme, antiféminisme et christianisme* [Women, Antifeminism, and Christianity], Paris, 1975.

dependent on his. It is simply unthinkable that Adam could in any way be subordinated to Eve or that she could be his equal. Such notions will only become thinkable under the action of the Spirit as he breaks through cultural stereotypes and chases away the ghostly fears, conscious or unconscious, of women who are not only "impure" due to their menstrual periods but also weak and dangerous. All of these specters only obscure the real question. In the spiritual context where consecrated celibacy appears to be the way par excellence toward Christian perfection, women become the primary source of temptation for men. In the West especially, but no doubt elsewhere too, the battle "between the spirit and the flesh," between God and man, has only too often been perceived as "a battle between man and woman."[3] The question of women's place thus runs throughout all of Church history, right from the beginning. "All these with one accord devoted themselves to prayer, together with the women and Mary the mother of Jesus, and with his brothers" (Ac 1:14). Such is the Church at the dawn of its life. Everything is simple for the men and women who are waiting in faith and hope for the return of the Lord, but the return of the Lord did not occur as soon as the first disciples had thought, and therefore the Gospel's eternal newness had to take root in historical cultures. And here is where the problems begin.

Tensions and Discontinuities

Saint Paul

Let's look first at the apostle Paul. His statements about women seem to me to be very characteristic of an ambivalence due to the tension between the already anticipated

---

[3] P. Claudel, preface to *Partage de midi*, 1948. See also D. de Rougemont, *L'Amour en Occident* [Love in the West], Plon, 1939 (out of stock); also available in 10/18, #34.

vision of the Kingdom and the necessary adaptation of the Gospel to specific historical and cultural settings. In the words of the ancient baptismal hymn, Paul proclaims, "For as many of you as were baptized into Christ have put on Christ. There is neither Jew nor Greek, there is neither slave nor free, there is neither male nor female; for you are all one in Christ Jesus" (Ga 3:27-28).

As the herald of freedom in the Spirit, St. Paul did not exclude women from the generous distribution of his gifts. But we see here that he is faced with questions of proper social conduct: "Is it decent for a women to prophecy in the Christian assembly?" Under what conditions is it permitted? What would be proper dress for her when prophesying? So Paul, being the founder and leader of the young Corinthian community as well as a man concerned about the reputation of other men, begins a reasoning process that is as subtle as it is obscure. His point is to justify the obligation for women to cover their heads with a veil (1 Co 11:2-16) by using the famous text of Genesis 2: the honor of the husband depends on the veil.[4] But all of a sudden, Paul breaks his laborious line of argument and states the essential element, even though it had been so far unthinkable: the reciprocity of men and women is a principle based on God's plan. "Nevertheless, in the Lord woman is not independent of man nor man of woman; for as woman was made from man, so man is now born of woman. And all things are from God" (1 Co 11:11-12). And so we see how the Spirit clears a new path through the thick forest of human prejudices!

Of course, the problem is not definitively solved. 1 Timothy 2:11-15, though written at a later time, prohibits women from teaching because that would be for them to take on arrogantly a form of domination over men. In his

---

[4] For the interpretation of this difficult text, see A. Jaubert, "Le voile des femmes" [The Women's Veil], *New Testament Studies* 18, 4, 1972, as well as "Les femmes dans l'Ecriture" [Women in the Scriptures], *Vie chrétienne* [Christian Life], March, 1979, pp. 49-51.

pastoral activity, the apostle took into account the situations and contradictions of everyday life. But the guiding line of Paul's thinking, though obscured by these apparent contradictions, is to be found in Galatians 3. Here we have a text that is one with the apostle's great christological vision of the new creation, of the Kingdom in which the relations of reciprocal domination are abolished and where freedom in Christ makes the Law null and void.[5]

The Fathers

The same tensions and discontinuities are found in the statements of the Fathers when taken as a whole, even though important nuances can already be seen in the approaches of the East and the West.

In their thinking, the Fathers of the fourth century especially the Cappadocians certainly reflected biblical personalism, but they were also under the influence of the platonic and stoic idea of the unity of humanity, an idea they saw as a seed of the Gospel. They also strongly affirmed the equality of men and women who are both created in the image of God and are called upon to progress toward his likeness. Beyond the multitude of individuals of both sexes and in his many faces, man (*anthropos)* is *one* in his origin in God his creator, and in his dynamic orientation that opens him up to and makes him strive toward communion with the total Christ, his Omega point: a communion in the Son of saved human persons who have become carriers of the Spirit.

Basil the Great saw in his sister Macrina his true spiritual master. Gregory of Nyssa was married, and St. John Chrysostom had the deaconess Olympia as his friend and confidant. Nonetheless, in his pastoral activities, St. John is often severely unfair toward the women of his time in that he accuses them of being responsible for the degradation of Christian mores. Moreover, even though the

[5] A. Jaubert, "Le voile . . .", p. 56.

institution of deaconesses was flourishing at that time in Byzantium, none of the Fathers of the Church ever imagined the possibility of women presiding at the eucharist. Was that because the idea of women priests was too closely linked with the pagan priesthood and sacred prostitution? Did the notion of women priests suffer from being associated with heresies like Montanism and Priscillianism in which women played an important role? Whatever the reason, this refusal contradicted patristic anthropology and was justified by the old argument of the subordination of woman to man who is her "head," that is her master. The priesthood, which would seem to imply a relation of superiority for those who enjoy it, could not therefore be conferred on women. This at least seems to be the argument of the *Apostolic Constitutions* from the fourth century; this document seems to express a general opinion.

The eastern Fathers did not attempt to justify rationally this discontinuity between their anthropological teaching and a practice that they believed went back to apostolic times.

In the West, especially starting with St. Augustine, theologians will go very much farther in their rational explanation of this ambivalence. Augustine affirmed that since Eve was created from Adam, she was also made *for* him, but how could she be useful to him except to guarantee him physical descendants? In all other areas, the help of a male companion was certainly to be preferred. Nonetheless, like Adam, Eve had a reasonable soul, but as a physical and sexual being, she was subordinated to him, until she was freed from her earthly envelop. It is at this point that the platonic dualism which marks Augustine's thinking is revealed.

Similar ideas, though in an aristotelian perspective, were developed by the great doctor of medieval scholastic theology, Thomas Aquinas. They were associated, however, with archaic and pseudo-scientific conceptions about procreation according to which the male was the only active agent. As far as their bodies were concerned, women were merely defective men. This physical infirmity reflected on women's intellectual powers and condemned women in this life to inferior tasks while waiting for rewards in the Beyond granted as a result of their virtues.

These anti-women speculations were propagated by clerics under the authority of the two greatest thinkers of the Christian West, and they have certainly contributed to the inferior status of women in the Church, especially in the Latin world. Theology seemed to justify this status and even considered it to be canon law. But in the East also, the deaconesses progressively disappeared, and from that time on, the presence of women at the altar seemed inadmissible.

On the basis of what we have noted above, it would be hazardous, however, to draw simplistic and uniform conclusions as to the real place of women in Christians communities of past times. In order to discover what that place was, we would need to make a more detailed and diversified study using different parameters. We would need to study the lives of women saints as well as other documents that would give us an idea of the existence of obscure but illustrious Christian women of the past. In a more convincing way than official theologians, many women believers have shown that "women too make up the Church;" they made the best of the conditions imposed on their sex in any given society and have succeeded at times even at shaking off its conventions. They have been martyrs, mystics, or simply mothers of families; they have been contemplatives or women of action, sometimes both at once; they have been missionaries, founders of orders or philanthropic organizations and have taken to heart the temporal destiny of their people and the Church. They did not espouse any theories but simply obeyed the call of Christ and the Spirit thus transcending all through Christian history the accepted stereotypes of their respective cultures. We can name several of them: Blandine of Lyons, Brigitte of Sweden, Theresa of Avila, Julian of

Norwich, Joan of Arc; princess Olga of Kiev and Nina of Georgia whose people called them "equal to the apostles."

I would especially like to call attention to an extraordinary person in the Russian Church, Juliana Lazarevskaya. She was a laywoman, wife, mother of 13 children, a landowner of the lower nobility who dealt in a very concrete way with the social and economic problems during a very troubled period of Russian history. She was both a heroine, showing compassion toward the poor whom she fed in times of famine by selling most of what she had, and an authentic mystic in the hesychastic tradition. The *vox populi* canonized her following her death in the first years of the 17th century.[6]

As we can see from this rapid survey, the question of women's place in the Church is an old one. The Church has preserved the essential in that it never ceased to baptize, chrismate and give communion to women. At the same time, however, the men who directed the Church did not escape from the contamination of the accepted ideas of their time, ideas which were transmitted by male-centered cultures and perpetuated a certain scorn for and fear of women. The Church's greatness, her grace, is that she transmitted through the centuries the eternal Word that judges her in her temporal and historically conditioned aspects. In these areas, the Church is not exempt from error and sin and therefore quite open to judgment. This Word with the Spirit who adapts the letter to our times and gives it life, calls the Church to an unending reformation. The *Ecclesia semper reformanda* of the 16th century reformers is not incompatible with Orthodox the faithfulness to the authentic Tradition. The Orthodox theologian Vladimir Lossky said that "Tradition is the critical spirit of the Church." Ought not this critical spirit be applied today to the superstructures that obscure the relation between

---

[6] T. A. Greenan, *Juliana Lazarevskaya*, Oxford Slavonic Papers, XV, 1982; E. Behr-Sigel, *Prière et Sainteté dans l'Eglise russe* [Prayer and Holiness in the Russian Church], Bellefontaine, 1982, pp. 109-113.

men and women in the Church, a relation that is in keeping with the Gospel itself?

The Condition of Women in the 20th Century

It is much beyond the scope of this article to try to analyze the many factors that all through the 20th century have led to a new awareness among women. We can cite, however, certain facts that indicate the radical transformation in the existence and status of women in modern Western societies. In women's relations with men, this transformation has brought along with it new experiences of reciprocity, of partnership, and a new sharing of responsibilities not only at home but also in public life.

The knowledge and control of the reproductive process together with a considerably extended life span have created a situation in which biological motherhood and the care given to young children no longer, as in former times or as in less developed countries, take up most of the time of adult women. For these women, motherhood is no longer a fate accepted with joy or resignation, sometimes in a spirit of rebellion. Motherhood is nowadays rather the result of a choice, a decision taken more and more in common by the couple. It becomes a part of a total life project which for the women too can have many facets: a profession that assures an income and material independence as well as—and this is more and more often the case—a personal growth and development and the realization of a vocation in the service of culture, society, and finally, why not, the Church. In traditional societies, women have their place, and it can be a royal one, in the home or in a religious community. There are a few exceptions, however, but they only prove the rule.

The entry of women into all levels of public life where they share with men the same responsibilities is a phenomenon of Western or Westernized societies. Women have become partners in professional, cultural and political life with the same intellectual tools as men. For a long time, these domains were closed to women because it was thought that intellectual training for women served no useful purpose. Now, however, women have become partners not only outside the home but also in the family cell. Increasingly, a more flexible sharing of jobs and responsibilities between the father and the mother is taking over from a rigid distribution of roles. Without aiming at a crippling suppression of differences, this role sharing openly takes into account other factors than just sex: individual situations, personal vocations that transcend but do not negate psycho-biological differences. To the unique experience of motherhood, so wonderful for the wife, is now added that of a parenthood which is lived in common. This transformation does not mean that men and women have become simply identical and interchangeable parts, but their differentiation has its place less in social functions than in qualitative ways of acting and reacting.

These experiences have nothing specifically to do with religion although it is worth noting that they have occurred in societies influenced by Christianity. They constitute a reality that the Church must take into consideration, as it took note in the past of the thinking of men and women to whom it announced the Gospel. Going even farther, might not the Church discern in these experiences the "seeds" (*logoi spermatikoi* as the Fathers said) sown by the divine Planter looking ahead to the coming of a new community where "men and women will come to exercise *in freedom*[7] their complementary characteristics in many types of relationship, partnership, and friendship?"[8]

The Church has the vocation to baptize this new freedom won by women so that it will not degenerate into anarchy and mere confrontation of selfishness.

---

[7] Underlined by the author, Elizabeth Behr-Sigel.

[8] P. Teilhard de Chardin, quoted from H. de Lubac, *op. cit.*, p. 81.

The Ecumenical Movement

The Churches have reacted differently and with greater or less speed to the challenge they have received by the emergence of a new feminine consciousness in the secular society. This challenge has also been felt inside the Churches themselves by their own women. For various cultural and spiritual reasons, the traditional Orthodox Churches of Eastern Europe and the Mediterranean basin have often been occupied with major problems in other areas and have not for a long time felt deeply concerned by the problem of women's place in the Church. Only in the context of ecumenical dialogue have they become aware of the importance of this problem for other Churches, as well as of its universal ethical import. Many communities that have come out of the Reformation as well as large section of the Roman Catholic Church in Europe and in North America have taken the opposite path and have quickly become sensitive to the evangelical call implied in this deep cultural change. Underneath the excesses of an aggressive feminism, "a Christian idea gone crazy," these communities have recognized the legitimate desire of many women to participate in the life of the Church as free and responsible partners, where Christ and the Spirit have called them to serve.

The problem of women's participation in the life and especially in the different ministries of the Church has thus been a part of the ecumenical movement right from the beginning.

Of the 400 Church delegates to the first assembly of Faith and Order in Lausanne in 1927, there were only seven women lost in the mass of male theologians and dignitaries. These women, however, inspired a prophetic motion which was accepted. It expressed "the serious concern of giving to women the place that is theirs in the

Church and in the councils of the Churches . . . a concern that must be kept in the minds and hearts of everyone."[9]

Since that time, a growing number of Protestant theological faculties, also some Orthodox ones in Greece and Romania, have welcomed women students who go on to receive diplomas that are generally required of candidates for the pastoral ministry in the Churches of the Reformation. Certain Protestant communities, especially in North America, have begun to ordain women. In France, the small Reformed Church of Alsace-Lorraine took this step in the middle of the 1930s when it gave some women the position of pastors. These cases were, nonetheless, isolated. At the constituent assembly of the World Council of Churches in Amsterdam in 1948, the problem of women's ordination was brought up as one of the questions that divide the Churches. Many other disagreements appeared then to be far more serious and were given priority.

In the decade that followed, the aspiration of women to participate more in the various ministries of the Church was channeled toward a section of the WCC innocuously called "Cooperation of Men and Women in the Family, Society, and Church," directed by a Frenchwoman, Madeleine Barot. In this section, Protestants and Orthodox worked peacefully together. It was only in the 1960s under the pressure of advocates of women's ordination, whose numbers had significantly increased, that women's ordination became a burning question in the WCC. It ceased being a theoretical theme and became from then on a question that was asked on the basis of concrete experience. This was underscored by the important motion voted by the assembly of the WCC at Upsala in 1968. It recommended the study of women's ordination in a theological and ecumenical perspective taking into account "the experience of a growing number of Churches that today ordain women."[10]

---

[9] *Ordination of Women in Ecumenical Perspective, op. cit.*, p. 22.
[10] *Ibid.*, p. 23.

This was the beginning of the debate in which two opposing camps were formed: on the one side, Protestants and a number of Anglicans for the most part in favor of the ordination of women; on the other side, the Orthodox who saw themselves as the spokespersons for the *catholic* Tradition for whom the ordination of women was "out of the question." The confrontations also revealed divisions inside different Christian communities, such as Anglicanism, which were at a turning point. Very soon, all the partners in the ecumenical dialogue, in which the Roman Catholic Church was henceforth to occupy a central place, were to be confronted with a question which became a test case of the members' desire to pursue the dialogue.

Being conscious of the high stakes at risk, the WCC and the Faith and Order Commission jointly launched in 1977 *The Study on the Community of Men and Women in the Church.* Going beyond the polarization on the single problem of women's ordination, the study tried to place it in its anthropological and ecclesiological context. An inquiry on the "day to day life of women in the different Christian communities" was sent by the thousands all over the world. Numerous local and international conferences were held, such as the ones at Strasbourg-Klingenthal on *The Ordination of Women* in 1979 and at Niederaltaich on *Theological Anthropology.*[11] They all converged at the great international meeting at Sheffield in July, 1981, where the subject was *The New Community.*[12] 140 participants, two thirds of whom were women, represented a hundred member Churches in the WCC. Catholic theologians, who were full members of the Faith and Order Commission and who had played a significant role in its preparation,

---

[11] A resumé of the first one is found in *Ordination of Women.* Many of the presentations given at Niederaltaich were published in *Midstream,* P. O. Box 1986, Indianapolis, Indiana, XXI, 3, July, 1982.

[12] *The Community of Women and Men in the Church,* compiled by Constance F. Parvey, Philadelphia, PA, 1982. E. Behr-Sigel, "Vers une communauté nouvelle" [Toward a New Community], *Contacts* 115, 3, 1981 and 119, 3, 1982.

actively participated in the work of the meeting. A dozen Orthodox delegates and observers were present as representatives of their Churches. Neither the Churches of Greece nor of Romania was represented, and only two Orthodox women theologians, an American and a Frenchwoman, followed the study and felt involved in its work. Was not this under-representation a sign of disinterest, even of disapproval? This impression was confirmed by the lukewarm welcome given to the Sheffield report by Orthodox members of the WCC's central committee assembled at Dresden in August, 1981. The section of the report about "ministries" was nonetheless drawn up in particularly prudent terms, and its intention was to invite the Churches to reflect without prejudice on the reactions they would give to the report. The Sheffield report was, however, accompanied by a *Letter to the Churches* whose "prophetic" accent surprised and shocked dignitaries used to a more measured language. The misunderstanding was finally cleared and the Sheffield report was sent to the leaders of the Churches.

The bridges were therefore not burned, and the dialogue continued between the Churches but also inside the Churches between the hierarchy and the Christian people which includes women. In Orthodox circles, the poor quality of the internal dialogue was officially recognized by metropolitan Meliton.[13] The same deficiencies had been evident in the dialogue started several years ago, but unfortunately not continued, between the pastors of the Church and Orthodox women.

It may be worthwhile to mention here the international conference of Orthodox women, jointly organized by the WCC and the patriarchate of Romania in September, 1976. It was held in the famous Agapia monastery, one of the most important centers of women's monasticism in

---

[13] A homily preached by metropolitan Meliton at the liturgy ending the 2nd preconciliar panorthodox conference, September 12, 1982, *Episkepsis* 15, September, 1982, p. 18.

Romania. About 50 women from all over the Orthodox world, representing the ancient patriarchates of the East as well as the new Churches of the American and European diaspora, gathered together to talk freely about their problems and their aspirations.[14] Several bishops were also present: among them was the present patriarch of Antioch, his Beatitude Ignatius IV, metropolitan Emilianos (Timiadis) of the Ecumenical Patriarchate, and metropolitan Antony (Plamadeala) of the patriarchate of Romania. The tone of the meeting was not in the least aggressive, and the intention to remain within the continuity of the ecclesial Tradition was openly affirmed. On the other hand, no fear of the modern world was shown, and the women at the conference expressed their desire to meet the challenges of the modern world with a clear mind. The roles traditionally given to women in the societies evangelized by the Orthodox Churches was respected. The conference was reminded that women are called upon to serve the Church as mothers of families and as nuns, but new tasks were also envisaged; the following bold statement was set forth: "Women must take part in the councils of the Church at the level where decisions are made; they must be encouraged to play an active role in those councils . . . at the level of the parish, the diocese, and the local Church."[15]

A creative restoration of the women's diaconate, "which existed in the ancient Church up to Byzantine times," was also proposed.[16] And finally, the Orthodox women at Agapia expressed their desire to see the Orthodox position on the ordination of women to the priesthood "clarified" and "made explicit." All this was put in the perspective of the ecumenical dialogue in which the Orthodox living in the West were existentially engaged. There was

[14] The presentation of the Agapia conference were published by the WCC, *Orthodox Women, Their Role and Participation in the Orthodox Church*, Geneva, 1977.

[15] *Ibid.*, p. 48.

[16] *Ibid.*, pp. 49-50.

unfortunately no second Agapia. Did the freedom of speech of the women at Agapia raise too many fears? The 1976 meeting did, nonetheless, bear some modest fruits. A reflection was begun jointly led by priests and laymen, theologians and non-theologians, men and women. Several publications, especially in the Orthodox diaspora in France, Great Britain, and the United States, printed articles bearing witness to the thinking that was going on.[17] The following reflections are inspired by the desire to continue in the direction and the spirit of the Agapia conference.

In talking about "Russian grandmothers," a Soviet Christian said that "women are the infantry of our Church," an infantry that is reborn in each generation. It is this infantry that "wrote the history of the Church, the best history that we have."[18] Perhaps the time has come for a public recognition of this great and humble service rendered by women, and this will require a real "ecclesial metanoia." I see a prophetic sign of this metanoia in the action of metropolitan Antony Bloom. When pope John Paul II was on a visit to England, metropolitan Antony accompanied him, and in the chapel dedicated to the 20th century martyrs in Canterbury Cathedral, he lit a candle in memory of mother Marie Skobtsov, an Orthodox nun who died in the Ravensbrück camp near the end of the war. Before the Second World War, she took on a real diaconal ministry on behalf of Russian émigrés in France.

Nonetheless, beyond this and other symbolic gestures, we need to clarify the ecclesial statements about women and eliminate the ambiguities and contradictions that we have found in them. This clarification is to be carried out within the dynamic and authentic Tradition and not in rupture with it. Tradition's dynamism comes from the Spirit sent by the Father and who rests on the Son. Like

---

[17] See the bibliography at the end of this book.

[18] V. Zielinsky, "Une nouvelle génération de croyants" [A New Generation of Believers], *op. cit.*

living water, the Spirit flows from the Son onto women and men and makes them God's daughters and sons, and the creation waits in groaning and labor pains for their revelation (Rm 8:19-22).

Jesus' Attitude toward Women

The standard measure for a Christian attitude toward women, that is, one that is fully human, is found in the Gospel, in Jesus' attitude toward them. We must of course be wary of projections and of letting our own ideas get in the way. As France Quéré has remarked,[19] we must not read the New Testament through the glasses of an American feminist. Jesus did not spend his time denouncing the mores of his contemporaries or their views about the role of women. The women mentioned in the Gospel usually occupy the place that was given to them by custom. They served at table like Peter's mother-in-law and took care of the house like Martha. Joseph did not wrap Jesus in swaddling clothes. But on the other hand, Jesus did not abide by any of the sexual taboos concerning women. He was not afraid to touch them or be touched by them, even when they were seen to be impure, like the woman with an issue of blood or the prostitute who wiped his feet with her hair. He let women touch him, in the physical and moral sense of the word. He spoke with them as he did with the Samaritan woman whom he met at Jacob's well, even though she was of a rather dubious character having had five "husbands" and presently living with a sixth. It was nonetheless to this woman that Jesus confided the revolutionary secret about worship "in spirit and in truth."

What a contrast between this liberty and the taboos of the Old Testament which still clutter up our sacristies and

---

[19] F. Quéré, *Les Femmes de l'Evangile* [The Women of the Gospel], Paris, 1982. See especially the last chapter "L'Eglise, Jésus, les femmes" [The Church, Jesus and Women].

our imaginations! Patriarch Ignatius of Antioch follows Jesus' example when he said the following:

> I must admit that I do not understand how certain prescriptions of the Jewish tradition, found in the Old Testament, can be applied to the life of the Church. I cannot imagine, for example, why a woman would be "impure" when her husband is "pure" even though they both live in marital communion with each other.[20]

Jesus did not deny the differences between the sexes. He fully assumed his own masculinity and referred to his mother as "woman" (Jn 2:4). At the same time he appealed to what, in each one of us, is beyond sex, beyond it but raising it up into a higher order. Jesus' call is addressed to the person, to the hidden man of the heart, *homo cordis absconditus*, who is faced with the ultimate choice of faith or unbelief. Each person, man or woman, is called upon to accept the radical requirements of love and sharing, of giving up his own self-centeredness in order to enter into the Kingdom of heaven which is communion with Jesus in the Spirit.

The Fathers of the Church

We are not going to speak again about the theological anthropology of the Fathers of the Church, especially the Eastern Fathers. Let us merely recall what is their main point: the biblical revelation of the creation of *one* humanity in a double polarity of male and female, "in the image and toward the likeness of the one transcendent God" in three Persons.[21] This is the divine, living, and energetic Word that is sharper than any double-edged sword (He

---

[20] "Il ne suffit pas de soupirer après l'Esprit" [It Is Not enough to Long for the Spirit], an interview with the patriarch Ignatius of Antioch, *Service orthodoxe de Presse* [Orthodox Press Service], #66, March 1982.

[21] See above chapter 2, section II "The Anthropology of the Fathers."

4:12) that cuts through heavy cultural prejudices. This is the real and authentic Tradition.

According to this same Tradition, the ecclesial community, and all other truly human communities, are called upon to bring about a unity that is in the image of the divine Uni-Trinity: a communion of persons who are defined not in opposition to one another but by the way each one gives himself to the others, by the way each one opens himself to the desire of the other, while at the same time cooperating with each other in love. This vision is suggested by the wonderful icon of the Holy Trinity by Andrei Rublev. I see in this icon the guiding image that can inspire every authentically human relation to move toward its ultimate goal, a goal which is determined by the order of grace. It is also the guiding image of the relation between man and woman in the Church.[22] The vision of *being-for-the-other* is opposed to the struggle for power, mutual oppression and exploitation, the violence that marks our fallen world, a violence that disfigures Eve's face as well as Adam's. For there is no salvation by women as such, as a certain pseudo-mystical feminism seems to proclaim. The unique Savior for men and for women is Christ in whom all baptized persons, men and women, have received the firstfruits of the new creation by the gift of the Spirit. Thus the heavenly vision which is carried in the icon must be for us a source of energy and light and not an alibi for passivity and a lack of imagination, energy and light for the transformation of our relations *here and now.* We must advance together in the Church toward him who comes. Together in a spirit of *conciliarity*, we must seek new forms, and especially a new quality, of cooperation between men and women, new forms which can answer contemporary aspirations.

The crystallization of women's aspirations around the question of women priests is often surprising to Orthodox who often see the question as a sign of clericalism, to be

---

[22] See above chapter 3, section III "Two Icons."

explained by a defective understanding of the universal priesthood to which all baptized persons are called: an offering in the Spirit of their thoughts, desires, and works of their hands and minds to the Father in communion with the unique sacrifice of the Son. It is a permanent offering, and the sacramental eucharist is its liturgical realization. What is more, whoever says *liturgy* says *common work*, and all clerics and laymen are called upon to participate in this work. "In the Church, all are ministers."[23] This is a true statement which in no way denies the existence of a specific ministry of a restricted number. It rather situates the specific ministry as a function, a service within the community and not over and above it.

"We offer to you what is yours." This is the offertory prayer of the Byzantine liturgy and though it is said only by the priest, it speaks significantly about what "we" offer. A Orthodox spiritual master has said this prayer:

> At this moment, we pray for the whole creation; consecrating all men and women as well as the whole world to God. We carry out the office of priest so that our priesthood might be the ministerial priesthood delegated by the Church or the "royal priesthood" that scriptures attribute to all believers.[24]

This royal priesthood is not merely limited to the activity of the eucharistic assembly. It extends into daily life, into the family and society, into all the various works of human culture. In the 19th century, this larger function of the royal priesthood was stressed by the great Russian

---

[23] N. Lossky, "Femmes et hommes dans l'Eglise, une approche orthodoxe de la question des ministères" [Women and Men in the Church: An Orthodox Approach to the Question of Ministries], a presentation given at the Faith and Order conference at Lima, 1982, *Service orthodoxe de Presse* [Orthodox Press Service], Supplément, #66.

[24] A Monk of the Eastern Church, *Notes sur la liturgie* [Notes on the Liturgy], Beirut, 1973, pp. 58-59.

theologian Alexander Boukharev who dreamed of a synthesis between Christian humanism and mystical prayer.

A spirituality centered on the constant invocation of the Name of Jesus became widely known through a collection of ascetical and mystical texts called the *Philocalia*, and Orthodoxy has been profoundly marked by these writings. The practice of the Jesus Prayer can accompany and support all kinds of work: "By setting the Name of Jesus on each person and on every thing in order to offer them to God, every man and woman becomes a kind of priest of the universe." The intuition of this universal and interior priesthood may explain why for the Orthodox Church the problem of women priests has not become as acute as in other Churches.

The struggle for the ordination of women to an ecclesial ministry is often carried on with great passion, especially in the West. The motives behind this struggle are nearly always expressed in ethical terms. We can sum up the argument in the following simplified way: The Church's acts and real attitudes must conform to its teaching. All the Churches teach the equality of men and women before God who "shows no partiality" (Ac 10:34; Rm 2:11; Ga 2:6; Ep 6:9; Col 3:25). By what right, then, do the Churches reject *a priori* the requests of women who honestly believe that they have been called to an ecclesial service that is conferred by ordination? Is the criterion of sex sufficient in itself to reject these petitions? Other arguments, of course, are advanced, some theological, anthropological, and pastoral. These arguments seem to me to have a certain weight especially where the problem is not simply theoretical. In parts of Europe, North and Latin America, there is a real demand upheld by a strong current of opinion within the people of God. This is not the case (can we say "not yet"?) within Orthodox communities. In an article already quoted in *Service orthodoxe de Presse* [Orthodox Press Service], metropolitan Antony of Souroge said that "the Orthodox Church has not yet woken up to this problem. It has come to us from outside." This is why Orthodox theologians have been slow to think about a question that seems to them to be "unreal."[25] They do not see what is existentially at stake. When the question of women priests was first put to Orthodox Christians in an ecumenical context, they felt they could give a negative answer without any deep theological reflection. They simply referred to Tradition quoting one or another canon that forbids the ordination of women, and that out of historical context.[26] Indeed, as metropolitan Antony said, "it is much easier to say that what has never been can never be rather that to rethink the problem and try to understand that there is in fact a problem."[27] The first official Orthodox reactions to women priests were characteristic of this attitude, one that metropolitan Antony called "lazy" but which reveals, in any case, a cultural lag.[28]

Thinking has, nonetheless, slowly changed among the Orthodox. A global rethinking of the problem in its various scriptural, theological, anthropological, and ecclesiological aspects has begun. This rethinking is still fragmentary but it does exist and is developing especially in those areas where Orthodox live in direct and permanent contact with Christians of other confessions for whom women priests is a burning issue. Nowadays even when Orthodox give negative answers to inquiries, their responses are more reflective and less one-sided. Orthodox thinkers are taking pains to make sure that questions and minority opinions get a hearing, such as those for which I dare make myself the spokesman. I try to do this in all humility and in the

---

[25] A. Schmemann, Preface to *Women and the Priesthood*, T. Hopko, ed., p. 7.

[26] The famous canon 11 of the council of Laodicæa, a council we know very little about, is very difficult to interpret and its meaning is rather obscure. This is the opinion of most specialists including Orthodox ones. See Fr. Afanassieff's article in *Women and Priesthood*, pp. 61-74.

[27] *Service orthodoxe de Presse* [Orthodox Press Service], Supplément, *op. cit.* ; *L'Actualité religieuse dans le monde* [Religious News of the World], #41, November, 1986.

[28] *Ordination of Women in Ecumenical Perspective*; See the articles by Prof. N. Chitescu and Fr. G. Khodr.

spirit of "conciliarity," that is, the *sobornost* of the Russian Slavophiles.[29]

In any case, the question of women's ordination is dealt with in a different way depending on whether it is an ordination to the diaconate or the priesthood.

The Diaconate

The restoration of the women's diaconate would probably not raise any problem. It existed and flourished during the patristic age. Its restoration is being promoted by such eminent Orthodox theologians as professor Evangelos Theodorou of the theology faculty, University of Athens, and bishop Kallistos of Diokleia in England.

The roots of this feminine ministry unquestionably go back into the apostolic Church[30] although it is difficult to be precise about its nature in the first centuries of the Christian era. This is not surprising since all the ministries of the Church at that time were fluid and not distinctly

---

[29] "We must make sure that all voices in the Church are heard, including those who may be few and weak, even if they consider Orthodox practice in this area to be questionable and the theological arguments up to now to be insufficient, fluid, and unconvincing.": Fr. T. Hopko, "The 'Reception' of the BEM and the Problems It Poses for the Orthodox," *The Ministry of Women, Service orthodoxe de Presse* [Orthodox Press Service], Supplément, #101.

[30] For a history of the ancient deaconesses, see, R. Gryson, *Le Ministère des femmes dans l'Eglise ancienne* [The Ministry of Women in the Ancient Church], Gembloux, 1972. Also C. Vagaggini, "L'ordinazione delle diaconesse nella tradizione greca e bizantina" [The Ordination of Deaconesses in the Greek and Byzantine Tradition], *Orientalia Christiana Periodica*, XL, 1, 1974, pp. 145-189; G. Martimort, *Les Diaconesses*, Rome, 1982. For the New Testament, see *Le Ministère et les Ministères selon le Nouveau Testament* [The Ministry and the Ministries In the New Testament], Paris, 1974, and the thesis of E. D. Theodorou, *Hè "cheirotonia," hè "cheirothesia" tôn diakonissôn* [Cheirotonia and Cheirothesia of Deaconesses], Athens, 1954. This document is only available in Greek, but the author has published a summary under the title of "Das Diakonat der Frau in der Greichische-Orthodoxen Kirche" [The Woman's Deaconate in the Greek Orthodox Church], *Diaconia*, 1986/2; M. J. Aubert, *Des femmes-diacres* [Women Deacons], Paris, 1987.

defined. For example, the apostle Paul called Phoebe *diakonos* of the Church at Cenchreæ, but exactly what service did she perform? Or the women named as deacons in 1 Timothy 3:11? The present state of our knowledge on this subject only allows us to put forward hypotheses. Clement of Alexandria and St. John Chrysostom saw them as "women diaconate," or "deaconesses," fellow workers (*syndiakonous)* with the apostles. One of the oldest witnesses about the specific functions of women in the first Christian communities comes to us from a pagan writer. Pliny the Younger, being the governor of a province of the empire, wrote to the emperor Trajan and mentioned the case of two women that the Christians called "servants" or *ministræ* the Latin equivalent of the Greek *diakonos*. These women were tortured to get information about the new religion. Unfortunately this testimony does not give any more information about the exact functions of these women.

A more clearly defined women's diaconate only appears in the third century, probably in Syria. We hear about this ministry from the *Didascalia of the Apostles* in which, for the first time, the title *deaconess* (*diakonissa* in Greek) was used instead of the word *diakonos* to designate this women's ministry.

The institution of deaconesses was flourishing in Constantinople at the time of St. John Chrysostom, and we have several of his letters written to Olympia the deaconess. The laws of the emperor Justinian counted the Byzantine deaconesses among the clergy. They were "consecrated" to their service by a rite which was still mentioned in the 14th century by the Byzantine canonist Matthew Blastares. He described this rite and considered it still to be lawful but fallen out of use.[31] Blastares stated that the rite was essentially the same, "apart from certain exceptions," for deacons and deaconesses. The service consisted of the laying-on-of-hands by a bishop and an

[31] S. Hackel, "The Byzantine Deaconess," *Sobornost* 7/7, 1978, p. 595.

invocation of the Holy Spirit on the handmaid of God called to the deaconate according to a very ancient ritual:

> O holy and all powerful God, your only Son, our God, was born of a virgin and thereby sanctified womankind giving to women and not just to men the grace and the outpouring of your Holy Spirit. Look now, O Lord, on your handmaid here present and call her to your service (*diakonia*). Send down upon her the gift of your Spirit, keep her in the Orthodox faith so that she may fulfill her function without reproach according to your good pleasure. For to you is given all honor, glory, and worship, to the Father, Son, and Holy Spirit to the ages of ages.[32]

What is the exact meaning of this laying-on-of-hands? Is it simply a "blessing" (*cheirothesis*) or an "ordination" (*cheirotonia*)? This distinction did not exist at the time that the women's deaconate was the most flourishing, that is, during the 4th and 5th centuries, but it entered into Byzantine legislation at a later period.[33]

Concretely, however, the ministry of deaconesses was different from deacons. Though deaconesses had a full ministry, being liturgical, pastoral, and philanthropic, they were essentially oriented toward the service to women.

During the patristic period, the deaconesses took communion around the altar with the clergy. They helped the priest during the baptismal unction of women, but did not have the right to actually baptize except in emergency cases. Before and after baptism, they taught women the rudiments of the faith as well as the duties of Christian women. They visited sick women and brought them

---

[32] Quoted from E. Theodorou, *op. cit.*, pp. 31-32. Also R. F. Littledale, *Offices From the Service Books of the Holy Eastern Church* and *Sobornost* 7/7, 1978.

[33] P. L. Fontaine, *Les conditions positives d'accès au sacerdoce aux premiers siècles* [The Positive Conditions for Being Ordained to the Priesthood in the First Centuries], Ottawa, Ontario, 1963, p. 37. The author has noted that the 15th canon of the council of Chalcedon uses both words *cheirothesis* and *cheirotonia* to designate the ordination of diaconesses.

communion. The deaconesses were generally chosen from among the "widows" or "virgins," but some were married as was the case for Gregory of Nyssa's wife. She became a deaconess after her husband was elected bishop.

As the baptism of adults became an exception, the women's deaconate fell into disuse. In Byzantium, it was progressively reduced to a honorary title and function and gradually disappeared, but not completely as E. Theodorou has pointed out. In Greece a holy bishop of modern times, St. Nectarius, ordained some nuns to the diaconate.

In Russia at the beginning of the 20th century when there was a religious renewal underway, the Russian Church considered restoring the women's deaconate. A certain group of Christian women, no doubt influenced by the example of Protestant deaconesses, saw in a new type of women's deaconate the possibility of uniting the prayerful spirit of traditional Orthodox monasticism with active service to one's neighbor in the world. The 1917 Revolution, however, put an end to any hope of institutionalizing this ministry. In Egypt, a similar spiritual renewal is pushing the Coptic Church to establish women's communities whose members would in fact exercise a diaconal ministry. Such a ministry seems to be open, partially at least, to women in the Orthodox Churches. It is perhaps a path that needs to be explored, but if we envision the women's deaconate as simply the restoration of ancient and outmoded structures, the project will certainly lead to a dead end. The feminine deaconate should in no way be seen as a substitute for their participation in the presbyteral ministry. Nor should it serve as an alibi for avoiding a serious theological reflection about the ordination of women to the priesthood.

We find the following exhortation in the *Didascalia of the Apostles*, a Syrian text of the end of the third century: "Honor the deacon as having the place of Christ; honor the deaconess as having the place of the Holy Spirit."

The close relation between the deaconess and the Holy Spirit can be explained by the feminine gender of the word *ruah*, which in Aramaic designates *breath* or *spirit*. Are we justified in concluding with Paul Evdokimov that the Holy Spirit is somehow feminine?[34] Paradoxically, Evdokimov finds his main argument against women priests in this theologoumenon. Does not the priesthood, however, have something to do with the gift of the Holy Spirit who is invoked over the priest? This sort of speculation must be handled very carefully. There can be no question of introducing sexuality into the Christian representation of the trinitarian God and of making the distinction of the divine Persons into a sexual difference.[35] In the same way, it seems to me at variance with Christian anthropology and soteriology to oppose the Spirit-carrying woman to the christic man-*vir*. This would be in opposition to Galatians 3:27-28 and would lead to the impoverishment of both men and women. From the recommendation of the *Didascalia*, I would like to retain the embryonic idea about a ministry that is essentially identical, conjoined, shared, and exercised by persons who are unique each in their own way. This *diakonia* exercised by men and women, of equal dignity would be a common service. Their ministries would be linked together in the distinction between the Son and the Spirit, between the Lamb and the Dove though they are eternally associated, immanent one to the other. Their distinction/association is for Christians the divine model and a permanent source of inspiration.

The Priesthood

Can a similar model be applied to the presbyterial ministry? On first look, this would seem impossible in the Roman Catholic Church as in the Orthodox Church. On

---

[34] P. Evdokimov, *La Femme et le Salut du Monde* [Woman and the Salvation of the World], p. 219; *La Nouveauté de l'Esprit* [The Newness of the Spirit], pp. 259-262.

[35] On this subject, see the relevant criticism of the German woman theologian, A. Jensen, *op. cit.*, pp. 136-37.

many occasions in the WCC and in bilateral ecumenical talks, the Orthodox opposition to women's ordination to the priestly ministry has been vigorously expressed, even to the point of calling into question the talks themselves. We are therefore quite aware of the risk we are taking by putting forward the hypothesis that this negative attitude might be softened, that a certain pluralism in this area might be compatible, from the Orthodox point of view, with the search for full ecclesial communion.

Let us first note that the arguments put forward today against the ordination of women are by and large no longer the same as those used in past centuries. Among contemporary Orthodox theologians, we hardly hear anymore arguments based on the inferiority of women and the hierarchy of the sexes (based on the rabbinical exegesis of the second creation story) or of the responsibility of Eve in the Fall. We hear, however, rather paradoxically, arguments based on women's spiritual charisms—which these theologians feel it is their duty to reveal to women. Such thinkers as Evdokimov call on women not to aspire to a ministry that is incompatible with their specific vocation.[36] These speculations, though, seem to us only to confuse the matter and have very little scriptural foundation. The apostle Paul noted the case of women who had received charisms, for example, the gift of prophesy, and he felt he had the right to regulate the public exercise of those gifts for the good order of the assembly. He never spoke, however, of feminine charisms.

We sometimes hear that women are to be the "orants," "the praying ones," or "religious souls" par excellence. But we do not see why this "gift" ought to be incompatible with the exercise of an ecclesial ministry.

Like the inferiority of women, the notion of female ritual impurity has disappeared from official theological

---

[36] P. Evdokimov, *La Femme et le Salut du Monde* [Woman and the Salvation of the World], pp. 247ff; "Les charismes de la femme" [Women's Charisms], *La Nouveauté de l'Esprit* [The Newness of the Spirit], p. 237.

statements, even though it may still haunt people's unconsciousness.

The fact that Jesus chose twelve apostles, only males, to carry the Good News to the nations remains, however, a weighty argument, but is it decisive? Like the patriarchs of ancient Israel, the patriarchs of the new Israel, the Twelve, were men. But in the writings of St. Paul, himself outside the group of twelve, the term *apostle* is applied to all those who "labor to announce the Gospel and among these, there were women." This enlarged use of the word *apostle* is accepted by the Church which glorifies the myrrh-bearing women of the Gospel as "apostles of the apostles."

It is nonetheless a fact that throughout their 2000 year old history, neither the Orthodox nor the Roman Catholic Churches have felt the necessity to ordain women to the presbyterate. Can they break with a tradition so old and venerable without running very serious risks? The life of the Church is continuity: "Jesus Christ is the same today, yesterday, and for ever" (Heb 13:8). This continuity of life, however, must not be mistaken for a simple and blind repetition of the past. It does not prevent the Church from going ahead under the inspiration of the Spirit "in newness of life" (Rm 6:4).

For a long time, I thought that the masculinity of the priest was justified by his function, in a way iconic, in the eucharistic liturgy. I am less convinced of that today. As the president of the eucharistic assembly, the presbyter-bishop represents Christ who is the one High Priest according to the order of Melchizedek and who "entered once for all into the Holy Place, taking not the blood of goats and calves but his own blood, thus securing an eternal redemption" (Heb 9:12). The question, nonetheless, must be asked: What is the meaning of this "representation" of Christ by the priest? According to the Orthodox understanding, the priest is not "another Christ." He is only the instrument that mediates the personal and invisible presence of Christ. St. John Chrysostom stressed that the only ones who act are Christ and the Spirit. Now the priest mediates the action of Christ not by his masculinity but by pronouncing the very words of the Savior over the holy gifts. This is the Tradition of the Church which Nicholas Cabasilas interpreted in the following way: "The priest recounts the story of the Last Supper . . . and by repeating these words, he prays and applies the very words of the only-begotten Son our Savior to the offered gifts."[37] The priest is thus the spokesman for the eternal Word. He lends his voice to the Word. Can this voice not be a feminine one?

Some might object that Christ was a man and that the Word took flesh in the body of a male human being. But if the eucharist is a memorial of the incarnate Son of God's sacrifice, it is also the anticipation of the messianic banquet of the Kingdom and communion with the Resurrected Christ who has ascended into the heavens, that is, entered into the divine sphere where the categories of masculine and feminine are, if not destroyed, at least totally transcended.

And finally in the liturgical action, and this seems to be important, the priest not only represents Christ, but by saying "we," he also lends his voice to the Church. He pronounces the epiclesis in the name of the gathered assembly, in communion with the universal Church. The fervent prayer of the liturgy of St. John Chrysostom asks for the outpouring of the Spirit "on us and on the gifts here present." Now according to the marriage symbolism that in fact runs throughout the Scriptures, a symbolism that is often invoked to justify the male priesthood, the Church as the people of God is the Bride who having received the Spirit, prays with him and in him: "Amen! Come Lord Jesus" (Rv 22:20).

What conclusions can we draw from these facts? The Church performs the eucharist and believes that Christ is living and present through the Holy Spirit. Christ acts as

[37] N. Cabasilas, *Explication de la Divine Liturgie* [Explanation of the Divine Liturgy], ch. XXVII.

the one High Priest who both "offers" and "is offered." The ordained minister does not *produce* the Lord's real presence. He is rather ordained to this service, "sent" in the succession of the first apostles and is only the witness of the presence. He pronounces the words of institution and is called upon to give himself totally to this action. He equally asks that the Holy Spirit be sent on the assembly and on the gifts offered. In the words of the Orthodox liturgy of St. John Chrysostom,[38] he "loans his tongue and his hands" to the Lord but also to his Church which is called to be the temple of the Holy Spirit. If this is the essence of the Church's faith as witnessed to by the words of the liturgy, is not the maleness of the priest thereby relativized? Might we not also say that, assuming a unity of faith, the greater or lesser importance given to this masculinity corresponds to different and relative accentuations accorded to it by various cultures?

We must add, however, that the problem of the ordination of women to the priesthood does not just concern the thinking of the faith in the clear light of the divine Logos. It also touches the darker and very powerful regions of the emotions, the unconscious, and cultural archetypes. It is up to the Church's wisdom, and to the wisdom of the Churches, to take all these factors into account so as not to scandalize the weak ones while remaining firm on the essential Gospel message of freedom.

A Disciplinary Pluralism?

St. Paul wrote that "all things are lawful for me, but not all things are helpful" (1 Co 6:12). Now for the Churches, what is helpful here may not be so elsewhere, in different times, places, and circumstances. The people of God does not live and advance everywhere at the same rhythms. Some are still at the end of the Middle Ages while others

[38] The epiclesis of the liturgy of St. John Chrysostom: "We pray to you and supplicate you: send your Holy Spirit on us and on the gifts here present."

are already living in the third millennium. On a problem like the ordination of women, might we not imagine different "helpful things" that the local Churches could determine for themselves? This autonomy would have to go hand in hand, however, with a concern shared by all the Churches to promote the liberty in the Holy Spirit and the dignity of all, men and women, inside the "new community." But would not such a pluralism of discipline in this area be compatible with the unity of faith and ecclesial communion?

CHAPTER SIX

Mary, the Mother of God: Traditional Mariology and New Questions*

The Attitude of the Orthodox Church Toward the Mystery of Mary

A Western Christian, whether Catholic or Protestant, who goes into an Orthodox church and attends a liturgical celebration cannot help but be struck by the manifestations of a very vigorous devotion to Mary. She is invoked as the Theotokos, the Mother of God, or literally the Birth-giver of God, and is present everywhere. Her name comes up in all the prayers. Candles are lit in front of her icons, sometimes in greater number than before those of Jesus Christ. However, Mary is hardly ever represented without her Son, from whom she is inseparable. The icon of the Theotokos is essentially an image of the incarnation of the divine Word. At all the feasts and celebrations in her honor, such as the Annunciation, the Dormition and others, the Mother of God, the Virgin Mary, is always

* This lecture was given on July 2, 1985, in Strasbourg, France, and was part of a larger conference organized by the World Lutheran Federation's Center of Ecumenical Studies on the theme of "Mary and the Place of Women in the Church."

solemnly invoked. Her name is praised at other occasions also, during each liturgy, in the prayers of the Hours, in the major feasts that refer to the main events of salvation history, Christmas, Easter, Ascension, and Pentecost. The following prayer is addressed to Christ throughout the whole Orthodox liturgy: "By the prayers of your holy Mother, save us." One of the strongest expressions of this veneration is the Acathist, a hymn to the Virgin. The word itself comes from the Greek verb *kathizomai* meaning "to be seated" with the alpha privative prefix added on. The Acathist is a long poem written in Mary's honor and is read or sung at the matins of Saturday, actually celebrated Friday night, of the 5th week of Great Lent. It is a glorification of the Mother of God which, according to the meaning of *acathist* is to be heard standing up.

In the Orthodox Church, there is a strong contrast, however, between the lyrical exuberance of the liturgical glorification of Mary and the sobriety of the dogmatic statements about her. The Orthodox Church has essentially two dogmatic statements about Mary: 1) reflecting the Gospel stories, the Nicene creed says that the Son of God was "born of the Holy Spirit and the Virgin Mary;" 2) Mary is Theotokos, a title given to the Jesus' mother by the Council of Ephesus in 431. Beyond these two statements, the Orthodox Church has made no dogmatic statements about Mary since patristic times. Orthodoxy has therefore had no "dogmatic development" about Mary as is the case in the Roman Catholic Church. There have been no new dogmas, such as the Immaculate Conception or the Assumption proclaimed by Rome in the 19th and 20th centuries. Nor has there been any systematic development of mariology in any scholarly theological works. In treatises on the faith of the Orthodox Church, such as the now classic book by Fr. Sergius Bulgakov, *Orthodoxy,* mariology has a modest place, only a few pages at the beginning of the chapter on the veneration of the saints.

We must note, however, that Orthodox mariology went through a creative renewal in Russian religious thinking at the beginning of the 20th century. In this current of thinking, mariology was interpreted in the light of the theme of Sophia or the Divine Wisdom, seen as the vision of the world and humanity in God. Mary is viewed as the personification, the earthly heart of the Divine Wisdom. Due to the translation of an important part of his works into Western languages,[1] Fr. Sergius Bulgakov has become the best known representative of this sophiological current which itself was introduced into Russian religious thought by the philosopher Vladimir Soloviev. Fr. Bulgakov was a master thinker, a sort of modern Origen, who tried to integrate the intuitions of his teacher Vladimir Soloviev into classical Orthodox mariology.

The Orthodox Church thus peacefully continues along the path of its traditional veneration of Mary, anchored as we will see in christology and primarily expressed in liturgical poetry. This approach contrasts with the Roman Catholic dogmatization of devotion to Mary. The Catholic approach makes the meaning of this devotion more precise but it also provokes negative reactions and rejections. Orthodox traditionalism does not, however, exclude creative rethinking, but this creativity has not resulted in new dogmatic formulations. The unique dogma about Mary is concentrated in the title Mother of God which the Church gave to Jesus' mother.

The attitude of the Orthodox Church toward the mystery of Mary differs therefore from both the Roman Catholic attitude (though being nonetheless rather close to it) and the generally held Protestant attitude. Simply stated, this is the Orthodox position: neither a restrictive dogmatization going hand in hand with a heavy intellectual elaboration, nor a rejection or neglect. The Orthodox devotion to Mary is rooted in the christological dogma and is expressed

---

[1] A succinct exposé of his sophiology was translated into English and published in London in 1937 under the title *The Wisdom of God.* A French translation by Constantine Andronikoff has recently been published by Age d'Homme: S. Bulgakov, *La Sagesse de Dieu*, Lausanne, 1983.

in the form of poetic symbols that are proposed, not imposed, for meditation, a meditation that probes their meaning and progressively discovers the richness of their significance.

History and cultural influences have certainly played a role in the formation of these different attitudes, but something much more fundamental is also revealed in the process. It is not my intention to systematize these oppositions since in its positive elements, each different approach may well contain a part of the truth which must be brought out and integrated into the catholic (*kath'holon*) fullness toward which we are moving.

Striving toward this exacting reconciliation that can only be the fruit of a common deepening, I will begin by recalling the christological meaning of the title Theotokos, Mother of God, that the Council of Ephesus gave to Mary. This title ties the statements about Mary to the rock of the Gospel statements about her Son, especially to the fundamental and clear proclamation *Iêsous Christos Kyrios*.

I will then try to show how everything that is said about Mary in the liturgical prayers of Byzantine rite Churches is organically tied to this basic fact while at the same time leaving a great freedom to persons and communities to interpret and appropriate the mystery according to times and places. We may therefore be able to see a light shining from this mystery that can also enlighten our contemporary research on the image of woman that is projected by the Church's teaching. Beyond that, light may also be shed on the place of the feminine principle in the history of salvation.

The Title *Theotokos* as Applied to Jesus' Mother: Its Christological Meaning at the Ecumenical Council of Ephesus

The application of the title *Theotokos* to Mary is ancient, but its origins are obscure. We find the term on a papyrus that probably goes back to the end of the third century. It is even possible that the ancient prayer "Under your protection, I take refuge, O Mother of God . . ." dates from this same period. After the Council of Nicæa I in 325, we have many texts that show that the title *Theotokos* was used to designate Mary. The title was used in nearly all theological camps; even the Arians used the expression. It therefore does not seem to have had a very precise theological meaning. Its connotation was instead emotional and devotional. *Theotokos* as a title for Mary only acquired its real theological and spiritual significance during the debates that preceded the ecumenical Council of Ephesus where popular piety and a major theological problem came together. On the surface, the theological problem seemed very abstract, but the real stakes were very existential. As Fr. George Florovsky a contemporary Orthodox theologian has written, the question was nothing less than "salvation through the incarnation of the Word."[2]

After the ecumenical Councils of Nicæa I and Constantinople I (381), the theologians were drawn from the question of the Trinity to the christological problems. Nonetheless, the scandal that the incarnation of God presented for philosophy was always at the center of the debates. At Nicæa, the questioning came from below: How can this man Jesus be God? At Ephesus, it came from above: How could the Son of God, the divine Word, have become Jesus? Inside the "great Church," no one any longer doubted Christ's true divinity which Nicæa had affirmed against the Arians, nor his real humanity as affirmed against the Docetists. The question was still asked: How must we understand the unity of Him who is constituted from two natures or from two perfect or complete beings and at the same time is said to be both God and man? The Cappadocians Fathers had worked out the distinction between *ousia* and *hypostasis*, substance and person, in the context of the debates about the Trinity, but this

---

[2] G. Florovsky, "The Lamb of God," *The Scottish Journal of Theology*, March, 1961, p. 16.

distinction had not yet been clearly applied to the problem of christology. The controversy therefore crystallized around the title *Theotokos*, Mother of God, which monastic circles were especially prone to give to Mary.

The leaders of the opposing camps were two eminent theologians: the patriarch of Constantinople, Nestorius, and the patriarch of Alexandria, Cyril. The first came from the theological school of Antioch, and his concern was to keep Christ's humanity from being dissolved in his divinity. In order to accomplish this, Nestorius felt that he had to distinguish what, in the incarnate God, belonged to the divinity and what belonged to the humanity without denying that the two were conjoined in the Savior. The key term here is "conjoined" (*sunapheia*), and it indicates that there was a union but not the significant exchange that is implied in the Greek word *perichoresis*, in Latin *circumincessio*. By its connotation, does not the word *conjunction* imply a certain division in Christ?

When he was challenged, Nestorius recognized that the conjunction of the two natures is expressed by a common *prosopon*, but what does this word mean exactly? A face, an individual, a person?

> In fact, Nestorius is very close to the separation in Christ of the divine Logos and the man Jesus who was assumed by the Logos. For Nestorius, Jesus was an individual human being that the divinity assumed in whom it found a perfectly adapted temple. In Christ there is a symmetry between the divine and the human, the two set side by side, but without any exchange of divine and human characteristics. This is the case whether we are talking about the birth, suffering, and death of a human subject or about the transfiguration of the flesh by the communication of the divine life.[3]

---

[3] O. Clement, *"Présentation de l'Eglise orthodoxe"* [A Presentation of the Orthodox Church], in *Formation théologique par correspondance* [Theological Formation by Correspondance], St. Sergius Orthodox Theological Institute, Paris.

The result was that Jesus' mother could not be called *Theotokos*, Mother of God, but at the most *Christotokos*, that is, Mother of the common *prosopon* who was the result of the conjunction of the eternal Logos and a mortal human individual.

Nestorius' adversary, Cyril of Alexandria, was a very passionate man and seems to have had a rather questionable personality. His vocabulary, like that of Nestorius, was not clear and precise. Nonetheless, the depth of his thinking put Cyril in line with Athanasius and the great Cappadocians, that is in the line of Orthodoxy itself. The title *Theotokos* as applied to Jesus' mother was for Cyril the sign and corner stone of a sound christology as we learn from one of his letters proclaimed at Ephesus during a turbulent and sometimes confused debate. Although the letter's language is no longer what we would use today, it correctly expressed the faith of the Church. I shall quote only one significant passage:

> We confess one single Christ and one single Lord. We do not worship a man *with* the Word because by saying *with*, we would introduce a hint of division. We rather worship one and the same [Lord]. . . . This is what the Orthodox faith teaches everywhere, what we find in the teaching of the Fathers. This is why they dared to call the holy Virgin *Theotokos* not because the nature of the Word, his divinity, took his existence from the Virgin but because from her was born this holy body animated by a reasonable soul to which the Word united himself through his person.

We must overcome the hurdle of Cyril's somewhat cryptic language; certain expressions which are ambiguous were to become clear only in the light of the interpretation of the Council of Chalcedon in 451, and discover the essential christological intention of the title *Theotokos* as used in the text for Mary. It is this christological orientation which is normative for the Church's faith. In a language closer to our own way of speaking, we can explain the meaning in this way: the only-begotten Son of the Father became incarnate in our Lord Jesus Christ. He is the unique subject not only of his divinity but also of his humanity. There are not two separate beings in Christ, even less a composite, compound being. He is rather a perfect man who is such because the Son of God became the Son of Mary without ceasing to be God. God is at once the supremely Other and Love without limits who overflows the boundary of his own transcendence and assumes with his creature a relation of personal identity that at the same time respects the otherness of his creature. He becomes man without ceasing to be the Other and without dissolving the creature in Himself. This relation goes beyond all intelligence but was established and offered by God and accepted by humanity in the person of Mary. The root of salvation and of the new creation is found in this relation.

Nestorius took offense at those preachers who applied the title of *Theotokos* to Mary and wrote the following to Proclus of Cyzicus, a partisan of Cyril of Alexandria: "It is one thing to say that God, who is the Word of the Father, conjoined himself to the Son of Mary . . . and another thing to affirm that God needed to be born at the end of nine months.[4]

Cyril's affirmation, contested by Nestorius, is indeed a scandal for enlightened minds, but is it not in the logic of the faith that transcends human logic? This is the meaning of Proclus' answer: "If God was not born of a woman, he would not have died. And if he did not die, he could not have defeated the one who holds the power of death."[5]

Gregory of Nazianzus summed up the soteriology of the Fathers of the Church by saying that "what was not assumed was not healed, and what was united to God was saved." Maximus the Confessor later on said that "Christ

---

[4] *Nestoriana*, "Die Fragmente des Nestorius," hgb. von F. Loofs, Halle, 1905, pp. 337-38.

[5] PG 55, 680-92, quoted by E Brière, "Rejoice, Scepter of Orthodoxy: Christology and the Mother of God", *Sobornost*, 1985, 7/1.

is fully God who saves the whole of man." God saved man; the Son took on an individual human existence in all its proper characteristics, except sin, including temporality, its main one. In the fallen state of humanity, the assumption of that human existence meant that the Word was born and that he died; in fact he was born in order to die.

But the root of salvation and the glorification of mankind is found precisely in this *kenosis*, in this ineffable humbling. By being born of woman, God made himself vulnerable and mortal. The cave where Jesus was born prefigures the tomb and is painted in somber colors on the traditional Orthodox icon of Christmas. "Trampling down death by death," by *his* death, "and upon those in the tombs, bestowing life." This is the Easter hymn of the Byzantine liturgy. The name *Theotokos* as given to Mary invites us to contemplate the whole mystery of God "the Lover of mankind," who "when the time had fully come, sent forth his Son, born of woman, born under the law, to redeem those who were under the law, so that we might receive adoption as sons" (Ga 4:4-5).

The people, and especially women, greeted the proclamation of Ephesus with enthusiasm. It opened wide the door for the glorification of Mary in the Church. Very often the simple people were far ahead of erudite thinkers in offering praise to Mary. At the same time, when the Council of Ephesus gave Mary her most significant title, *Mother of God*, it set the limits of this veneration by anchoring mariology in christology. We might say rather that the council made clear the basis and the meaning of Mary's glorification: Mary is inseparable from her Son, and it is her motherhood, both physical and spiritual, as received from God *through the Holy Spirit*, that gives her all her glory. Her glory reflects on all humanity, and the Mother of God reveals mankind's highest vocation. But in the heart of that humanity, her glory especially reveals to us women our vocation.

The Liturgical Glorification of Mary

Thus everything that is said about the Mother of God in the Church finds its real meaning in relation to the central mystery of salvation: God is with us, *Emmanuel*. The Orthodox Church has never felt it necessary to formulate other dogmas with the purpose of setting out the content of the Ephesian proclamation in reference to Mary. Everything the Church believes about Mary is based on dogma of Ephesus and set forth in the poetic and symbolic language of its liturgical hymns of praise and glorification.

The function of this language is not, however, simply decorative and ornamental even though a certain rhetorical style can be detected. The liturgical language is beautiful, but its essential *raison d'être* is not æsthetical. This body of poetry is a vehicle for carrying a theological, theanthropological, and spiritual message which can be read at various levels. Fr. John Meyendorff has written that "the boundless expressions of marian piety and devotion . . . represent a legitimate and organic way of placing the somewhat abstract concepts of fifth and sixth century Christology on the level of the simple faithful."[6] At the same time, their symbolism leaves the door open to new and deeper appreciations, in the participation in common prayer and the communion of the saints.

The Mother of God's place in the Byzantine liturgy has been the object of many scholarly studies. I will note only certain aspects in a cursory survey.[7]

---

[6] J. Meyendorff, *Byzantine Theology: Historical Trends and Doctrinal Themes*, Fordham University Press, New York, p. 165.

[7] Among others, we can cite J. Ledit, *Marie dans la liturgie byzantine* [Mary in the Byzantine Liturgy], Paris, 1976. A Monk of the Eastern Church, *L'An de Grâce du Seigneur* [The Year of Grace of the Lord], I and II, Beirut, 1972-73. This work is solid and deep and meant to edify the faithful. A. Kniazev, "The Great Sign of the Heavenly Kingdom," *St. Vladimir's Theological Quarterly*, 1969/1-2.

The Annunciation

It goes without saying that the liturgical glorification of Mary is linked above all to the incarnation. The role of the Mother of God is underscored in the realization of God's great plan. The Annunciation is the marian feast par excellence in the Orthodox Church. Moreover, the exaltation of this Annunciation, Mary's Magnificat, is sung at each office of matins. Like Christmas, the Annunciation is a feast of the Son of God who became man and of her by whom the humanization of the divine Word took place, God's irruption into human history.

The triple meaning of this feast is oriented both toward the glorification of God and of Mary with her son looking toward the salvation of mankind. It is expressed in the following hymn from the matins of the Annunciation:

> Today is revealed the mystery that is from all eternity. The Son of God becomes the Son of man, that, sharing in what is worse, He may make me share in what is better. In times of old, Adam was once deceived: he sought to become God, but received not his desire. Now God becomes man, that He may make Adam God. Let creation rejoice, let nature exult: for the Archangel stands in fear before the Virgin and saying to her "Hail," he brings the joyful greeting whereby our sorrow is assuaged. O Thou who in Thy merciful compassion wast made man, our God, glory to Thee.[8]

Mary's glorification is basically the glorification of the merciful God who loves man, who loved his creature so much that he emptied himself for his salvation. The incarnation is the continuation of the good work of the creation, the good work Adam's sin turned away from its

---

[8] *The Festal Menaion*, Mother Mary and Kallistos Ware, trs. and eds., Faber and Faber, London, 1959, p. 460.

goal. The meaning of the incarnation is universal and cosmic.

The feast of the Annunciation, as it is celebrated in the Byzantine rite, has an obvious triple, even four-fold, meaning: theological, anthropological, soteriological, and finally mariological. Mary is never considered alone, outside her specific vocation in the history of salvation. In this history, the one God in three Persons is the real actor but Mary, he associates his creature with the great play.

The Church's hymnography celebrates with wonderment the woman who was called upon to "contain Him that nothing can contain." It also calls the community of faithful to turn toward the God of love who ineffably lowered himself to become man so that mankind could realize the vocation for which it was created: to participate in the divine life. All creatures are called upon to join in the jubilation of the announcement that God's project is about to be realized:

> Let the heavens be glad and the earth rejoice: for the Son who is coeternal with the Father, sharing His throne and like Him without beginning, in His compassion and merciful love for mankind has submitted Himself to emptying, according to the good pleasure and the counsel of the Father; and He has gone to dwell in a virgin's womb that was sanctified beforehand by the Spirit. O marvel! God is come among men; He who cannot be contained is contained in a womb; the Timeless [One] enters time; and strange wonder! His conception is without seed, His emptying is past telling: so great is this mystery! For God empties Himself, takes flesh, and is fashioned as a creature, when the angel tells the pure Virgin of her conception: "Hail, thou who art full of grace: the Lord who has great mercy is with thee."[9]

---

[9] *Ibid.*, Stichera from Lauds of the Annunciation, p. 443.

In this perspective, Mary is not a goddess representing feminine gentleness alongside of or opposed to a fearful masculine God. In the person of a woman, a human mother, Mary represents humanity associated with the accomplishment of God's loving plan. In this woman, in this mother sanctified and made fruitful by the Spirit, the divine Agape took a human body. Mary's virginal conception of Christ did not raise her above mankind. From the often expressed Orthodox point of view, Mary remained in intimate solidarity with all mankind. Her virginal motherhood indicates that the Lord took the initiative for man's salvation, and that his entry into history transcends the laws of fallen human nature without at the same time destroying the creature. According to the symbolism found in Byzantine hymnography and iconography, the Virgin is often symbolically represented as the burning bush that burned with the divine fire but was not consumed (Ex 3:2).

At the same time, the conception of Mary's Son without seed from Adam, that is, from mankind wounded by sin, marked the beginning of a new line of humans whose founder is the Son of God become the Son of Man. This conception unites those who believe in him, "who were born, not of blood nor of the will of the flesh nor of the will of man, but of God" (Jn 1:13), to their real Father, to the "Father who is in the heavens."

The liturgical glorification of the Mother of God is theocentric and christocentric. It is always set in the perspective of the history of salvation but also concerns her personally as one who possesses the gift of freedom. Mary is not a passive instrument, not simply the womb through which the Word passed in taking flesh. Her glory does not consist solely in the fact that she nursed the Son of God. For the feast of the Annunciation, as for all the great marian feasts, the Orthodox Church reads two texts together: Luke 10:38-42 and 11:27-28. They explain what is Mary's "good portion" and why we can call her "blessed."

As in the case of Mary of Bethany who sat at the Lord's feet and listened to his words, Mary of Nazareth received in faith the Word of God that the angel brought her. Because of the way Mary received the Word in faith, she was able to give flesh to him. He took his humanity from her. By the free consent of her faith, Mary the daughter of Sion, daughter of Abraham the believer, participated in the realization of God's project.

The hymnography of the Annunciation stands squarely in this line of interpretation when it insists on Mary's agreement as an indispensable condition of the incarnation. Because of her faith, Mary became God's first co-worker. This is the meaning of the praises that the angel addressed to her: "Hail, thou through whom joy will shine forth . . . Hail, thou restoration of fallen Adam . . . Hail, thou redemption of the tears of Eve."[10]

The participation of the humble handmaiden in God's work is that of a created freedom as seen in the mysterious synergy, cooperation, dear to eastern Christian thought; the divine and human wills work together. In order to give a complete picture, we would have to quote all of Nicholas Cabasilas' homily, but we will give only a significant passage:

> God dressed himself in humanity, and the Virgin became the Mother of the Creator. God did not inform Adam when he wanted to take Eve from his side but deprived Adam of feeling by putting him to sleep. On the other hand, God announced his plan to the Virgin and waited for her act of faith before he could accomplish his work. When he created Adam, God spoke to his Son: "Let us make man," he said. But when the time came to introduce this admirable counselor, as St. Paul said, his firstborn Son, into the world and thus form the second Adam, he allowed the Virgin to participate in his work. As Isaiah said, God pronounced this very serious decision and the Virgin ratified it: the incarnation of the Word was not only the work of the Father, of his Power and of the

[10] *Ibid.*, the 6th ode of matins, p. 454.

Spirit wherein the Father decided, the Spirit descended and the Power of the Father covered the Virgin with its shadow. *The incarnation was, however, also the work of the will and the faith of the Virgin.*[11] As such a plan could not have come about without the these three, in the same way, *the divine counsel could not have been realized without the agreement and the faith of the All-Pure One . . .*

When God instructed and persuaded the Virgin in this way, he made her his Mother and borrowed the flesh of a conscious and consenting woman so that just as he was conceived because he wanted to be, Mary conceived by an act of her free will and *became mother by a free choice. She was thus not just a simple passive instrument in the hands of an artist, but she rather offered herself and became the co-worker with God* for the providence of mankind, thus associated with the glory that was to be the result.

So, just as the Savior was not man and with man only in the flesh but also in soul, intelligence and will as well as in all that is associated with man, in the same way, he had to have a perfect mother who prepared his birth not only in the body but also in spirit, will, and her whole being so that the Virgin might became mother of body and soul and carry all mankind to the ineffable birth-giving.[12]

Mary's consent goes beyond her own person and is in fact the agreement of all mankind, at least in desire and hope. The Church sings the following hymn at Christmas:

What shall we offer Thee, O Christ, who for our sakes hast appeared on earth as man? Every creature made by Thee offers Thee thanks. The angels offer Thee a hymn; the heavens a star; the Magi, gifts; the shepherds, their

---

[11] Underlined by the author.

[12] N. Cabasilas, quoted in *Bulletin de la Crypte* [The Bulletin of the Crypt], 131, March, 1985.

wonder; the earth, its cave; the wilderness, the manger: and we offer Thee a Virgin Mother. O pre-eternal God, have mercy upon us.[13]

Other aspects of the liturgical glorification of Mary are organized on the basis of and around this fundamental fact: Mary participated, according to grace in the work of salvation, in the incarnation of the Son of God, and through her, all mankind also participated in it.

The Meeting in the Temple

For the commemoration of the Presentation of Jesus in the Temple, also called the Holy Meeting, the Church associates Jesus and Mary in the following hymn: "Let us also go . . . to the meeting of Christ and welcome him. Make your room beautiful and welcome Mary, the gate of heaven."

The faithful are thus called upon, like Simeon and Anne, to welcome the mother and child. That means as well: welcome the child who is the Son of God in the spirit of Mary's faith and humility. The gospel reading for the feast recalls Simeon's prophecy to Mary: "a sword will pierce your soul" (Lk 2:35). In these words, the Orthodox Church senses the mystery of Mary's participation, and with her that of all believers, in Christ's passion. Mary gave birth to the God-Man in the cave of Bethlehem whose darkness already announces the tomb. This same Mary will also be present at the passion and cross. She is the compassionate One par excellence, she who interiorizes the passion of her Son and who shares it spiritually.

The theme of the Mother of God's "compassion" is expressed with poignant intensity in the offices of the three last days of Holy Week. The hymns sing of the Mother of God at the foot of the Cross (*Stavrotheotokia*). In her lamentation at her Son's suffering, Mary is a witness to its

---

[13] *The Festal Menaion*, vespers, p. 254.

reality as well as to the reality of the humanity and the passion of One of the Holy Trinity, but hers is a witness of participation and communion. Following in the Mother of God's footsteps, the Orthodox believer feels called upon to accept suffering and death as a grace of participation in Christ's suffering and death. We have in the *strastoterptsy*, those who like Mary have suffered their personal passion with Christ and in him, a particularly touching expression of Russian Orthodox spirituality.

The Dormition

Along with the Annunciation, the other major Orthodox marian feast is the Dormition. The hymnography of the feast is based on an apocryphal tradition and recalls very clearly the natural death of the Mother of God. On the other hand, the hymns intimate that after her death, Mary was mysteriously glorified in her body.

> Open wide your gates and . . . receive the Mother of the never-failing light. . . . For on this day, the heavens open to receive her. . . . The angels praise the most holy falling asleep that we celebrate with faith. . . . Let every son of the earth dance in spirit . . . and celebrate with joy the venerable assumption of the Mother of God.

These are some of the characteristic expressions of the hymns of the feast.

The Orthodox Church has not made Mary's assumption the object of any dogmatic definition. To reject Mary's bodily glorification, however, would be a blasphemy in the eyes of the Orthodox. In the words of the Monk of the Eastern Church, the word *assumption* stands for a reality "that is outside and above history."[14] The assumption of the Mother of God is an "eschatological sign."[15] In Mary,

---

[14] A Monk of the Eastern Church, *L'An de Grâce*, II, p. 158.
[15] A Kniazev, *op. cit.*, p. 21 ff.

the Mother of the never-failing light, who is raised up to heaven in the wake of her Son's Resurrection and Ascension, believers are called upon to contemplate the glorification of all creatures at the end of time when all things will be accomplished, when "God will be all in all," in the words of the apostle Paul.

Mary's assumption anticipates this end (the *telos)* for which all mankind was created, and by it we participate through faith in this end while still groaning in the labor pains of the new creation's birth. Mary was raised to heaven, in contrast to Christ who raised himself up toward the Father, and is for us a sign of hope. She is our promised land, the great sign of the coming in power of the heavenly kingdom.

Mary's Nativity

The feast of Mary's birth as well as that of her Presentation in the Temple are also based on apocryphal traditions especially found in the pseudo-Gospel of James, but they carry, nonetheless, a deep spiritual meaning. According to these traditions, Mary was born of Joachim and Anne in answer to her father's prayer. Joachim had withdrawn into the desert while Anne had not been able to have children for a long time. At the vespers of the feast, the Church reads Old Testament lessons that are applied to Mary according to a typological interpretation. Mary is the ladder set up between heaven and earth that Jacob saw in his dream when he spent the night at Luz (Gn 28:10-17). She is *bethel*, the "house of God" which is the name Jacob gave to the rock on which he laid his head during the night. Proverbs 9:1-11 is another reading that points to Mary as "the house with seven columns" built by Wisdom. This identification will be developed and deepened by the Russian sophiological school of the 19th and 20th centuries, running from Vladimir Soloviev to Sergius Bulgakov.

As with the birth of Samuel in the Old Testament and John the Baptist in the New, Mary's birth was in no way "miraculous," but it was a sign of the living God's victory over human sterility. Mary's birth is also considered as the final fruit of a long period of preparation, as the realization of promises made to the righteous ones of the Old Testament. The liturgical hymns celebrate Mary as the "flower of Jesse" and the "flowering branch of his root." God progressively purified her ancestors. This is an idea that was especially developed by Gregory Palamas, a Byzantine theologian of the 14th century, in relation to Mary's birth.

In a larger and universalist perspective, Mary is the daughter of Eve. In the words of a hymn, "For behold, she who was made from the rib of Adam plainly declares her daughter and descendant blessed. 'For,' says she, 'unto me is born deliverance, through which I shall be set free from the bonds of hell.' "[16] We have here the beginnings of the theme of Mary the new Eve that Irenæus of Lyons in the second century as part of his meditation on the mystery of salvation. From St. Iranæus' point of view, which is also that of the Byzantine liturgy, the parallel between Mary and Eve is in no way humiliating for Mary. She does not thereby become the model of passive obedience as some shallow exegesis would try to make us believe. Mary is an image of liberation. In St. Irenæus' words, "What the Virgin Eve bound by her unbelief, Mary freed by her faith."[17] Mary is of Adam's descendants, that is, one with all humanity, but she is the part that God reserved for himself from the beginning. This is how the Byzantine mystic Simeon the New Theologian explained it.[18]

Even though Mary's holiness from her birth is solidly affirmed by the Orthodox Church, the notion of her immaculate conception is foreign to the Orthodox vision about Mary. The Orthodox Church has not dogmatized on this subject, but in addition, the dogma of 1854,

---

[16] *The Festal Menaion*, p. 104.
[17] St. Irenæus, *Against Heresies*, III, 22, 4.
[18] Archbishop Basil Krivocheine, *Dans la lumière du Christ* [In the Light of Christ], Chevetogne, 1980, p. 336.

proclaimed by the Roman magisterium, provoked negative reactions on the part of Orthodox theologians. The motivations behind this rejection are no doubt complex and in part perhaps psychological, being linked to an anti-Roman reflex. The notion of Mary's immaculate conception, as a theological opinion (*theologoumenon)* has been tolerated in the Orthodox Church in the past and even defended by certain respectable theologians.[19] If we do not find the exact expression *immaculate conception,* we do find a very closely related belief in Patriarch Photius and Gregory Palamas. George Scholarios, +1456, the first patriarch after the fall of the Byzantine empire, openly taught the doctrine of the Immaculate Conception. Today, however, nearly all Orthodox theologians reject the idea. They feel that the Latin Church's formulation of the dogmas incompatible with Mary's full solidarity with the human race. Is there not a risk, they ask, of making her a demi-goddess, a intermediary being between God and mankind? The real problem is probably in the different conceptions or accentuations about original sin.[20]

The Presentation

The feast of Mary's Presentation in the Temple also has its source in the apocryphal Gospel of James. According to the legend, Mary was led at the age of three into the Temple in Jerusalem and lived there. The Orthodox Church has not taken a stand on the historicity of the event itself. Nonetheless, the offices of the day develop the feast's spiritual meaning through various hymns and readings.

First of all, we have Mary's holiness which is symbolically indicated by the entry of the little girl into the Holy of Holies of the Temple. One of the most frequent names

---

[19] See L. Gillet, "The Immaculate Conception and the Orthodox Church," *Chrysostomus* VI, 5, London, 1984.
[20] Meyendorff, *op. cit.*, pp.147-48.

given to the Mother of God in the Orthodox Church is *Panaghia*, the All-Holy One. The prayer that the faithful most often address to Mary celebrates her holiness which is greater than that of the angels: "More honorable than the cherubim and more glorious beyond compare than the seraphim . . . true Theotokos, we magnify you."

What is the nature of her holiness? Does not this proclamation contradict another statement in the eucharistic liturgy addressed to the whole people of God, the faithful and the clergy, before communion: "One is holy; one is the Lord, Jesus Christ, to the glory of the Father." (1 Co 8:6 and Ph 2:11)? The answer to this question is found in the second theme of the hymns and readings of the Entry of Mary into the Temple. This theme compares the Temple of stone with the living temple, the Mother of God. The kontakion of the feast designates Mary as the temple of the Holy Spirit: "The all-pure Temple of the Saviour . . . is led today into the house of the Lord, and with her she brings the grace of the divine Spirit."[21] Mary is a human person filled with the grace of the Spirit when he overshadowed her so that she could give birth to the God-Man. Mary's holiness therefore surpasses that of the Jerusalem Temple. Her holiness situates her beyond the *sacred* that is signified by the Temple: "The living temple sanctifies the constructed temple."[22]

Most Orthodox theologians reject the dogma of the Immaculate Conception in the sense of an exemption from original sin in view of Christ's merits. They nonetheless insist that Mary was sanctified by the Spirit who overshadowed her: the first time was at the Annunciation which represents her personal Pentecost and then in the middle of the apostles, "disciples and women" (Ac 1:14) when the Church was born. In this perspective all danger of Pelagianism has been set aside. There is no risk of attributing too great a role to nature and to human will at the expense

---

[21] *The Festal Menaion*, p. 185.
[22] A Monk of the Eastern Church, *op. cit.*, I, p. 72.

of divine grace. Certain Fathers of the Church, among them St. John Chrysostom, were very aware of this risk and insisted on the human weakness of Mary. In Orthodox thinking, the All-Holy One is a human person wholly sanctified in her body and soul by the Spirit.[23] Mary is the Spirit-bearer, *pneumatophoros*, par excellence, the women in whom the creative and redeeming work of the one God in three Persons has attained its objective, its ultimate accomplishment. In her, God's project of becoming man, of becoming *sarcophoros*, so that mankind might become Spirit-bearer, *pneumatophoros*, is already realized by anticipation. Mary is an eschatological sign; she is walking ahead of mankind and indicating the end toward which everyone is moving. Her intercession is therefore particularly sought by those who aspire to "acquire the Holy Spirit," in the words attributed to St. Seraphim of Sarov, a Russian mystic of the 19th century.[24]

The Feast of the Protection, "Pokrov"

And finally we need to note the marian feast that is particularly dear to the Russians, the Protection or Intercession of the Mother of God, *Pokrov.*

The feast goes back to an apparition of the Mother of God in the church of Blachernes in Constantinople during the fifth century. Mary was accompanied by a cloud of saints lead by John the Baptist. The vision was seen by a fool-for-Christ, Andrew and his companion Ephrem. Mary

---

[23] By a different path than that taken in Latin theology, this conception affirms Mary's holiness as a work of grace in her.

[24] Seraphim of Sarov, who had only one icon in his cell, that of the Tenderness of the Mother of God, appears to be a modern spiritual son of Symeon the New Theologian. St. Simeon claimed to have received the illumination of the Spirit where he personally met Christ after having heartily prayed to the Mother of God. On Seraphim of Sarov, see I. Gorainov, *Saint Séraphin de Sarov*, Paris, 1980, and Vsevolod Rochcan, *Saint Seraphim: Etudes et Documents*, Bellefontaine, 1987. St. Symeon the New Theologian, see B. Krivocheine, *op. cit.*, pp. 333 ff.

took off her veil, *pokrov*, and extended it over the two men and Constantinople as a sign of protection.

We need to get beyond certain exaggerations of popular piety which might suggest that Mary is a source of grace or that she pleads for humans before a coldly righteous and vengeful God. Beyond these deformations, we need to see the idea of the communion of the saints as it is stated in the Apostles Creed, Mary being its personification. This conception of her role is illustrated by the icon of the Deisis that is found in Orthodox churches on the upper part of the iconostase above the Royal Doors. On this part of the iconostase, two processions of suppliants converge toward Christ the judge of the world who is seated in the middle. On the left, the procession is led by John the Baptist, the image of manly holiness, we might even say of Old Testament holiness; on the right, the Mother of God leads the procession as a representation of the Church radiant with the newness of the Spirit.

The righteous God is not, however, a coldly righteous and vengeful God that Mary, by her intercession, tries to make more indulgent. The Monk of the Eastern Church has written the following about the meaning of the feast of the Protection:

> The Mother of God covers us with her veil, but this veil is nothing other than Jesus' own tunic. It was this tunic that the sick people touched in order to be healed. When it seems that Mary touches us, it is in fact Jesus.[25]

The Virgin of Tenderness[26] is the name given to another famous icon and reveals in a feminine form the philanthropy of God which takes a bodily form in her. The veil of the Virgin of the Intercession is the image of the Spirit's

---

[25] Lev Gillet, "Marie, Mère de Jésus" [Mary, the Mother of Jesus], *Contacts*,108, 1979/4.

[26] See the commentary on this icon in M. Evdokimov, *Lumières d'Orient* [Lights from the East], Limoges, 1981, p. 176.

motherly tenderness as he hovers over the chaos of our world, just like he hovered over the primeval waters at the creation (Gn 1:2).

Mary as the Image and Personification of the Church

As in the Roman Catholic Church, the Orthodox tradition links Mary and the Church but hesitate to proclaim her "Mother of the Church" as pope Paul VI did at Vatican II. By making such an identification, the Orthodox Church would fear putting on the same level our adoption in Christ by the Father and our adoption by Mary. In the words of Fr. Alexis Kni-azev,[27] "Mary . . . is rather the personification of the Church and not the Mother of the Church, a title that seems to give her a power and a force that belong only to Christ the Savior. " We prefer to talk of Mary's motherhood *in* the Church rather than of her being Mother *of* the Church.

This distinction becomes clearer in a vision of salvation and of ecclesiology that always associates but never confuses the economy of the Son and that of the Spirit.[28]

Mary is the human person wholly sanctified by the Spirit who descended on her personally first at the Annunciation and then again at Pentecost in the middle of the disciples. She is thus the image and personification of the *Spirit-bearing* Church, the womb of the new humanity.

> Mary is the cause of what preceded her, that is, the Son's long work of preparation throughout the Old Testament period. . . . At the same time, she precedes what comes after her. . . . By her men and angels receive grace. No

---

[27] A. Kniazev, "Notes sur la IIIe session du Concile du Vatican: Marie, Mère de l'Eglise" [Notes on the Third Session of the Vatican Council: Mary, the Mother of the Church], *Le Messager orthodoxe*, 27-28, 1964, pp. 57-59.

[28] On this subject, see V. Lossky, *Essai sur la théologie mystique de l'Eglise d'Orient* [in English: *The Mystical Theology of the Eastern Church*], pp. 176 ff.

gift is received in the Church without the help of the Mother of God, the firstfruits of the glorified Church.[29]

Mary is the face of the Church, the bride of Christ according to the marriage symbolism inherited from the Old Testament and applied by Paul to the relationship between Christ and the New Testament people. She is the "heart" of the Church, its mysterious center that gives it force, orients it toward its final goal which is that ". . . God may be everything to everyone" (1 Co 15:28 and Col 2:11). In the Church and for the Church, she is the sign that anticipates this goal; she is a sign of the Kingdom of God already come, of the creation already saved, while still waiting for "Him who comes."

The Mother of God has already passed from death to life and remains in solidarity with the creation which is still groaning in labor pains. She participates in those pains spiritually. There is a mysterious link between Mary and the "woman clothed with the sun . . . and on her head a crown of twelve stars" who is described in Revelations. Many of the Church Fathers have identified this woman with the Church pregnant with daughters and sons of God who cries out "in her pangs of birth, in anguish for delivery" (Rv 12:1-2). Beyond the institutional limits of the Church, the Mother of God contains in herself potentially all of saved humanity. She prays for all, for the revealing of the total Christ in whom everyone and all will be reconciled, as we see in the icon called by the name of The Virgin of the Sign. It represents the Mother of God in the orant position, standing with her hands raised to heaven. In her womb, she carries Christ the God-Man, Redeemer of everything that is human and of all mankind.

In modern Orthodoxy, the credit of having tried to unravel the meaning of this great but silent sign goes to the school of Russian sophiology of the beginning of the 20th century. We have already mentioned Vladimir

---

[29] *Ibid.*, p. 191. He sums up in these terms a homily of Gregory Palamas.

Soloviev who founded the school along with his disciples Paul Florensky and Sergius Bulgakov. Using different and sometimes garbled expressions, these thinkers saw Mary as the earthly personification of the heavenly Wisdom (*sophia*), that is of the idea of world and of humanity in God, a dynamic and living idea with infinite possibilities of being personified. Sophiology has come under criticism, even condemnation by Church authorities, for some of its expressions.[30] It nonetheless expresses a deep intuition of popular piety. Vladimir Lossky, who also was a critic of Fr. Bulgakov's thinking, wrote that the mystery of the Church—that energy field in which mankind is called to realize its divine vocation—is expressed "in two perfect persons: the divine person of Christ and the human person of the Mother of God."

This is why, concludes Lossky, the Church exhorts us to glorify the Mother of God:

> Let us praise, O faithful Believers, the one who is the glory of the universe, the gate of heaven, the Virgin Mary, the flower of the human race and the birth-giver of God. She is the heaven and the temple of God; she has destroyed the boundaries of sin; she is the liberation of your faith. The Lord who was born from her fights for us. Be bold, O people of God, for he has beaten down the enemy, he who is all powerful.[31]

Mary as the Face of the New Humanity: Mary's Femininity

To sum up what has been said up to this point, I can say that in the Orthodox vision Mary is essentially the humble

---

[30] On this subject, see, E. Behr-Sigel, "La Sophiologie du Père Serge Boulgakov" [The Sophiology of Fr. Sergius Bulgakov], *Revue d'histoire et de philosophie religieuse*, 1932/2, pp. 130-157. This study was reprinted in *Le Messager orthodoxe*, 57, 1972/1.

[31] The dogmaticon of the first tone from the Oktoekos, quoted by V. Lossky, *op. cit.*, pp. 191-92.

handmaiden in whom the Lord accomplished wondrous things. He has associated her as a free person, freed by grace, with the realization of his loving plan by making her the worthy mother of the Son of God, the sovereign and guide of the people of God as this people moves toward the Kingdom. In a human person totally sanctified by the Spirit, she is the sign of the coming of the Kingdom and of the creation totally glorified in hope.

But what is the meaning of Mary's femininity in this vision? It is obvious and at the same time difficult to explain. In the Orthodox tradition, Mary is neither a guardian goddess nor the model for women. Theologians and the simple faithful contemplate in her the vision of the new humanity. She is the archetype and the guide of those men and women who aspire to give birth to Christ in their hearts and who ask her to intercede for them and to call down on them the gift of the Spirit. Both men and women are "of her race," in the words which she spoke to Seraphim of Sarov.[32] Maximus the Confessor in the seventh century taught that by being born of the Virgin, the separation of human nature into males and females is overcome.[33] At the other end of the chain, Fr. Sergius Bulgakov, when talking about the icons of the Mother of God, underscored the "ascetic symbolism of the iconography" in relation to the naturalism of Western images of the Virgin, especially Raphael's madonnas.[34] What stands out most strikingly in these paintings, whose æsthetic value Fr. Sergius recognizes without any difficulty, is "femininity, the woman, sex." In the tradition of the Church, Mary is the revelation of the "virginal eternal" which is "above sex" which belongs to the "tunics of skin." The "feminine," that

[32] E. Behr-Sigel, *Prière et Sainteté dans l'Eglise russe* [Prayer and Holiness in the Russian Church], p. 121.

[33] Maximus the Confessor, *De ambiguis*, PG 91, 1308-09.

[34] S. Bulgakov, "Pensées sur l'art" [Thoughts on Art], *Le Messager orthodoxe*, 57, 1972, p. 63.

is, that aspect of woman participating in sin, is absent from the ever-virgin Mary.[35]

Does this mean that the Theotokos, as the instrument of a supernatural birth, was conceived like a non-sexual angelic being? In the atmosphere of a monastic spirituality in which ascetical motivations predominate, in which sex, and especially women, was often seen as synonymous with sin, the piety surrounding Mary has not always escaped the temptation of "angelism." In relation to Mary, this "angelism" seems to me to be a real heresy that is closely related to christological Docetism. The result is that the Mother of God is radically separated from ordinary women who can neither recognize themselves in her nor be recognized in her. The contemporary Orthodox theologian, Paul Evdokimov, believed that he found in certain Church circles a tendency toward contempt for women going hand in hand with a phenomenal rise in the veneration of the Mother of God. We have in this phenomenon, however, something morbid and foreign to the Church's vision which teaches precisely the full humanity of the Theotokos: a perfect human being, superior to the angels, who integrated the sexual polarity into the totality of her personal existence; in her, however, the sexual polarity is transcended without being abolished or denied. This is the message delivered in a silent but eloquent language by the great icons of Mary's feasts.

In the 20th century, we have been living a double rebirth of Orthodox theology and iconography. In Russian religious thought, this renaissance has been accompanied by an effort to rethink creatively the "feminine" as a spiritual principle and as a basic category of human existence. This is true for the relation with the Other as well as with the others, with God and neighbors. Mary is the perfect expression of this principle which has its foundation in the very life of the Trinity itself. This idea has shaped the various studies undertaken within a current of

---

[35] *Ibid.*

thinking whose best known representative in the West, after Fr. Sergius Bulgakov, is Paul Evdokimov. This line of thinking has ancient roots and very diverse expressions. The sophiology of Fr. Sergius Bulgakov, following after that of Vladimir Soloviev, has no doubt played the role of catalyzer, even if the most recent representatives of the school take a certain distance from their formidable forbearer.

A global and deep analysis of this whole line of thinking is yet to be undertaken, and such an enterprise goes far beyond the realm of this presentation. I would only remind you, however, that for Paul Evdokimov, whose thought was far from being rectilinear, the transcendent foundation of the feminine archetype as personified in the Theotokos, is not found in the heavenly divine Humanity, Bulgakov's Sophia, but in the personal motherhood of the Spirit, the *rouah* which is feminine in certain Semitic languages.

Even though these speculations are motivated by a generous heart, they also carry with them certain dangers especially in a polemical atmosphere, such as the opposition to the ordination of women, when they are turned into simplistic systems. Is it not dangerous to turn the masculine and the feminine principles into personal realities to the detriment of the basic category of *person* as the image of God in man (*anthrôpos*)? The question must nonetheless be raised.

Conclusion: Some New Questions

What is the model of womanhood set forth in the Orthodox vision of Mary, the Mother of God? What are the chances that the Orthodox understanding of Mary's role in the history of salvation might be accepted in other Churches? In conclusion, I will try to provide some partial answers to these two questions since they have been asked of me. It must be understood that they are only remarks that are intended to launch a common reflection that we must all pursue.

As I hope you have seen in what has been said up to this point, the first question has rarely, and then only very recently, been discussed in the context of Orthodox theological thinking. This does not mean, however, that the question does not have *its* place in the life and reflection of the Church. It just means that it is not the main question that occupies Orthodox thinkers. It seems to me that in the Orthodox vision Mary is not seen mainly as the model for women or as the archetype of womanhood in the banal or sociological meaning of the term.

This point is convincingly made by meditating on an authentic icon of the Theotokos. She is the one by whom the Lord of the heavens came into the world as a brother of men, and in her person we have the revelation of the highest vocation not just of women but of all humanity. The signification of Mary is both unique and universal, both cosmic and eschatological. In her, the end (*telos)* of all creation is announced and proclaimed. She personifies the call to holiness that is addressed to each person and to all. This call is to give birth, by the Spirit in oneself and for the world, to the new creature in Christ. The greeting that the angel addressed to the young girl in Nazareth was in fact only said to Mary, the future mother of the divine incarnate Word, but through her the greeting was addressed to all mankind, both men and women.

It is of no small consequence, however, that this new creation, having Mary as its human root, has a women's face. It has a meaning that goes beyond the obvious biological necessity. We see in Mary the representative of the "poor ones of Israel," she who gives birth to the Son of God. In her, the Lord "has scattered the proud in the imagination of their hearts, . . . put down the mighty from their thrones, and exalted those of low degree." These are the words of the Magnificat that is sung at matins in the Byzantine rite. Among those of low degree, we must count women with whom Mary, the "lowly handmaiden" is in solidarity. In her and with her, believing women know that they are saved, honored, and glorified.

Even though the link that ties Mary to Orthodox women is sometimes obscured by a misplaced exaltation, the consciousness of that relation remains very much alive. The awareness of their special relation to Mary strengthens Orthodox women's feeling of dignity, whatever may be their social standing in the more or less patriarchal societies in which the historical Orthodox Churches have their roots. Through Mary and in line with the biblical tradition, these Orthodox women are respected in their maternal function. They also feel called, following in Mary's steps, to a total consecration to Christ which according to the Church's teaching can be realized in various ways: marriage, monasticism, ways that have existed in the past and that are yet to be discovered.

It is significant that a profound theology of marriage potentially implied in the marriage service has been elaborated in contemporary Orthodoxy precisely in relation with the line of thinking that tends to give great value to "womanhood" as a spiritual principle that is also present in God.[36]

The image of Mary set out by the Orthodox liturgy and mariology is explained by such great spiritual masters as Symeon the New Theologian and Nicholas Cabasilas. For them, Mary is a woman that God associated with the realization of his loving plan, "not as a passive instrument in an artist's hands, but as a complete person, free and instructed by God himself. By his call to Mary to be become a "co-worker,"[37] God solicited the free acceptance of "her will and faith."

Even though patriarchal cultural stereotypes have obscured this image, it nonetheless shines in the depth of

---

[36] The main spokesman in the West for this Orthodox theology of marriage is Paul Evdokimov who was influenced by the theologian prophet A. Boukharev (1822-71) whose intuitions fertilized the Russian religious renaissance of the 20th century. See E. Behr-Sigel, *Alexandre Boukharev*, pp. 85-89.

[37] N. Cabasilas, quoted from *Bulletin de la Crypte* [The Bulletin of the Crypt], 131, March, 1985.

the Church's consciousness. Freed from the sludge that surrounds it, this image can enlighten our groping studies concerning the place and ministries of women in the Church. A Russian spiritual master of the 19th century exhorted one of his disciples, who was later to become priest, to see in each woman both the icon of Christ imprinted in her by virtue of his humanity and "the icons of her by whom the Lamb of God stooped to become incarnate."[38] In his mind, this was the only attitude that could meet the challenge of an embryonic feminism taking form in the Russian intelligentsia. He felt that the Church should not condemn this feminism but rather baptize, purify, and enlighten it.

Beyond its meaning for women, Mary's womanhood can have a meaning for *anthropos*, all mankind. In their relation to God the source and giver of life, all persons and mankind in general, are called upon to adopt an attitude of openness and altruistic self-abandonment which makes them transparent to the radiance of the Other. Our language calls this attitude "womanly" because women perhaps are more spontaneously disposed to it. It is of little importance whether this attitude comes from nature or culture or is related to their maternal vocation or to their centuries old social standing. It is often the case, however, that a man (*aner*) does not discover this openness to the Other and to others except through a woman: mother, sister, wife, lover. The femininity of the Mother of God shows us the basic structure of humanity in its highest vocation, the call to holiness. As a result, women have their proper responsibilities in the Church, but it seems to me that there is not a proper distribution of roles and ministries based on sex. As St. Paul taught, this distribution is based on charisms, which though they may be colored differently by sex, are essentially gifts from God to a *person* for the building up of the community.

---

[38] E. Behr-Sigel, *Alexandre Boukharev*, p. 104.

Concerning Mary's role in the history of salvation, her place in the liturgy and Christian piety, Catholics and Protestants often seem to be radically opposed to one another. We can legitimately ask, however, if the terms *Catholic* and *Protestant* do not in fact cover quite a variety of attitudes and beliefs. This apparent opposition is no doubt the reason why Mary has had such a small place in the ecumenical dialogues that have taken place over the past 20 years. Even so this difficulty must be faced one day.[39] Is it possible that Mary's role as formulated and live in the Orthodox Church could help find a way out of this impasse? I would like to think so. The difficulty must not, however, be underestimated and requires an answer with many shades of meaning. I will simply mention some paths that need to be explored.

I think we should begin by distinguishing various levels: dogma, theology, liturgical expressions, and popular piety. Even within our different Churches, these different levels are apparent.

On the dogmatic level, the Orthodox Church soberly holds to what is said about Mary in the ecumenical Nicene creed and to the title *Theotokos* given to her by the Council of Ephesus and confirmed by the Council of Chalcedon. It is important to remember that this title is essentially a christological statement. This platform, which is shared by all the Christian communities that see themselves in continuity with the Church of the first centuries, is the basis of all Orthodox piety concerning Mary. The Orthodox Church would not feel itself in full communion of faith with a community that rejected this heritage. The Orthodox consider the acceptance of this heritage to be a matter of faithfulness to the deposit of the apostolic faith; it is necessary to be faithful to the God who became man to save humanity.

---

[39] The recent papal encyclical *Redemptoris Mater* invites such a reflection. See E. Behr-Sigel, "Marie: une question incontournable" [Mary: An Unavoidable Question], *Actualité religieuse dans le monde*, #44, 15, IV, 87.

The fact that the Orthodox Church has never felt it necessary to dogmatize beyond the proclamation of Ephesus indicates that it preserves "a scale of theological values which always" gives "precedence to the basic fundamental truths of the Gospel."[40] This does not mean that the Orthodox Church rejects or ignores the spiritual message carried by the Roman dogmas about Mary of the 19th and 20th centuries. From the point of view of form, the *dogma* of Mary's assumption is a problem for the Orthodox; its content, however, is accepted as long as the idea of Mary's natural death is not eliminated. The Orthodox liturgical texts are very clear on this point. Orthodox theologians are on the whole much more critical, however, about the dogma of the Immaculate Conception. It seems to me though that they could be invited to accept such a dogma as a special Western theological elaboration that does not bind the faith of the universal Church even though it may not be in contradiction to that faith.

The Orthodox Church does not require an explicit acceptance of the dogmas about Mary either of her faithful or of those who want to become members. It rather counts on the pedagogy of the liturgy to introduce them into the mystery of Mary. The Orthodox Church prefers to teach and initiate the faithful progressively to this mystery by using the images and symbols of liturgical poetry rather than the restricting conceptual approach. The symbol does not define; it rather suggests and gives food for thought. Poetic expressions are better suited to a reality that belongs essentially to the age to come. As the Reformed theologian Denis Muller[41] has noted, the partial opacity of a symbol, and in a general way all poetic language, constitutes its richness and opens it to a plurality of personal understandings that point to *catholic* truth. The Orthodox refusal to restrain the spontaneity of popular

---

[40] J. Meyendorff, *op. cit.*, p.148-49.

[41] D. Muller, "Parole de Dieu, langage et symbole" [The Word of God in Language and Symbol], *Irénikon*, LVIII, 1985, pp. 199 ff.

devotion to Mary through the use of dogmatic formulas might facilitate dialogue with Christian communities that have developed historically in opposition to the exaggerations and deviations of the veneration of Mary characteristic of the end of the Middle Ages.

At the same time, the exuberance of the liturgical poetry about Mary found in Byzantine Orthodoxy risks putting off, even shocking, the sobriety of Reformation Christians. Is not the use of apocryphal traditions especially in conflict with one of the basic principles of the 16th century Reformation, the *Sola Scriptura*? According to this principle, the Scriptures, as determined by the canons, are the unique basis of the Church's faith.

A real effort at understanding the *other* is required of both sides. Orthodox theology ought no doubt to explain more clearly than it has up to this point exactly how it understands the use of apocryphal material and the limits of that use. On the other hand, ought not thinkers in the Reformation tradition renounce some of their *a priori* principles and admit the possibility and existence of a Gospel piety about Mary? Scientific exegesis is a common ground for both sides and might contribute to a rapprochement of points of view.[42] In its present-day orientation, this kind of exegesis gives more importance to the meaning of facts then to the materiality. In fact, the *facts* are in any case often scientifically unattainable.

From a different perspective, feminist theology, as worked out in America but elsewhere also, is attracting the attention of circles that have traditionally been opposed to the veneration of Mary. They are finding a new interest in the figure of Mary the Mother of God, who, according to a Protestant woman author, "is so important for our history, our great history."[43] In these same circles, however,

---

[42] M. Carrez, "Identité protestante et identité chrétienne" [Protestant Identity and Christian Identity], *Les quatre fleuves*, #20, Beauchesne.

[43] F. Dumas, "Marie, cette inconnue" [Mary the Unknown], *Réforme*, 17-25, August, 1985.

women often feel uneasy when faced with the sugary, sentimental, and moralizing image of Mary that is often advocated by certain Westerners, especially pastors. The Orthodox vision of Mary, as expressed by Nicholas Cabasilas or the great icons of Mary, can be of great help here. At the same time, the fact that Orthodox mariology is solidly grounded in christology can also help to avoid paganizing tendencies. The ideological use of Mary by certain currents of feminist theology have not always avoided such tendencies.

Even though these new signs of the shining of Mary's mystery are coming from outside the institutional limits of the Church, I hope that the Orthodox Churches will be able to welcome them with discernment and without small-minded fear.

APPENDIX

Questions about Men and Women in the People of God*

The following document made public in Paris in 1979, is an attempt to make a survey of the Orthodox position about men-women relations in the Church. It is the result of a discussion that was inspired by the international consultation of Orthodox women at Agapia, Romania in 1976 (see Service orthodoxe de Presse *#11). This text is intended to serve as a starting point for a wider reflection within the Church. Thirty-six persons signed the document–men and women, clergy and laity.*[1]

The question about the place of women in the people of God has been asked with great seriousness, and sometimes passion, great passion, in the communities that have come out of the Protestant Reformation as well in certain

* Published in *Service Orthodoxe de Presse* #40, July-August, 1979.

[1] Since 1979, the date this document was published, the Orthodox reflection on the place and service of women in the Church has advanced and deepened. In November 1988, the Ecumenical Patriarchate convoked an inter-Orthodox consultation at Rhodes on this theme. Some 60 lay and clerical theologians were present, 18 of whom were women. This consultation bears witness to the hierarchy's awakening to the importance of the challenge posed by this question, a question which for a long time the bishops felt they could ignore. A second and significant international consultation of Orthodox women was organized by the World Council of Churches and held at the Orthodox Academy of Crete in January, 1990. See the bibliography for documents relating to these consultations.

Roman Catholic circles. But, the question seems to have left the Orthodox indifferent. They say, with a good conscience, that "it does not concern us. Because we honor the Mother of God, women have no problem finding their right place in our Church." This feeling is correct and generally sincere, but it can also be used as an excuse for refusing to face certain realities. The feminist question is seen as foreign to Orthodoxy, and for a long time it has been of little interest except to some Orthodox theologians involved in ecumenical dialogues. In the name of the *catholic* Tradition of the Church, these theologians have vigorously condemned the ordination of women to the pastoral or priestly ministry as it is accepted and practiced in the various Protestant and Anglican Churches, even though some of these Churches, like the American Episcopal Church, consider themselves close to Orthodoxy. On the whole, ecumenically oriented Orthodox theologians have not shown themselves to be very motivated in finding a positive way of expressing women's aspirations. As far as we know, only Paul Evdokimov as an Orthodox theologian has taken up the challenge that the modern feminist movement has issued to the Church.[2] However, for some time now, there has been an increasing number of signs, still timid though, that indicate a change in mentality. There are efforts to rethink the relations between men and women in the Church, and from inside the Orthodox Tradition, in the light of the Gospel.

The first consultation of Orthodox women was held in 1976 at the Agapia monastery in Romania.[3] It was organized by the World Council of Churches with the blessing of the heads of all the large Orthodox Churches and the ancient Eastern Churches, Coptic, Armenian, and

[2] See the important books of Paul Evdokimov, *Sacrement de l'Amour* [Sacrament of Love], Editions de l'Epi, and *La femme et le salut du monde* [Woman and the Salvation of the World], Desclée de Brouwer, 1979. Even though some points are somewhat outdated, this second book remains a basic text.

[3] *Service Orthodoxe de Presse* #11 and #12.

Jacobite. Even though the results of this consultation were modest, a decisive turning point had been reached. Women came together from every part of the Orthodox world, from the East and the West, from the Third World and the industrialized European and North American countries. They were treated as privileged guests but did not enjoy complete freedom of expression. They nonetheless dared to speak out, not to demand rights in a hostile tone, but to express their desire to serve the Lord in the Church as free and responsible persons, daughters like the sons created in God's image.

Following in the wake of this first dialogue, books and articles were published[4] and local meetings organized. These first dialogues, like subsequent ones, have been between women, between men and women, and between lay people and the hierarchy whose authority and charisms we respect. One of these dialogues took place in Paris where an informal working group was set up. Lay men and women were brought together; some were from traditional Orthodox families while others were converts who had come to Orthodoxy as adults. Some priests also joined us. All of them were deeply committed to the life of our Church. The first goal was simply to meet together in a

[4] The WCC has published in English a small book that contains the main texts of Agapia, *Orthodox Women*, Geneva, 1977. A mimeographed French version can be obtained from *Service Orthodoxe de Presse*. See also *Sobornost* #7/6, 1978, with the text of the presentation by Elisabeth Behr-Sigel, and *Contacts* #100, 1977, "La Femme–vision orthodoxe" [Woman: An Orthodox Vision]. *Unité chrétienne* has published in its #53, 1979, the course given by Elisabeth Behr-Sigel at the ecumenical chair of the Catholic faculties Lyons, France. See also the publication, following Agapia, of a small periodical called *Images* by a group of students at St. Vladimir's Seminary in New York as well as two important studies by Fr. Thomas Hopko, "The Male Character of the Christian Priesthood" and V. Kesich, "Saint Paul Anti-feminist or Liberator?", *St. Vladimir's Theological Quarterly* #1/1975 and #3/1977. See also the German Orthodox periodical *Orthodoxie Heute* #62-63, 1977, with an article by A. S. Elverson. And finally see the very well thought out and positive contribution of Archimandrite Kallistos Ware in the collection *Men, Women, Priesthood*, London 1978. This list is by no means meant to be exhaustive.

climate of complete freedom, to ask questions, and to talk about problems that had been silenced for too long. Are our parishes and communities really places where the "Spirit blows"? Are they places where mutual relations in particular between men and women can be established? Are they places where the divino-humanism our times so badly need is operative? Or, in the words of a young Greek woman theologian who spoke at an ecumenical conference, are they "the last bastion of traditionalist conservatism"? These questions of course do not have simplistic answers.

Situations and sensitivities are not everywhere the same, even if we limit ourselves to the Orthodox reality in France and Western Europe. We are therefore only at the beginning of our inquiry and reflection. Nonetheless, certain convergent lines are beginning to appear. At the point where we find ourselves, we thought it desirable to share our questions, worries, and modest discoveries with others. We therefore submit them to the Church here in this place and look forward to receiving answers and reactions. We want to move ahead *together*.

One misunderstanding must be cleared away: we are not a bunch of modernists who are unconcerned with the Church's Tradition which is Spirit and Life. We are, however, witnesses of the evolution of mores in the modern Western society[5] and especially of the changes concerning the status of women, but we reject the idea that the Church can abandon any part of its message, of the "deposit" (1 Tm 6:20) it has received, in order to adapt itself to the ever changing and relative thinking and values of a historical culture, even though that culture may be our own. On the other hand, Church history, the apostle Paul, and the Church Fathers up to and including our own time have all shown that the authentic Tradition is both

[5] By "Western" we mean a cultural rather than a geographic entity, even, in its roots, spiritual. It is in the name of this spiritual West that Iranian women protest not against the veil itself but rather the obligation of wearing it.

transcendent to all cultures and at the same time capable of absorbing certain elements from many cultures. This Tradition is able to discern the good wheat from the weeds, the vain wisdom of this world from the *logoi*, those seeds of the one Gospel that have been deposited by the "Spirit who blows where he wills." We very much need this discernment today faced as we are with the aspirations for an authentic liberation of women, aspirations, however, which are sometimes confused or perverse, but which have their root in the liberating message of Christ. There is no question whatsoever of having the Church "kneel down before the world," as Jacques Maritain said, but rather of converting ourselves, men and women members of the people of God, more and more and ever anew to the Lord of the Church. Our goal is that this Church in its historical and empirical existence may become what it is in its deep reality: the holy Bride, "without stain or wrinkle . . . purified by water and the Word" (Ep 5:26-27).

Already *here and now*, the daily life of the Church is being filled with light by its deep spiritual reality which, as the Deisis icon explains in the language of icons, is a Church that "has never unilaterally masculinized its approach to mystery;"[6] a Church in which the humblest woman, seeing and hearing herself in the light of the Theotokos and the Magnificat, can know that her dignity is recognized; a Church that offers a profound theology of marriage and in which the existence of a married clergy assures that women are not excluded from the sacred.

Having this great richness, it is all the more regrettable that certain elements survive in our communities, elements that survive more from inertia than from real convictions based on faith. These elements include rites, usages and prohibitions that discriminate against and are offensive to women, or simply incomprehensible to the young generation. We are thinking specifically about the exclusion of women from sacramental communion during certain times

[6] *Contacts* #100, p. 255.

of their biological cycle and after childbirth, which however is a blessing; the prohibiting of women from entering the sanctuary behind the iconostase, even excluding baby girls, a prohibition based on custom and not on the canons. The very beautiful rite of reception of a child into the ecclesial community is not the same for a girl as for a boy. The priest carries the baby boy behind the altar while the little girl is only carried in front of the iconostase! We are told that these are but minor usages without any great importance and that they will fall into disuse by themselves. Our perception, however, is that they do die hard and that their common tendency is not insignificant. Rather than coming from the Gospel, do these usages not have their roots in ancient beliefs, taboos, and fears about women? Are they not legalistic or magic conceptions, beliefs, taboos, and fears about things "pure" and "impure"? Did not Christ in his earthly life always stand against these things? He was born of a woman, allowed himself to be touched by women in general, but specifically by the woman with an issue of blood and the prostitute who according to the Law were impure. To the surprise of his disciples, he had a theological discussion with the heretical Samaritan woman at Jacob's well. He also admired the faith and granted the prayer of the pagan Syro-Phoenician woman as well as calling all men and women to worship the Father "in spirit and in truth."

We must naturally avoid scandalizing the weak ones, so we are told by those who want to justify maintaining these customs. This is the argument we hear even though these customs are foreign to the Gospel and to the light-filled anthropology of the Fathers. They in fact go far beyond the Old Testament and have their roots in ancient anxieties. Ought we not rather to be concerned about scandalizing those, more numerous than we might think, who are shocked by the clash between this literal legalism, fed by the ghosts of an immense and collective unconsciousness, and the liberating dynamism of the Gospel?

These exclusions and prohibitions, based on sex, are grounded in the prescriptions of Leviticus 12:1-7 and 15:1-28, but they do not even have the excuse of being faithful to the literal text of the Scriptures. Under certain conditions, these prohibitions were applied to men as well as to women in the Old Testament, but in our times, only those aspects that apply to women have been retained, as though there was an intention of deeply ingraining a feeling of impurity solely based on womanhood. Has the time not come today to throw away the "old wine skins" of this out-of-date symbolism which is the source of so many misunderstandings, and pass over with Jesus "to the other side" (Mk 4:35), to the shore of that freedom which, for Gregory of Nyssa, was the essence of the image of God in us?

If it is important to cleanse the Church of the sludge and dust deposits that for so many centuries have disfigured it, must we not also explore new and ancient ways that would allow women to use their charisms and aptitudes in the service of the Church better and more freely. In this area also, do we not still hold onto frozen stereotypes that have become outmoded a long time ago? Motherhood is certainly and profoundly imprinted in a woman's being, but should we limit "motherhood" only to biological motherhood, as wonderful as that is, or to the education of children which in fact is the task of the couple and of society, or to spiritual motherhood which is a charism that does not exclude other activities?

Paul Evdokimov wrote that the Churches "make use" of women who are in charge of an ever increasing number of tasks but who merely carry out the orders of others and have little to do with conceiving or directing projects. Is not women's work simply material work, such as cleaning? This kind of work has its usefulness and dignity, but it does not exclude other responsibilities. Women are often given the task, too often only women, of teaching young children, a responsibility wrongly considered to require little competence. But why, in certain cases, do we not also give women the job of teaching theology on an academic level, if they have the necessary qualifications and competence? Are women integrated enough into the fabric of the Church's conciliarity? Are they present in the circles where the Church's thinking about spiritual, ethical and institutional problems is done? Are they helping to solve the problems the Church faces today? When a local Church studies problems concerning women as well as men, such as contraception, abortion, or divorce, are women consulted? During a recent consultation between Orthodox and Anglican theologians on the ordination of women to the priesthood, the Anglicans asked if at least one or two Orthodox women theologians could be present.

Even though this request was in no way an attempt to undermine the authority of Orthodox bishops present at the conference, it was refused. There are, nonetheless, in Greece and elsewhere, women who have received theological training from established faculties and institutes.

In the Orthodox Church, a layman can be called upon, occasionally or with the status of a permanent ministry as is often the case in Greece, to comment on the gospel reading during a liturgical service. Why cannot this practice be extended to women who have received an adequate theological formation and the charism of the word? We often hear St. Paul's rule: ". . . the women should keep silence in the churches" (1 Co 14:34). But the interpretation of this verse taken out of its context is very difficult, and it contradicts 1 Corinthians 11:5 where we hear about how women can "prophesy" as long as they wear a veil, that is, are decently dressed according to the culture of the time.[7]

Among the ancient ways that could possibility be explored and restored today is the women's diaconate. It

[7] On this subject and on the so-called misogyny of St. Paul, V. Kesich, "Saint Paul Anti-feminist or Liberator?", *St. Vladimir's Theological Quarterly* #3/1977, pp. 123-147; A. Jaubert, "Le rôle des femmes dans le peuple de Dieu, recherche de critères en référence à l'Ecriture" [The Role of Women in the People of God: Search for Criteria in the Scriptures], *Ecriture et pratique chrétienne* [Scriptures and Christian Practice], Cerf, 1978.

existed in the ancient Church, especially in Syria and later in Byzantium up to the twelfth century.[8] In a recent article in the Anglican-Orthodox periodical *Sobornost,*[9] Fr. Sergius Hackel, an Orthodox priest in Great Britain, gave the translation of a description of the rite of a deaconess' ordination. The text itself is from a Byzantine theologian of the 14th century, Matthew Blastaras. Fr. Hackel noted that Blastaras emphasized both the "dignity" of the deaconess' ministry and its "limitations." We would rather say its "specificity." The deaconess' ministry was in no way confused with that of the bishop-presbyter and remained subordinated to it in the sense of the trinitarian *taxis.* We still need to study more closely, however, the origin and evolution of the women's diaconate in the light of earlier documents such as the *Didascalia of the Apostles,* end of the third century, and other still little known Syrian sources.

Whatever may be the actual history of the women's diaconate, its restoration, if that ever happens, must not be simply an archæological reconstruction. It will have a meaning only if it is rethought theologically on the one hand and restructured according to the needs of our world and the Church today. All this must be done under the creative inspiration of the Spirit. The most important aspect of the ordination prayers quoted by Fr. Hackel seems to us to be the following: the Church recognized that "the Lord does not reject those women who offer themselves to him in the service of his holy dwelling." In turn, the Church "accepts them in the rank of ministers (*leitur-*

[8] The canonical and historical aspect of the question has been studied by Professor E. Theodorou in his doctoral thesis, *Cheirotonie or Cheirothesis* Athens, 1967, in Greek. Also see P. H. Lafontaine, *Les Conditions positives de l'accession aux ordres* [The Positive Conditions that Led to Orders], Ottawa, Ontario, 1963, and R. Gryson, *Le Ministère des femmes dans l'Eglise ancienne* [The Ministry of Women in the Ancient Church], Gembloux, 1972.

[9] *Sobornost* 7/7, 1978, pp. 595-96.

goi) and calls down on them the grace of the Holy Spirit for the carrying out of their ministry."

These reflections are incomplete and fragmentary; we are very conscious of this fact. But can they not serve nonetheless as a starting point for a common reflection and action? We propose them to conciliar thinking, that is, thinking done in a spirit of humility, openness, and mutual listening. In the diversity envisioned by the Creator, let us aim at building up "the body of Christ until we all attain to the unity of the faith and of the knowledge of the Son of God, to mature manhood, to the measure of the stature of the fullness of Christ" (Ep 4:13-14).

The preceding text was signed by Fr. Jean-Marie and Nadine ARNOULD, Catherine ASLANOFF, Jean BALZON, Nicolas and Nadia BEHR, Elisabeth BEHR-SIGEL, Fr. Boris BOBRINSKOY, Anne-Marie BOTTON, Fr. Jean and Lynn BRECK, Barbara CHPIGANOVITCH, Olivier and Monique CLEMENT, Jerome CLER, Michel and Marie-Claire EVDOKIMOV, Vsevolode and Daniele GOUSSEFF, Jacques and Monique GUILLON, Jeanne de la FERRIERE, Bruno and Chantal LIANCE, Nicolas and Veronique LOSSKY, Nina PECHEFF-EVDOKIMOFF, Serge and Helene REHBINDER, Fr. Jean RENNETEAU, Germaine REVAULT D'ALLONNES, Vladimir and Irene SCHIDLOVSKY, Michel and Catherine SOLLOGOUB.

BIBLIOGRAPHY

In English

Behr-Sigel, Elisabeth, "Women Too in the Likeness of God," *Midstream* XXI/3, July 1982; "Orthodox Tradition as Resource for the Renewal of Community," *Women and Men in the Church*, Constance Parvey, editor, WCC, Geneva, 1983.

Belonick, Deborah, *Feminism in Christianity*, New York, 1983.

Bishop Maximos Aghiorgoussis, *Women Priests?* Holy Cross Orthodox Press, Brookline, Mass., 1976.

Hopko, Thomas, "God and Gender: the Orthodox Christian View," and Elisabeth Behr-Sigel, "The Ordination of Women: an Ecumenical Problem," *Church and Culture: Orthodox Women's Consultation January 16-24, 1990*, The Subcommittee on Women in Church and Society, WCC, Geneva. To be published in 1990 or 1991.

Kesich, V., "St. Paul: Anti-Feminist or Liberator?", *St. Vladimir's Theological Quarterly*, 1977, #3.

Malacky, D., "Woman in God's Creation," *St. Vladimir's Theological Quarterly*, 1977, #3.

Orthodox Women: Their Role and Participation in the Orthodox Church, Report on the Consultation of Orthodox Women, Agapia, Roumania, WCC, Geneva, 1977.

Topping, Eva C., *Holy Mothers of Orthodoxy: Women and the Church*, Light and Life Books, Minneapolis, Minn., 1987.

Women and Men in the Church: A Study of the Community of Women and Men in the Church, Department of Religious Education: Orthodox Church in America; Syosset, New York, 1980.

Women and the Priesthood, Thomas Hopko, ed., St. Vladimir's Seminary Press, Crestwood, N. Y., 1983. The following articles are contained in this volume:

Preface, Alexander Schmemann;

"Man, Woman and the Priesthood of Christ," Bishop Kallistos Ware;

"Women and the Priestly Office According to the Scriptures," Georges Barrois;

"Presbytides or Female Presidents," Nicholas Afanasiev;

"The Characteristics and Nature of the Order of Deaconess, Kyriaki Karidoyanes FitzGerald;

"On the Male Character of Christian Priesthood," Thomas Hopko; "The Spirit of the Female Priesthood," Deborah Belonick;

"Women and the Priesthood: Reflections of the Debate," Thomas Hopko.

Zion, Basil, *Eros and Transformation: Marriage and Sexuality in the Eastern Christian Perspective*, University of America Press, Lanham, Maryland, 1990.

In French

Behr-Sigel, Elisabeth, John Erikson and Evangelos Tehodorou, "Les Femmes dans l'Eglise orthodoxe," *Contacts* (Special issue on the Rhodes Consultation), 1989/2.

—, "Femmes et Sacerdoce," *Contacts* 150, 1990/2.

—, "Hommes et femmes dans l'Eglise," and Olivier Clément, "Féminisme russe et Mère de Dieu," *Contacts* 111/1979, an answer to an inquiry of the World Council of Churches.

—, "La femme dans l'Eglise orthodoxe," and Paul Evdokimov, "Le devenir féminin selon Nicolas Berdiaev," *Contacts* 100/1977.

—, "L'ordination des femmes: un problème oecuménique," *Contacts* 150/1990.

Chitescu, N. and G. Khodr, *De l'ordination des femmes*, World Council of Churches: Faith and Order, 1964.

Evdokimov, Paul, *La Femme et le Salut du monde*, Casterman, 1958, 2nd edition Desclée de Brouwer, 1979.

—, *La Nouveauté de l'Esprit*, Bellefontaine, 1977.

—, "Femmes et hommes dans l'Eglise: Une approche orthodoxe de la question des ministères," *Service orthodoxe de Presse: Supplément* 66.

Goritcheva, T., "Délivrée des larmes d'Eve, réjouis-toi," *Femmes et Russie*, Paris, 1980.

Hopko, Thomas, "De la spécificité masculine de l'ordination sacerdotale," *Service orthodoxe de Presse*, #5, February, 1976.

In German

Behr-Sigel, Elisabeth, "Ordination von Frauen? Ein Versuch des Bedenkens im Licht der lebendigen Tradition der orthodoxen Kirche," *Warum keine Ordination der Frau?*, Unterschiedliche Einstellungen in den christlichen Kirchen, Freiburg i/Br., 1987.

Jensen, Anne, "Wie patriarkalisch ist die Ostkirche?", *Una sancta*, 1985/2.

Theodorou, Evangelos, "Das Diakonat der Frau in der Griechisch-Orthodoxen Kirche," *Diaconia*, 1986/2-3.

Other Book by Elisabeth Behr-Sigel

The Place of the Heart: Initiation into Orthodox Spirituality (to be published 1991 by Oakwood Publications).

Other Books by Oakwood Publications

The Art of the Icon: A Theology of Beauty – Paul Evdokimov, 367 pp., 367 pp., 10 color illus. A "summa on beauty" giving the biblical and patristic vision of beauty applied to contemporary movements in art; plus a "theology of the icon" with commentaries on ten specific icons.
ISBN 0-9618545-4-5

The Icon: Image of the Invisible – Egon Sendler, 238 pp., 150 b/w, 36 color photos. A unique study of the theology of the icon, the æsthetics and the technique of icon painting with excellent reference guides, Greek/Slavic alphabets. ISBN 0-9618545-0-2

Dynamic Symmetry Proportional System as Found in Some Byzantine & Russian Icons of the 14th to 16th Century – Karyl Knee, 90 pp., illus. Application of the theory of dynamic symmetry to ancient Egyptian and Greek art and Orthodox iconographic art. ISBN 0-961845-2-9

The "Painter's Manual" of Dionysius of Fourna – Paul Hetherington, 128 pp. A translation of the most ancient of classic "Greekstyle" narrative descriptions of saints, Bible events, parables and decoration of churches. Compiled on Mt. Athos from 1730-1734. ISBN 0-9503163-0-X

An Iconographer's Pattern Book: Illustrated in the Stroganov Tradition –Fr. Christopher Kelly, 300 pp., 450 illus. (patterns) of saints, feast-day, councils. Ancient headnotes translated with color descriptions, special notes. Source reference from 15th century. ISBN 0-9618545-3-7

The Image of God the Father in Orthodox Theology & Iconography – Fr. Stephen Bigham, 150 pp. illus. The history and theology of depicting God the Father in images. ISBN 0-9618545-7-X

The Christmas Icon: A Theological and Hidstorical Study – Georges P. Drobot, 330 pp., illus. The theological and historical background of the dogma of the incarnation. The canonical Christmas (Nativity) icon to present each element's historical and theolgical context.
ISBN 0-961845-5-3

Icon Painter's Ssketchbook: An Anthology of Source Material – Gregory Melnick, 300 pp. A gathering of original sourcematerial on icon painting, technique, rules, theology, etc. Translated from original Slavonic and Greek.

Icons & Iconpainting – Dennis Bell (videotape, VHS), depicts in sight, sound and music the history of icons, showing techniques of painting, colors and application of paints. ISBN 1-879038-02-1